DISCOURSE ANALYSIS

A SOCIAL-PHILOSOPHICAL GROUNDING

KYRKOS DOXIADIS

DISCOURSE ANALYSIS

A SOCIAL-PHILOSOPHICAL GROUNDING

KYRKOS DOXIADIS

Common Ground

First published in Champaign, Illinois in 2011
by Common Ground Publishing LLC
as part of The Humanities series

Copyright © Kyrkos Doxiadis 2011

All rights reserved. Apart from fair dealing for the purposes of study, research, criticism or review as permitted under the applicable copyright legislation, no part of this book may be reproduced by any process without written permission from the publisher.

Library of Congress Cataloging-in-Publication Data

Doxiadis, Kyrkos.
Discourse analysis : a social-philosophical grounding / Kyrkos Doxiadis.

    p. cm.

Includes bibliographical references and index.
ISBN 978-1-86335-916-0 (pbk. : alk. paper) -- ISBN 978-1-86335-917-7 (pdf. : alk. paper)
1. Discourse analysis. I. Title.

P302.D68 2011
401'.41--dc22

                        2011008014

Cover image: Phillip Kalantzis-Cope

This book was previously published in Greek under the title: *Analysi logou: Kinoniko-filosofiki themeliosi* in 2008 by Plethron.

Table of Contents

Preface x

Part I : Discourse in Contemporary Thought

Chapter 1: The concept of discourse in Laclau and Mouffe 3

Chapter 2: Discourse and objectivity 13

Chapter 3: The intervention of Žižek 23

Chapter 4: Derrida and the concept of "presence" 37

Chapter 5: Language, writing, representation 49

Chapter 6: Subjectivity and finitude 61

Part II : The Ontological Priority of the Material Component

Chapter 7: The materiality of language 75

Chapter 8: Discourse and the non-discursive 89

Chapter 9: On referentiality 99

Chapter 10: Archaeology of knowledge and discourse analysis 107

Chapter 11: The four axes 117

Part III : The Ethical Priority of the Conceptual Component

Chapter 12: The concept of the subject 127

Chapter 13: Hypostatisation and representation 137

Chapter 14: Foucault and freedom as a moral value 145

Chapter 15: Psychoanalysis and linguistics 153

Chapter 16: Desire and understanding 167

Part IV : Applications

Chapter 17: Chinatown 179

Chapter 18: Two award-winning films 201

Index 205

It is very strange to be localised in a body, and this strangeness can't be minimised, despite the fact that a great deal of time is spent puffing ourselves up and boasting about having reinvented human unity, which that idiot Descartes had cut in two. It is completely useless to make great declarations about returning to the unity of the human being, to the soul as the body's form, with large dosages of Thomism and Aristotelianism. The division is here to stay.

Jacques Lacan

Preface

On the front cover of the paperback edition of Naomi Klein's *The shock doctrine*, there is only one of the many laudatory comments the book has received: John le Carré's. Several others are inside and on the back cover. That le Carré's plaudits would deserve pride of place is hardly questionable; he is one of the most highly esteemed authors of our time. His enthusiasm itself is also hardly surprising politically; after the end of the cold war, le Carré's politics have taken an impressively decisive left turn. On the other hand, there is an almost uncanny feeling provoked by a non-fiction book on politics being praised on its front cover by a novelist. Le Carré is not merely a famous person who happened to like the book; he seems to be speaking *as an expert*. And an expert he is; if one considers the sheer amount of research on which the writing of his novels is apparently based. Moreover, his topics are the same with Klein's: capitalist greed and political ruthlessness. So where is the difference, if any? An attempt to deal with questions of this sort is probably the basic motive behind this book.

Discourse Analysis: A social-philosophical grounding has two main, closely interrelated goals. Its main negative goal is to point to a fundamental misconception shared by several trends in contemporary thought. The main positive one is to provide a grounding for the methodology known as "discourse analysis", using conceptual tools derived from contemporary philosophy and the broader field of theoretical social/human sciences.

The first goal is primarily dealt with in Part One. In my opinion, certain key figures in that extremely broad and very loosely defined area of contemporary thought labelled "poststructuralism" have served, each in their own fashion, to undermine a fundamental distinction which—however complicated and blurred it may be—remains crucial for critical thought: that between subjectivity and objectivity. To demonstrate my point, I have chosen several theoretical notions as targets of my critique, amongst which are the following: (a) Ernesto Laclau and Chantal Mouffe's tendency to confuse the object of knowledge with the real object, and thus to treat "discourse" as an all-encompassing entity that includes material/objective social relations and practices together with discursive/subjective ones (Chapters 1 and 2). (b) Slavoj Žižek's treatment of the Lacanian "real" in a way that would be more suited to the "imaginary", and the consequent interiorisation of antagonistic relations by means of the Hegelian notion of "pure antagonism" (Chapter 3). And (c) Jacques Derrida's critique of the "metaphysics of presence", and the inextricably related substitution of the concept of "representation" with that of "writing" (which is conceived as *non*-representation)—which have significantly contributed to a tendency in contemporary thought virtually to abandon the materialist task of the critique of representation (Chapters 4, 5 and 6).

In Parts Two and Three, the above task is approached anew, on the premise of what I describe as a "materialist dualism". The question is how to provide a new materialist foundation for ideology critique, that would escape from its various implicitly or explicitly idealist Hegelian variations, as well as from the economic reductionism of base/superstructure Marxism. The method proposed draws very loosely on Michel Foucault's "archaeology of knowledge", which, in my view, is not so much a quasi-positivist approach to the history of ideas as has sometimes been suggested, but rather an approach to "discourse" based on certain fundamental philosophical properties that pertain to it.

Discourse analysis and ideology critique are treated as a materialist reworking of the Kantian dialectic in the following sense: a main starting point is the importance of (fundamental) finitude in Kantian philosophy (pointed out by Heidegger) and in modern thought generally speaking (demonstrated by Foucault in *The order of things*). This concept of finitude is in turn employed in an effort to constitute a new, non-economistic materialism, that can serve as a basis for a critique of hypostatised infinity and of the various forms this acquires in a multitude of modern discourses and ideologies, from scientific discourse to historical novels, and from monotheistic religion to liberalism and Marxism. Throughout this book, the emphasis is on the analysis of representation as taxonomic discourse, in a way that exposes the complicity of the latter in sustaining hypostatisation, from Cartesian philosophy to present-day films.

In short, the "dualist" part of "materialist dualism" consists in that the critique of hypostatisation is a practice that on one hand is based on the ontological priority of the material component of discourse, while on the other supporting the ethical supremacy of the freedom of critique, and of thought in general, by constantly demonstrating the non-objective character of the latter. Psychoanalytic theory and theoretical linguistics are also utilised, though not as mere "complements" filling the "gaps" in the Foucauldian approach to subjectivity, but rather in terms of the philosophical importance of certain key concepts for explaining hypostatisation and maintaining the distinction between subjectivity and objectivity.

Part Four is an "application" of the above considerations to an analysis of three important films, not in any mechanistic sense of the term, but as a way of "putting to the test" both the "technical" aspect of the proposed methodology and the theoretical/philosophical premises on which it is grounded.

Part I
Discourse in Contemporary Thought

Chapter 1
The concept of discourse in Laclau and Mouffe

a. *The fact that every object is constituted as an object of discourse has* nothing to do *with whether there is a world external to thought, or with the realism/idealism opposition. An earthquake or the falling of a brick is an event that certainly exists, in the sense that it occurs here and now, independently of my will. But whether their specificity as objects is constructed in terms of "natural phenomena" or "expressions of the wrath of God", depends upon the structuring of a discursive field. What is denied is not that such objects exist externally to thought, but the rather different assertion that they could constitute themselves as objects outside any discursive condition of emergence.*

b. *At the root of the previous prejudice lies an assumption of the* mental *character of discourse. Against this, we will affirm the* material *character of every discursive structure. To argue the opposite is to accept the very classical dichotomy between an objective field constituted outside of any discursive intervention, and a discourse consisting of the pure expression of thought. This is, precisely, the dichotomy which several currents of contemporary thought have tried to break.*[1]

---

1. Ernesto Laclau and Chantal Mouffe, *Hegemony and socialist strategy: Towards a radical democratic politics* (translated by Winston Moore and Paul Cammack), London: Verso, 1985, p. 108.

The main negative target of this text is to demonstrate a fundamental illusion that characterises "several currents of contemporary thought". The positive target is to provide a grounding for the methodology known as *discourse analysis* using conceptual tools of contemporary philosophy and the broader field of theoretical social sciences. It goes without saying that the negative and the positive targets are not unrelated.

Let us start from the negative target, and let us take as an example the previous sentence: "It goes without saying that the negative and the positive targets are not unrelated." It is a commonplace of logic, but also of everyday language, that "relation" does not simply mean "identity". Two things may be different or even opposite and yet very closely related. A large part of contemporary critical thought appears to ignore this simple truth. I am referring to the distinction between thought/subjectivity on one hand and matter/objectivity on the other. It is wrongly assumed that, since the rigorousness of the distinction has been challenged and the complexity and closeness of the relations between these two realms of existence has been demonstrated, this is tantamount to the *abolition* of the distinction.

I have chosen the above extract from Laclau and Mouffe for three reasons. The first one is general, the other two more specific. The general reason has to do with the uniquely significant place of Ernesto Laclau in contemporary critical and left-wing thought. It is, in some sense, a crucially functional place, if one takes into account the fact that Laclau's work forms a point of intersection, or *junction*, so to speak, in at least two especially important ways. On one hand: very consistently left-wing and socialist in his affiliations, a spiritual offspring of the Gramscian but also of the Althusserian component of the European communist tradition, and at the same time genuinely open and receptive towards influences by non-Marxist, non-leftist theoretical trends. And on the other hand: the central thematic of his theories is most directly political, in the strictest sense of the term: political movements, questions of democracy and socialism; but he constantly enriches these theories with conceptualisations that he "borrows" from fields like linguistics, psychoanalysis, philosophy (in the narrow sense) and cultural studies, which, however, he thoroughly elaborates, so as to incorporate them organically into his own approach and thematic. It is no accident therefore that this thinker has constituted and still constitutes a reference point for a very wide spectrum of contemporary thought, either as source of influence, or as target of critique, or—quite frequently—as both.[2]

---

2. Several years ago, in 1997, he was in Athens and was dining with a group of Greek academics, consisting of quite a large variety of specialists in the social and political sciences, and of diverse theoretical orientations and affiliations. He discovered to his surprise that there wasn't a single person among the group that had not devoted at least an article or a book chapter to his work. Of course I am not suggesting that group was an especially representative statistical sample; I am merely mentioning the event as an indication of what I am trying to say regarding Laclau's particular significance.

The more specific reasons have to do with the particular extract. It was chosen as a quite revealing case of a view that tends to abolish the distinction between subjectivity and objectivity, or thought and matter, and chosen for two reasons. In the first part of the extract, it is most distinctly apparent that this view is never presented as a naïve contemporary version of some extreme idealism or solipsism. Objective/material reality (an earthquake, a brick falling) is recognised as something existing independently of thought, that is, of subjectivity. This means that the distinction, before being abolished, is declared as acceptable.

The second part of the extract, however, shows us the way in which the distinction is essentially abolished. One has to do with an *actual* or *functional* abolition, which continues to deny itself on a manifest level. The (functional) way that the distinction is abolished mainly consists in the use of a certain concept, of a certain term, which includes both aspects, objectivity and subjectivity, matter and thought, *in a fashion that abolishes the difference between them.* This term, in Laclau and Mouffe's case (but elsewhere too), is the term *discourse*.

Let us see how Laclau and Mouffe define "discourse", somewhat earlier in the same text:

> "In the context of this discussion, we will call *articulation* any practice establishing a relation among elements such that their identity is modified as a result of the articulatory practice. The structured totality resulting from the articulatory practice, we will call *discourse*."[3]

This means that any social totality, as long as it emerges as an effect of a practice that modifies the identity of the elements that constitute it, will be included under the category of discourse. A social class is discourse, therefore, so is a political party, as well as what the authors call "hegemonic formation". I am not suggesting of course that Laclau and Mouffe are in any sense proposing some simplifying scheme that uncritically reduces everything to "discourse". In fact, one has to do with an exceptionally complex procedure, by way of which, in Laclau and Mouffe's conceptualistion, objectivity and subjectivity, material conditions and mental processes, *coexist* in what the authors call "discourse" or "discursive formations" *without being directly identified with each other*.[4] Besides, in many sociological and political-scientific approaches at least since Weber, one often finds a coexistence of subjective and objective elements in the research field under consideration, without this necessarily amounting to a leveling of differences between the two.

The question, however, in the particular case of Laclau and Mouffe, as well as of other directly related theoretical approaches, is why has this specific word been chosen: *discourse*? As a first impression that might suggest the oddity of this choice, let us assume for a moment that the authors had

---

3. *Ibid.*, p. 105.

4. *Ibid.*, pp. 93-148.

chosen an approximately *inverse* term, to describe *the same multi-complex, subjective and objective, mental and material, socio-political entity*. For example: *economy*, or *production*.⁵

The problem does not lie *only* in the arbitrary broadening of the term *discourse* towards the direction of objectivity, but *also* in the fact that, as it is most clearly stated in the extract I quoted at the beginning, a *unilaterally material* quality is attributed to this term. They respond, in other words, to the assertion about the "mental" character of discourse not by suggesting an alternative conception that would include both realms of existence, but by insisting that we have to do with an *exclusively*—or at any rate a *predominantly*—material entity. That is to say, on one hand, they choose a term that at least till recently was largely in concurrence with the *subjective/ideational* aspect of human activity, and on the other, they maintain that this term refers to a *material* entity. It would be equivalently paradoxical if they had chosen the term "economy", for example, while insisting that this applies to an *ideational* entity.⁶

The oddity of Laclau and Mouffe's undertaking is not that they stress excessively some doubtlessly material/objective *aspects* of discourse at the expense of its ideality/subjectivity; but rather in that they consider *the material/objective world itself as discourse, to the extent that it simply fulfils some preconditions:* "The objective world is structured in relational sequences [...] which, in most cases, do not actually require any meaning at all: it is sufficient that certain regularities establish differential positions for us to be able to speak of a discursive formation."⁷

---

5. This was actually the case, in some sense, with the broadness that Althusser had attributed to the term *mode of production* – see especially Louis Althusser and Étienne Balibar, *Reading Capital* (translated by Ben Brewster), London: New Left Books, 1970, and Kyrkos Doxiadis, *Subjectivity and power: On the theory of ideology* (in Greek), Athens: Plethron, 1992, p. 81 ff.

6. To support their view, they refer to the authority of speech-act theory and of Wittgenstein - Laclau and Mouffe, *op. cit.*, p. 108. As to the former, nowhere in that theory can one find an *assimilation* of *speech* acts to any other acts. Searle begins his famous book on speech acts in a fashion that renders crystal-clear their *specificity as acts*: "How do words relate to the world? How is it possible that when a speaker stands before a hearer and emits an acoustic blast such remarkable things occur as: the speaker means something; the hearer understands what is meant; the speaker makes a statement, asks a question or gives an order?" - John R. Searle, *Speech acts: An essay in the philosophy of language*, Cambridge: Cambridge University Press, 1969, p. 3. As to the latter, they use an extract where Wittgenstein includes in the term "language game" both language and the "actions into which it is woven", and they draw the conclusion this means that Wittgenstein *assimilates* the former to the latter. Neither in this particular formulation of Wittgenstein nor in any other similar ones can such a conclusion be inferred - Ludwig Wittgenstein, *Philosophical investigations* (translated by G.E.M. Anscombe), Upper Saddle River, New Jersey: Prentice Hall, n.d., pp. 3-5.

7. Laclau and Mouffe, *op. cit.*, p. 109.

"Discourse" therefore is not merely the material/objective world, but this world even when it has been *purged of any of its noetic/subjective dimensions*. So why do Laclau and Mouffe insist on using the term "discourse"? A possible answer has been given in the preconditions mentioned in the above extract, and could be summed up in the *at once relational and differential character* of what they term discourse. Laclau and Mouffe's entire theoretical problematic around discourse has a *distinctly linguistic* conceptual starting point. They just isolate those properties of language that could indeed be said also to pertain to the structures of the material/objective world—difference, relativity, regularity—and apply them to what they call discourse, about which they maintain it has a predominantly if not exclusively material existence. Some questions however remain to be answered: first, why do they consider it necessary to ground their conceptualisation in linguistics? And second, why do they consider it necessary to use the term "discourse" instead of confining themselves to terms like "structure", "system", or even the more "dynamic" term "articulation", which they also use and which are semantically more neutral in the sense that they do not refer only to language but to objective/material entities as well?

They themselves feel obliged to answer the second question. Discourse, they claim, as a central category of their analysis, enriches the "field of objectivity" of social relations, in a way that could not be achieved if they remained in the frame of conceptualisation of the natural sciences. Concepts like "metaphor" and "contradiction" (which are intelligible only within the framework of the category of discourse) could not be applied to the explanation of natural phenomena but are indispensable for the analysis of a "wide range of relations among objects in the social and political field".[8]

But why is this so? Is it not because the socio-political field differs from the natural one precisely in that it is incessantly *conceptualised from within*? Every example they give in order to explain the concept of *equivalence*, which they themselves propose as a further conceptual elaboration of *metaphor*[9] (the colonialists/colonised antagonism in a colonised country, the antagonism of urban/agrarian culture in millenarian movements, Disraeli's politics in nineteenth century Britain[10]) definitely includes an important subjective/noetic component. It is true that throughout the development of their arguments they do not miss the opportunity to stress, not that they *abolish* the noetic dimension but that they *do not accept the "dichotomy"* between thought/meaning on one hand and reality/matter on the other. What is the *positive* argument they put forth to support this view? In other words, apart from their wish—which they share with "several currents of contemporary thought"—to dispense with the "very classical dichotomy", what is the *motive* for this theoretical innovation?

---

8. *Ibid.*, pp. 109-110.

9. *Ibid.*, p. 110.

10. *Ibid.*, pp. 127-130.

How "innovative" is the abolition of the dichotomy anyway, especially in the intellectual tradition from which they initially originate, i.e. Marxism? The dominant Marxist paradigm before Althusserianism was Hegelian Marxism, particularly in its Lukácsian version, where a predominant place was held by the *totality* in which thought and action, or mind and matter, were unified. On the other hand, it is certainly true that Laclau and Mouffe wish to adopt a view which radically differs from the Lukácsian position, where class reductionism leaves no room for the logic of "articulation"—in contrast to the Gramscian concept of *hegemony*[11] (which actually forms the main topic of their book). Surely Lukács and, more generally, Hegelian Marxism constitutes a common negative target not only of Althusserian Marxism but also of every theoretical trend related to structuralism and/or poststructuralism, with which Laclau and Mouffe were to varying degrees affiliated. And it is in this sense anything but unpredictable that they should choose both the term "discourse" and a linguistic theoretical starting point (to arrive finally at the first of the two questions raised above).

We could therefore presume that the linguistic conceptualisation and the consequent insistence on the use of "discourse" as a central analytical category together constitute an attempt *to preserve the Marxist concept of totality even after departing from hitherto dominant Hegelian-Marxist class reductionism*, in order to allow it to form a suitable theoretical framework for the further utilisation of Gramscian "hegemony".

What would a—*non-"essentialist"*—preservation of the concept of totality first and foremost consist in? It would consist in conceiving the realm of the social as a whole—but as a whole which is complex, multi-dimensional, open, incomplete, subvertible, pluralistic: all these are properties that systematically emerge in Laclau and Mouffe's approach, and that differentiate it from the traditional Hegelian-Marxist conception of totality. So they have recourse to linguistic conceptual tools in order to constitute their own theoretical scheme of totality, which they name after a term that in turn derived *also* from linguistics: discourse.

A possible objection one might have, apart from the question of the use of the term "discourse" itself, would concern the legitimacy of transposing concepts that pertain to language to realities including many non-linguistic elements: that is, to socio-political relations in their generality. However, this objection could well be removed, insofar as the transposition is successful. The "loans" between different academic disciplines do not always prove to be arbitrary or unfortunate.

Laclau and Mouffe themselves address the problematic character of introducing "the linguistic model [...] into the general field of the human sciences". They seem however to imply that the problem was already inherent within linguistics itself, at least in the work of the founder of (theoretical) linguistics—namely, Saussure—and had to do with the conception of lan-

---

11. *Ibid.*, pp. 68-69.

guage as a closed system.[12] But let us see rather more extensively the way in which they themselves employ the linguistic problematic in their theory.

The interesting thing is that the "closedness" of language is not to be found in Saussure himself but in a point of *critique against* Saussure raised by Émile Benveniste, in his text "The nature of the linguistic sign", to which Laclau and Mouffe positively refer a few pages earlier and once again in a footnote a bit further down. Benveniste maintains that the Saussurian concept of *value*, that is, the fact that signs depend entirely on their relations to other signs,[13] implies relations of *necessity*: "Everything is so *necessary* in it [in the (linguistic) system] that modifications of the whole and of details reciprocally condition one another."[14]

Why do Laclau and Mouffe refer positively to Benveniste on this particular point? Because they utilise this very property of necessity that characterises language (according to Benveniste) in order to describe the necessity that also characterises, in their view, *what they call discourse*; however, "discourse" in the sense of a completely articulated closed system. And such a discourse, according to the authors, exists nowhere, because the articulation process is never complete. Necessity is coexistent with *contingency*, which constantly threatens to subvert it.[15] In this way they provide themselves with the possibility—and here is the crucial point in their theory of discourse—to introduce *by way of a contrast*, so to speak, to the (linguistic) concept of *difference*, the concept of *equivalence*: "...the logic of equivalence is a logic of the simplification of political space, while the logic of difference is a logic of its expansion and increasing complexity".[16] As it can also be seen in the examples I mentioned, Laclau and Mouffe consider equivalence as the *revolutionary-subversive* dimension of the socio-political field, while difference is treated as the *conservative-stabilising* one: "...the more unstable the social relations, the less successful will be any system of differences and the more the points of antagonism will proliferate".[17]

But the "loans" from linguistics are not forsaken with the concept of equivalence either. As we have already seen, they base it on the concept of metaphor, and they compare its relation to difference with the relationship between the two dimensions of language: "Taking a comparative example from linguistics, we could say that the logic of difference tends to

---

12. *Ibid.*, pp. 112-113.

13. Ferdinand de Saussure, *Course in General Linguistics* (translated by Wade Baskin), Glasgow: Fontana/Collins, 1974, pp. 111-122.

14. Émile Benveniste, *Problèmes de linguistique générale, 1*, Paris: Gallimard, 1966, p. 54 – English translation (Mary Elizabeth Meek): *Problems in general linguistics*, Coral Gables, Florida: University of Miami Press, 1971, p. 48; Laclau and Mouffe, *op. cit.*, p. 106, and p. 114, fn. 23.

15. *Ibid.*, pp. 113-114.

16. *Ibid.*, p. 130.

17. *Ibid.*, p. 131.

expand the syntagmatic pole of language, the number of positions that can enter into a relation of combination and hence of continuity with one another; while the logic of equivalence expands the paradigmatic pole—that is, the elements that can be substituted for one another—thereby reducing the number of positions which can possibly be combined."[18]

Without oversimplifying Laclau and Mouffe's argumentation, we could in fact say that their whole reasoning revolves around two constantly and closely intertwined but also antagonistic dimensions, which correspond to the two dimensions of language:

- *"syntagmatic" dimension (combination):* difference, continuity, interiority, necessity, complexity, stabilisation.
- *"paradigmatic" dimension (substitution):* equivalence, discontinuity, exteriority, contingency, simplification, subversion.

Since Laclau and Mouffe insist on being based on the linguistic problematic, I believe we are ourselves entitled to investigate somewhat further the linguistic origin of the premises for their theoretical approach.

The syntagmatic dimension of language is the dimension of linguistic *value par excellence*—the dimension of that fundamental property of language, which consists, according to Saussure, as we pointed out above, in the complete interdependence between signs that is required so they can exist as signs; that is, so there can be a relation of *signification*, a relation between *signifiers* and *signifieds*. (Linguistic) value is the property of language that explains how the "horizontal" (i.e. syntagmatic) dimension determines the "vertical" (i.e. paradigmatic). To put it more simply, how meaning is produced (that is, how signification takes place) by way of relations of *combination* between different elements (that is, between signs).

We should note here that, in Saussure as well as in Martinet, the *associative* or *paradigmatic* relation also concerns the relationship between *signs* and not only between *signifier and signified*.[19] This means that in Saussure *value also* includes paradigmatic or associative relations. However, in a text which is considered to be a *landmark* in the semiological problematic, Roland Barthes essentially equates *paradigm* with the *fundamental relation of meaning*—the *signifier/signified* relation. Not unjustifiably: the signifier/signi-

---

18. *Ibid.*, p. 130. On the pair of terms *paradigmatic/syntagmatic relations*, see André Martinet, *Éléments de linguistique générale*, Paris: Armand Colin, 1980, p. 27. The equivalent terms in Saussure are *associative/syntagmatic relations* – Saussure, *op. cit.*, pp. 122-127. On the two dimensions of language, see Roman Jakobson and Morris Halle, *Fundamentals of language*, The Hague: Mouton, 1956, pp. 53-82. Jakobson, instead of the terms *paradigm/syntagm*, uses the alternative terms *metaphor/metonymy*. For a systematic interconnection between all relevant terms, I refer to Christian Metz, *Psychoanalysis and cinema: The imaginary signifier* (translated by Celia Britton, Annwyl Williams, Ben Brewster and Alfred Guzzetti), London and Basingstoke: Macmillan, 1982, pp. 174-191, holding however some reservations as to the rigorousness of certain conceptual distinctions.

19. Saussure, *op. cit.*, and Martinet, *op. cit.*

fied relation is indeed a relation of *substitution*. The fact that there can *also* be a relation of substitution between signs (*as well as between signs and referents*) merely accounts for the use—in this latter case—of the alternative term *metaphor*.²⁰ In this sense, strictly speaking, linguistic value also includes metaphoric relations, insofar as these are relations between signs. Relations between signs however (*as well as relations between signs and referents*) are always *initially* relations of combination. We could therefore accept, without excessively forcing the terminology, that a relation, to be metaphoric, must *first* be syntagmatic – more aptly, with reference to the corresponding to metaphor term that denotes combination, must *first* be metonymic.²¹

The fact that *basically* the syntagmatic dimension of language coincides with linguistic value is manifest in the way that Saussure himself treats the two terms. About value he says:

Language is a system of interdependent terms in which the value of each term results solely from the simultaneous presence of others, as in the diagram:

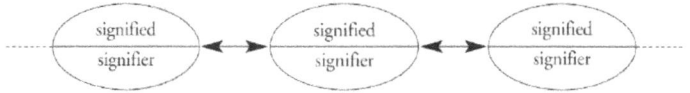

And about the syntagmatic relation, a few pages further down:

The syntagmatic relation is in praesentia. *It is based on two or more terms that occur in an effective series.*²²

It is quite clear: The "simultaneous presence" in value, even if we accept that it *also* includes the "associative" relations *between signs*, that is, the relations between "terms *in absentia* in a potential mnemonic series",²³ cannot be radically distinguished from the relation "*in praesentia*", that is, from the co-presence "in an effective series". Saussure himself would not be able to support the radicalness of the distinction, since at the first systematic presentation of the linguistic "sign" he particularly stresses the fact that language (i.e. signs) can exist as internal speech.²⁴

---

20. See Roland Barthes, *S/Z* (translated by Margarita Koulentianou), Athens: Nissos, 2007, my Afterword, p. 356 ff.
21. When referring to the "horizontal" dimension generally speaking, between the terms "syntagmatic relations" and "metonymic relations" I prefer the latter, because the term "syntagmatic relations" implies a conception of language that detracts from its referentiality, while the term "metonymic relations"—as well as the term "metaphoric relations"—more explicitly includes not only relations between signs but also relations between signs and referents.
22. Saussure, *op. cit.*, pp. 114-115 and 123.
23. *Ibid.*, p. 123.
24. *Ibid.*, pp. 65-66.

I said above that the *closedness-necessity* of the relations of value that Laclau and Mouffe employ referring to Saussure[25] does not exist in Saussure but in a text of *critique* towards Saussure by Benveniste[26] (which is also utilised by Laclau and Mouffe). Not only does not necessity exist in Saussure, but the target of Benveniste's critique is precisely the *non-existence* of necessity in Saussure.

Saussure formulates the well-known principle of the "arbitrariness of the linguistic sign".[27] Benveniste's basic objection has to do not with arbitrariness *per se* but with *between what things* is there a relation of arbitrariness (that is, lack of causality). Saussure claims that arbitrariness exists between signifier and signified – between the acoustic image of the sound of a word and the concept of the word. Benveniste amends him and says that what he really means is that arbitrariness exists between the sign (signifier and signified taken together) and the referent (the real object to which it refers). Benveniste's critique is both right and wrong. Right because, as one can see from the examples he mentions, this is indeed what Saussure meant (what Benveniste says he really meant). He is wrong however when in amending him he claims that between signifier and signified there prevails not merely a relation of causality but one of necessity: acoustic (or visual) images on one hand, concepts on the other. The dual nature of the linguistic sign has to remain dual. If this is abolished and we conceive of the sign as a thoroughly unified entity, it will cease to exist as a sign. But I will come back to this.

What is important at this point is that Benveniste's (false) view on the relation of necessity between signifier and signified is also the premise for his assertion that the relations of value, as long as they are the ones that determine the relation of signification, are also relations of necessity.[28] Laclau and Mouffe therefore base their case on something that in my view consists in a wrong theoretical intervention (on the part of Benveniste) and that definitely does not exist in Saussure. And most important: they conceal (not intentionally, I suppose) the *basic part* of Benveniste's false view, and they claim the *opposite*: That in the paradigmatic dimension of language, i.e. in the signifier/signified relationship, there prevails not a relation of nessecity but one of *contingency*: "The sign is the name of a split, of an impossible suture between signified and signifier."[29] A view with which I agree, *but for more or less the inverse reasons*.

---

25. Laclau and Mouffe, *op.cit*, pp. 112-113.

26. Benveniste, *op. cit.*, pp. 49-55 – English translation: pp. 43-48.

27. Saussure, *op. cit.*, pp. 67-70.

28. Benveniste, *op. cit.*, pp. 53-55 – English translation: pp. 47-48.

29. Laclau and Mouffe, *op. cit.*, p. 113.

Chapter 2
Discourse and objectivity

As we have seen, Laclau and Mouffe *oppose* the paradigmatic dimension of language to the syntagmatic, and accordingly what they call *equivalence* to *difference*. Difference indeed is a term that should be considered as belonging *mainly* to the syntagmatic dimension, for the same reasons as the fact that the latter is, as we have seen, the dimension of *value par excellence*. Saussure's whole explication of the concept of value is perhaps best summarised in his view that "in language there are only differences".[30] Language as production of significance emerges exclusively from the *combination of different* elements. The term *equivalence*, on the other hand, is introduced by Laclau and Mouffe so that they can connect their own conception of the notion of *antagonism* to their basically linguistic conceptualisation. They derive (as we have seen) *equivalence* from *metaphor* (which, even though it is differentiated from the "pure" paradigmatic relation—the signifier/signified relation—as we pointed out above, it still belongs to the paradigmatic or "vertical" dimension of language as long as it is based on *substitution*), in order to compare antagonism as well to the latter.

The term "equivalence" initially appears in their text when they analyse the "popular front" politics of the Third International, without using strictly linguistic terms. But at that stage already they counterpoise equivalence to difference, with reference to the concept of *substitution*. They main-

---

30. Saussure, *op. cit.*, p. 120.

tain that the logic of popular fronts unites different social forces within the system of (different) class positions ("the working class, the peasantry, the petty bourgeoisie, progressive fractions of the national bourgeoisie") on the basis of "their *equivalence* in the common confrontation with the dominant pole". It is not therefore a matter of *identity* between different social classes or class segments, but rather a matter of *substitutability* among them, as to their common opposition to the dominant pole.[31] Equivalence does not abolish difference, neither does it ignore it, it transcends it.

Further on, in their purely theoretical chapter, this is what they have to say about antagonism itself: "If language is a system of differences, antagonism is the failure of difference: in that sense, it situates itself within the limits of language and can only exist as the disruption of it—that is, as metaphor."[32]

So the vertical dimension of language, either as the signifier/signified relation, or as metaphor, or as equivalence-antagonism, is its disruptive and subversive element, its liminal element, which is opposed to the "stabilising", horizontal dimension of language as value, as system of differences.

The analogy between language and society is clear: metaphor is the subversive limit of language, antagonism itself is the subversive limit of society: "…if […] the social only exists as a partial effort for constructing society […] antagonism, as a witness of the impossibility of a final suture, is the 'experience' of the limit of the social. Strictly speaking, antagonisms are not *internal* but *external* to society; or rather, they constitute the limits of society, the latter's impossibility of fully constituting itself."[33]

The ease with which Laclau and Mouffe move over from language to society and vice versa reveals the reason they insist on the use of the term "discourse". They are in a position virtually to substitute the realm of the social with that of discourse, because both, according to their approach, are based on a common premise, for which "equivalence", either as antagonism or as metaphor, forms its limits and the non-completion of its constitution. In the case of language as well as in the case of society, one has to deal with "*closed systems of differences*", which, however, can never be completed as such, since antagonism (and/or metaphor) exists. Furthermore, closedness, necessity, determinateness are virtually *equated with objectivity*. Laclau and Mouffe abolish the distinction between discourse/language on one hand and society on the other, because they have a *conception of objectivity that includes both*. Objectivity for the authors is a *determinate ensemble of relations between objects*. We should note that this is so for both *conceptual* objects, as in the case of contradiction, and *real* objects, as in the case of (real) opposition. Both contradiction and (real) opposition sustain a determined system of differences, because both presuppose the existence of terms with "full identity" or "full presence"—something which does not hold for antag-

---

31. Laclau and Mouffe, *op. cit.*, pp. 62-63.

32. *Ibid.*, p. 125.

33. *Ibid.*, p. 125.

onism, given that with the latter the terms are never complete, since "the presence of the 'Other' prevents me from being totally myself".[34]

Apart from any objections or accordances one might have with the above theoretical scheme of Laclau and Mouffe, what matters at this point is the way in which they conceive of objectivity. Schematising though not distorting, we could say that objectivity for Laclau and Mouffe is *the common property of conceptual and real objects and not merely the property of the latter*. It is quite important to stress this, because I believe that here we can find a key to understanding the abolition of the distinction between subjectivity/thought and objectivity/materiality which I mentioned earlier.

Let us go back to the extract I cited at the beginning. Having in mind how they conceive of objectivity, this extract can now be better illuminated. What they would in no way accept is the view that some objects "could constitute themselves as objects outside any discursive condition of emergence"; while they have no particular problem with the fact that some objects "exist externally to thought". But if for them the property *per se* of objectivity is not the latter but the former, that is, if objectivity is not existence independent of thought or concepts, but the process of *constitution* of objects, whether conceptual or real objects, then they are definitely right to insist that there is no objective field outside discourse. We can now also understand what they mean when they claim that antagonism, as they conceive it, as the subversive limit of the closedness and determinateness of language and society, is far from being an objective relationship.[35]

At the same time however, this conception of objectivity verges far too closely on the limits of tautology. I will presently explain why.

The very concept of the *constitution* of objects as *fundamental* to the property of objectivity, in other words, the fact that for something to be objective it is not enough to exist as an object but that it has to be *constituted* as such, virtually leads to the identification of objective entities with the objects *of knowledge*. There is no other meaning in the concept of *constitution*. And we should not be misled by the already mentioned distinction between "real" and "conceptual" objects. The former are objects of knowledge that *correspond* to realities, while the latter are objects of knowledge that *correspond* to concepts.

The explanation they give in the example of the earthquake in the extract cited at the beginning is crystal-clear as to this point. What matters for Laclau and Mouffe is not the earthquake in itself, about which they accept that it does indeed take place independently of our thought, but *how the "earthquake" is constituted as an object of knowledge*. That is: does one have to do with the "earthquake" of seismology or with the "earthquake" of devout religiousness? That both seismologists and devout believers may be similarly shaken by the same earthquake does not seem to bother them that much as to how they conceive of "objectivity".

---

34. *Ibid.*, pp. 124-125.

35. *Ibid.*, p. 125.

Is there knowledge without discourse? Obviously not. In Foucault (as we will see further down), and not only in his case, the two terms are roughly synonymous. To maintain that the objects of *knowledge* cannot be constituted outside discourse is virtually equivalent to contending that the objects constituted by discourse cannot be constituted outside it. Here is the tautology.

We will further investigate the causes and consequences of this tautological scheme. But let us first go back for a while to the linguistic premises of Laclau and Mouffe's arguments.

I said that I agree with their view about the non-existence of necessity in the signifier/signified relation "*but for more or less the inverse reasons*". Laclau and Mouffe *counterpoise* the *indeterminacy* that characterises the signifier/signified relation to the *necessity* that characterises, as they believe (in *half* agreement, as we have seen, with Benveniste), the relations of difference of the language system. However, their view on necessity is *equivalent* to their view on objectivity. They distinguish it from natural necessity (which they place in quotation marks, thereby perhaps keeping their distance from it), and they define it (their own necessity, once again identifying language and society in this matter) as a "system of differential positions in a sutured space".[36] That is, they virtually equate necessity with *closedness-determinateness*, which in their view characterises language and society as systems of differences, as well as objectivity in general in the above sense of the *field of objects of knowledge*.

It is *in opposition* now to *this* necessity and objectivity that they conceive of both the *signifier/signified* relation and what they call *antagonism*. In the schematic classification of the two oppositional and intertwined dimensions, I therefore believe we could add the following:

- "*syntagmatic" dimension (combination):* objectivity, determinateness.
- "*paradigmatic" dimension (substitution):* antagonism, indeterminacy.

It is in a sense quite to be expected that in this scheme the (more or less) opposite of objectivity is antagonism—not subjectivity. When objectivity is conceived as the property of objects of *knowledge*, then obviously its opposite cannot be subjectivity. The subject *of knowledge* is indeed oppositional to the object *of knowledge*, but both coexist within the broader field of knowledge; which is in turn coextensive with that of subjectivity—but not, as it seems, in Laclau and Mouffe.

Is subjectivity to be found anywhere in Laclau and Mouffe's problematic? There is the *subject* (as subject *in general*, not as subject of knowledge); but there is no *subjectivity*. The above distinction is no sophistry: The way in which Laclau and Mouffe expressly conceive of the subject radically disconnects it from subjectivity: "Whenever we use the category of 'subject' in this text, we will do so in the sense of 'subject positions' within a discursive

---

36. *Ibid.*, p. 114.

structure."³⁷ Which means that the subject simply follows the—doubtlessly multi-complex and incomplete—fortunes of *articulation* and of what they call *discourse*: in terms of both the objective, i.e. necessary/determinate, and the contingent/indeterminate dimension.

We now go back to the signifier/signified dimension. The "split", the "impossible suture" that characterise this relation are the metaphoric terms that Laclau and Mouffe employ to describe its indeterminacy. It is an indeterminacy which, as we have seen, according to them, forms one of the fundamental properties of the "paradigmatic", i.e. the antagonistic dimension of discourse and articulation. My view is that indeterminacy—*that is, in this case, arbitrariness*—in the signifier/signified relation does exist but is of secondary importance. The *principal* terms are the terms that are metaphorically used by Laclau and Mouffe: *split, impossible suture.*

What is it that distinguishes a word in a computer's memory from the same word in a human being's speech or thought? I suppose we could agree that, in the first case, one has to do with an objective entity, not in Laclau and Mouffe's sense of a *constituted* object *of knowledge*, or anyway not *only* in that sense, but (also) in the sense of *something existing independently of our thought*: We accept—*axiomatically, as materialists*—that if a neutron bomb exploded, which was strong enough to eliminate all human life on the planet, while leaving intact the "inanimate" material things, that particular word in the computer's memory would continue to exist as it does now: as a quantum of electric energy.

This—*objective, by definition*—form of existence of the word in a computer's memory is *the digital equivalent of the signifier, according to the original, Saussurian definition of signifier*; that is, the digital equivalent *of the acoustic (or visual) image of the word in the human brain.*

Let us start from something about which we could easily accept it is indeed common to both the above entities: their materiality. It is merely a question of a different *type* of materiality. In the first case, we have to do with a materiality defined by computer science or electronic technology, while in the second case it is a materiality defined by neurobiology.

Once again axiomatically, as materialists, we accept that the only objective entities, that is, the only entities existing independently of our thought, are material entities. However, this is not necessarily equivalent to accepting that *all* material entities are objective, that is, that *all* material entities exist independently of our thought. As it will become apparent further down, I also happen to believe this latter principle, but it is admittedly more difficult to accept and no simple appeal to materialism would suffice in this case.

In the case of the (Saussurian) signifier, the "neutron bomb test" is certainly not sufficient. If the human species were eliminated, (Saussurian) signifiers would doubtlessly disappear together with human thought. If we accept that signifier and signified are the two sides of a coin, or, to use Saus-

---

37.*Ibid.*, p. 115.

sure's own simile, the two sides of a sheet of paper,[38] then it is indeed rather difficult to accept that one side, i.e. signifiers, could exist independently of the other: independently of signifieds, i.e. of concepts, of thought *per se*.

We could however conceive of another hypothetical example, without neutron bombs and computers: a group of European anthropologists carries out fieldwork in some completely isolated village somewhere in Africa, where an idiomorphic dialect is spoken, which resembles no other language or dialect. The anthropologists tape record several natives' conversations, and, after they depart from the village, a fatal epidemic occurs and every single villager—which means every single person who spoke that language—is eliminated. Until (and *if*) the anthropologists manage to decode this dialect, every time they listen to the recorded conversations of the eliminated villagers, the acoustic images of the words they hear will be *solely* (Saussurian) signifiers. They will have the materiality of the sound inscribed in the human brain, and they will exist independently of the signifieds, that is, the concepts or the thought (*per se*) of the deceased natives.

I gave this somewhat "eccentric" example in order to demonstrate the possibility of *complete* independence of signifiers from signifieds. *Partial or relative* independence occurs quite frequently: each time one hears an unknown word, whether from another language or from one's own, and before (and *if*) one finds out what it means. *In one's own* brain, the acoustic image of the word exists independently of its signified or concept.

For persons who hear an unknown word and for as long as it remains unknown to them, as well as for the anthropologists for as long as they are incapable of decoding the recorded speech of the natives, what they have in their head is *objective*, since it exists independently of concepts, *but it is not language*. In order for the latter to exist, what is required is the *coexistence* of both sides: acoustic images/signifiers *and* concepts/signifieds. In other words, something that characterises most, if not all, manifestations of human activity, perhaps in the case of language it is more apparent than anywhere else: *the non-reducible coexistence of objectivity and subjectivity*. "Non-reducible" in a double sense: neither can one side exist without the other (in order for language to exist), nor, however, can one side be identified with or assimilated by the other: the two sides are *at once closely interdependent and imperatively distinguishable*. And it is *in this* sense that the term "impossible suture" that Laclau and Mouffe use to describe the signifier/signified relation is indeed most apt.

Not however *in opposition* to the "horizontal" or "syntagmatic" dimension of language, which, according to the authors' contention, who agree here with Benveniste (but not with Saussure), is characterised by closedness and determinateness, but *together* with it. The "split", that is, the *radical discontinuity*, between objectivity and subjectivity does not mark only the indeterminacy that pertains to the "vertical" dimension of language, i.e. to the relations of *substitution*, but also the indeterminacy of the dimension of

---

38. Saussure, *op. cit.*, p. 113.

"value", i.e. of the relations of *combination*. Language is not a closed system, whose closedness is constantly threatened or subverted by some external "subversive limit" called metaphor or equivalence or antagonism; it is *to start with* open and "external" by itself. It is just a matter of an indeterminacy that is not absolute: it *coexists* with causality, but *in both* dimensions of language. In the vertical one: there is *some* correspondence, however unstable and variable, as to the *substitution* between signifiers and signifieds, otherwise meaning would not be feasible. In the horizontal: regarding the *combination* between signs, there are *some* rules: of logic, syntax, grammar, spelling and pronunciation.

The coexistence of causality and indeterminacy in language certainly has to do with its dual nature, objective and subjective, which is inherent in both dimensions. And if we absolutely had to decide which property *mainly* characterises language, we would choose the latter: indeterminacy, since indeterminacy is *primarily* (though not exclusively) a property of subjectivity, while causality *primarily* (though not exclusively) coexists with objectivity, and since language is *primarily* subjective and *secondarily* objective: signifiers *justify their existence* by the existence of signifieds—if the latter do not exist, the former are no different from the acoustic image of any sound.

The non-reducible coexistence of objectivity and subjectivity, and consequently of causality and indeterminacy, with the priority of the latter over the former, is something that accompanies language not only in its two dimensions but also in all its practical manifestations. In language as discourse (we will see further down more extensively the relation and differentiation between the two), as well as in the various forms of the latter's embodiment in social practice, this coexistence does not cease to pertain to all sectors of human activity, *without however replacing them*: the priority of subjectivity is withdrawn from the moment we move towards realms where material/objective factors are more important than language and discourse. More extensive elaboration of the above distinctions will be carried out further down.

I believe the reasons for which Laclau and Mouffe conceive of language as an *initially* closed and determinate system are of two sorts. One reason has to do with how they treat the concept of *difference*, which pertains to the horizontal dimension of language. But I will also deal with this matter further down. The other reason though is directly related to what interests me at this point, and which is what I have been reproaching them for right from the start: the *abolition of the distinction between subjectivity and objectivity*, which is to be found in their problematic regarding both language itself and socio-political practice more generally.

As we have seen, this abolition basically consists in confusing the "objectivity" of the objects *of knowledge*, which are *primarily* subjective entities, with the objectivity of objective entities *per se*, which is what exists independently of thought, subjectivity and knowledge—a confusion manifested in the substitution of the latter with the former. This substitution amounts to a twofold misleading gesture: *On one hand,* objectivity forfeits what defines it as such, which is existence independently of thought. *And on the other*, subjectivity is deprived of its fundamental property, that is, its indeterminacy.

In what Laclau and Mouffe call "discourse", which on one hand is based on their conception of language and on the other includes the whole sociopolitical formation, the *mainly objective* relations of *real causality/necessity* are substituted with the *mainly subjective* relations *of cognitive determination*. What perhaps also contributes to this confusion is the very term "determination", which may mean either of the two. And in this way, the latter forfeit their *inherent indeterminacy*. There is nothing contradictory in the above formulation: in a fashion similar to that in which the object of knowledge is distinguished from the real object in that the former is mainly subjective but it is called an object because it *corresponds* to the real object, the relations of cognitive determination are distinguished from the relations of real causality/necessity in that they are mainly subjective *and therefore primarily indeterminate* but they are called relations of determination once again because they *correspond* to the real relations of causality/necessity (also called relations of determination).

We are thus led to a peculiar sort of hypostatisation. Laclau and Mouffe do not hypostatise in the way that classical idealism does. They do not transform some ideational existence—God, Nation, History—into something objective, in the sense of something existing independently of thought, *precisely because they have conceived of the "objective" as something that is constituted by thought, i.e. by discourse*. On the other hand though, given the above confusion, they remove from a particularly significant dimension of this "objective"—which in fact, as we have seen, is mainly subjective—its most important property as subjective (indeterminacy), only to re-introduce this (indeterminacy) as something *external*, as the *limit*, as the *other dimension* of language, of discourse, of articulation: "metaphor", "equivalence", "antagonism".

Furthermore, even as "other dimension", as "from without" subversive indeterminacy, indeterminacy is not reinstated as the indeterminacy *of subjectivity*. How could it anyway, since, as we have pointed out, subjectivity does not enter anywhere in their problematic. As we have seen, the antagonistic dimension is the opposite of "objectivity" without being subjectivity. As the opposite of "objectivity" in the sense of *determinateness*, the antagonistic dimension cannot but be *(simply) indeterminacy*; indeterminacy merely for the sake of indeterminacy. What is the philosophical significance of this indeterminacy? I will presently proceed to examine this issue.

The answer was—initially—already given, when we pointed out how Laclau and Mouffe distinguish "antagonism" from contradiction and (real) opposition. The absence of "full identity" or "full presence" in the terms of the antagonism, given that one term's presence precludes the other's completeness, is the concrete form that "antagonistic" indeterminacy assumes in Laclau and Mouffe's approach. This is the *positive* content of this "indeterminacy", which thereby already warns us as to its implicit Hegelianism.

Even though at that particular point the authors do not expressly refer to Hegel, we cannot ignore the fact on the other hand that, at the beginning of the chapter where they expound the problematic of the two dimensions of articulation and "discourse", they posit Hegel's philosophy at the historical but also theoretical *starting point* of this problematic.[39] This surely has to do with the fact that Hegelianism in its several variations has permeated most dominant currents of Marxist thought, but as they themselves explain what matters is that the "ambiguities and imprecisions" that constitute the basis of the problematic were already there "in Hegel himself".[40]

What is quite striking in the whole approach of Laclau and Mouffe, and which is not necessarily *directly* connected to the question of the distinction between subjectivity and objectivity, is the radical way in which they differentiate themselves from most of the other thinkers who have some affinity to poststructuralism, in one particular issue regarding language and the text, which has to do precisely with the two dimensions. In the classification of terms I set out above, most poststructuralists would see things more or less the other way round. They would treat the "vertical" dimension as the more "conservative", and it is there that they would assign closedness, interiority, determination, stabilisation, while with the "horizontal" dimension, the dimension of *difference par excellence*, they would place openness, exteriority, indeterminacy and subversion.[41] It is a diversion which is doubtlessly provoking, given that in that same text they positively refer to those particular theorists in order to support their views. We will see further on more extensively the limits as well as the deeper significance of this positive correlation—it is surely not merely a matter of some "theoretical misappropriation" on the part of Laclau and Mouffe (and anyway the correlation that they themselves invoke is not always only positive—as we will see further on with the case of Foucault).

---

39. Laclau and Mouffe, *op. cit.*, pp. 94-95.

40. *Ibid.*, p. 95.

41. See Roland Barthes, *op. cit.*, my Afterword, p. 359 ff.

Chapter 3
The intervention of Žižek

Five years after the publication of *Hegemony and socialist strategy* (1985), Laclau put out his book *New reflections on the revolution of our time* (1990). As an appendix, he added a text by Slavoj Žižek, which he himself (Laclau) prefaced as follows:

"In October 1987 I participated, together with Chantal Mouffe, in a conference in Ljubljana, organized by the Institute for Marxist Studies of the Slovenian Academy of Arts and Sciences, on 'New Social Movements as a Political Dimension of Metaphor'. As the conference coincided with the publication of the Slovenian edition of *Hegemony and Socialist Strategy*, it was partly devoted to the discussion of the latter. Among the various contributions there was a remarkable piece by Slavoj Žižek which touches on central aspects of the issues discussed in the present volume. We reproduce it as an appendix, with the kind permission of its author."[42]

Žižek's text opens with a "spurning", so to speak, of all "conventional" readings of *Hegemony and socialist strategy*, which place it together with post-structuralism, either in agreement with the latter—and consequently with the book—or in order to use this as a basis for critique. It is of some importance that Žižek in this rather facile fashion passes over the critique that had been carried out on the basis of "we cannot dissolve all reality into a

---

42. Ernesto Laclau, *New reflections on the revolution of our time*, London: Verso, 1990, p. 247.

language-game, etc.", in order to concentrate on what he considers to be the more crucial contribution of the book, which consists in that it has, "so to speak, reinvented the Lacanian notion of the Real as impossible", and in that it has "made it useful as a tool for social and ideological analysis".[43]

The use of the Lacanian concept of the real by Žižek himself is not something that concerns us here. The more crucial contribution of Žižek in my view consists in demonstrating that Laclau and Mouffe are indeed differentiated from poststructuralism *precisely as to the issue that was pointed out above*—as well as in investigating the significance of this differentiation.

Žižek's intervention mainly consists in the further theoretical elaboration of the vertical dimension in Laclau and Mouffe, that is, of the dimension of "antagonistic" indeterminacy. Let me say right from the start: this is a theorist who is Hegelian to the core, and who Hegelianises in his stride, by way of his "readings", any theoretical discourse that catches his fancy—starting with Lacan. The thing is though that in Laclau and Mouffe's case the Hegelian design is already there. In a both latent and erroneous form, however—as if it had been waiting for Žižek to arrive two years later both to unveil it and amend it. I believe the laudatory presentation of Žižek's text by Laclau himself quite easily allows us to draw such a conclusion.

The "amendment" mainly consists in the *interiorisation* of the antagonistic relation. While for Laclau and Mouffe the relation of antagonism is characterised by exteriority, and, what is more, this is something that distinguishes it, as we have seen, from the horizontal dimension, the fact that they insist talking about absence of "full identity" that the presence of one term of the antagonism causes to the other, provides Žižek with the opportunity to claim that it is a matter of an "intrinsic, immanent impossibility" for full identity, and that the antagonistic term is merely the way in which we "'project' or 'externalize'" this impossibility.[44]

The "unveiling" on the part of Žižek is I think best summarised in the formulation with which he characterises the scheme of antagonism in Laclau and Mouffe after his own corrective intervention: "That would be the last lesson of the famous Hegelian dialectics of the Lord and the Bondsman, the lesson usually overlooked by Marxist reading: the Lord is ultimately an invention of the Bondsman, a way for the Bondsman to 'give way as to his desire', to evade the blockade of his own desire by projecting its reason into the external repression of the Lord."[45]

Appearances notwithstanding, we could not reproach Žižek for extreme idealism. He does not deny the existence of the real other, the real opponent, and consequently the existence of real antagonism, he just distinguishes

---

43. *Ibid.*, p. 249. For a more recent exchange between Laclau and Žižek, see Judith Butler, Ernesto Laclau and Slavoj Žižek, *Contingency, hegemony, universality: Contemporary dialogues on the left*, London and New York: Verso, 2000.

44. Laclau, *op. cit.*, pp. 251-254.

45. *Ibid.*, p. 252.

it from the process of the non-completion of identity. In Žižek—and in Laclau and Mouffe to the extent that they accept this reading of their theory—the antagonistic other is something like Cavafy's "barbarians". They exist, but they function as an *alibi* for the *interior* impossibility of completion. In this sense, as Žižek characteristically puts it, "the moment of victory [over the enemy—or, in Cavafy's terms, the moment we realise that the barbarians are not coming] is the moment of greatest loss", the "moment called by Hegel 'the loss of the loss'", the moment we feel that "we *never had* what we were supposed to have lost".[46]

Something else that Žižek adds to Laclau and Mouffe's approach is the way he conceives of the notion of the subject. As we have seen, in Laclau and Mouffe the subject exists only as "'subject positions' within a discursive structure". For Žižek there is a more "radical" concept of the subject, which he insists that he bases on Lacan, and which is precisely "this internal limit, this internal impossibility", the "experience of 'pure' antagonism as self-hindering, self-blockage [...] preventing the symbolic field from realizing its full identity".[47]

It is of some importance at this point to comprehend the way in which Žižek utilises Lacanian conceptualisation. In a manner equivalent to that in which Laclau and Mouffe base their approach on the "syntagmatic"/horizontal and the "paradigmatic"/vertical dimension of Saussurian linguistics, Žižek transfers some terms from Lacanian psychoanalysis and correlates them with the above two dimensions. He moves one step further though, to the abolition of the distinction between subjectivity and objectivity. As we have seen, the "contribution" of Laclau and Mouffe in this direction mainly consisted in the confusion, as to the horizontal dimension, between the objects *of knowledge*—a field *primarily* subjective—and the objectivity of material entities. Žižek takes this confusion for granted, and further consolidates it, on the one hand by identifying the Lacanian symbolic with this (horizontal) dimension (when in fact the Lacanian symbolic is discourse and language in general, not merely one of their dimensions), and, on the other hand, perhaps more importantly, by apparently including within this "symbolic field" what he calls "social *reality* of the antagonistic fight". He considers the latter as equivalent to "antagonistic subject-positions", and he distinguishes both these and their "social *reality*" from "pure antagonism", which in its turn marks *par excellence*—like the term "antagonism" in Laclau and Mouffe—the "vertical" dimension. Which is the Lacanian term that Žižek correlates with the "vertical" dimension? Given the strongly subjective tinge of his conceptualisation around "pure" antagonism, one would expect that this term would be the "imaginary". But Žižek chooses the term "real".[48]

---

46. *Ibid.*, p. 252.

47. *Ibid.*, pp. 253-254.

48. *Ibid.*, pp. 253.

So "antagonistic subject-positions" together with the "social *reality* of the antagonistic fight" are included in the "symbolic field", while the Lacanian "subject" in common with "pure antagonism" make up the "real". I will not be concerned here with investigating whether one can actually find relevant or equivalent conceptualisations in Lacan's exceptionally abstruse and multiply interpretable work. Nor is it my intention to take on certain psychoanalytic or social-theoretical orthodoxies about questions of the "correct use of terminology". I will disregard the issue of "correct or false" terminology in order to allow myself to move on to what in my view are more important matters—after merely expressing here a slight bafflement regarding the dimension of the "real". If Lacan indeed had in mind something *so* radically different from the current, "everyday" sense of "reality" and "real relations", why did he pick the word "real"?

Žižek's position is based on some "definition" Lacan gives of the real: "The real is the impossible".[49] And he specifies in a Hegelian manner the "impossible" so that it means "internal impossibility" of "realising" full identity. So the (Lacanian) "subject" according to Žižek is "real" in the sense that it marks precisely this non-realisation: "The subject is a paradoxical entity which is so to speak its own negative, i.e. which persists only insofar as its full realization is blocked—the fully realized subject would be no longer subject but substance."[50]

At the cornerstone of Žižek's reasoning there is a fundamental misapprehension, which is irrelevant to the correct or incorrect use of Lacanian terminology. Let us say that the question concerning this misapprehension is "purely philosophical". To know if this misapprehension is intentional or unwitting is impossible (not in a "Lacanian" sense impossible, simply impossible). Žižek starts the presentation of Laclau and Mouffe's positions in *Hegemony* by mentioning how the two thinkers conceive of the "subject", before moving on to modify their view in the way we saw above:

> "The main thrust of its [*Hegemony's*] argumentation is directed against the classical notion of the *subject* as a substantial, essential entity, given in advance, dominating the social process and not being produced by the contingency of the discursive process itself: against this notion, they affirm that what we have is a series of particular subject-positions (feminist, ecologist, democratic...)

---

49. Jacques Lacan, *Le Séminaire, livre XI: Les quatre concepts fondamentaux de la psychanalyse, 1964*, Paris: Seuil, 1973, p. 152 ff. For an alternative interpretation of this statement by Lacan, see the Translator's note in: *The four fundamental concepts of psychoanalysis* (translated by Alan Sheridan), Harmondsworth: Penguin Books, 1979, p. 280. On the Lacanian terms *imaginary* and *symbolic*, see Jean Laplanche and J.-B. Pontalis, *The language of psycho-analysis* (translated by Donald Nicholson-Smith), London: The Hogarth Press and the Institute of Psycho-Analysis, 1973, pp. 210 and 439-441. On recent literature regarding the Lacanian *real*, see Yannis Stavrakakis, *The Lacanian left: Psychoanalysis, theory, politics*, Edinburgh: Edinburgh University Press, 2007.

50. Laclau, *op. cit.*, pp. 253-254.

the signification of which is not fixed in advance: it changes according to the way they are articulated in a series of equivalences through the metaphoric surplus which defines the identity of every one of them."[51]

It is quite obvious; here Žižek refers to something which is indeed a common target of many "post-structuralist" views (quotation marks here are Žižek's – one assumes, so as to dissociate himself but ultimately Laclau and Mouffe as well), and which consists in demonstrating the constitution of the subject: more particularly, as also Žižek himself puts it, in *criticising the classical notion of the subject as a substantial entity*—a target which, even though it only became a frequent theme of critical thought in the post-war period, draws its origin in the critique that Kant carried out on the *"psychological paralogism"*, and which forms perhaps the central issue within the more general framework of the *critique of hypostatisation*.[52]

With the modification that he attempts to effect on Laclau and Mouffe's approach, Žižek does not of course intend to reinstate the classical concept of the subject. What is it then that he is trying to do with it?

Let us go back to one of his already cited formulations: "the fully realized subject would be no longer subject but substance". With reference to what has just been mentioned, what could this mean? Where does Žižek stand as to the critique of hypostatisation?

If we take what he says at face value, we have to assume that the "full realisation of the subject" would coincide with the *full constitution of the subject in the symbolic field*: "...the Lacanian notion of the subject aims precisely at the experience of 'pure' antagonism as self-hindering, self-blockage, this internal limit preventing the symbolic field from realising its full identity".[53] In other words, a fully constituted (in the symbolic field) subject *would not be a subject, it would be a substance, i.e. a hypostasis*. In this formulation, we can discern a correct conceptualisation and an abysmal confusion. Let us start with the former.

Indeed, *subject* and *substance or hypostasis* are counterposed by definition—at least if we agree that the subject is defined as an entity which thinks, which forms concepts, and that hypostasis or substance is what exists independently of thought and concepts, in other words, that which is an objective entity *in a primary sense* (that is, not in the sense of an object *of knowledge*). And one of the main hypostatisations, that is, one of the main

---

51. *Ibid.*, p. 250.

52. Immanuel Kant, *Kritik der reinen Vernunft*, Frankfurt: Suhrkamp, 1974 (first edition: 1781, second edition: 1787), pp. 341-399 – English translation (J.M.D. Meiklejohn): *Critique of pure reason*, London: Dent, 1934, pp. 233-249. See also Kyrkos Doxiadis, "Foucault and ideology" (translated by Yvonne Kosma), in *Society, ideology, morality* (in Greek), Athens: Plethron, 2001, p. 30 ff.

53. Laclau, *op. cit.*, p. 253.

illusions that make up hypostatisation and critical thought since Kant has sought to expose as illusions, is *to consider the subject as a hypostasis*.[54]

However, the very concept of the *constitution* of the subject, that is, to treat the subject as *constituted*, presupposes that one has *refuted* the subject as hypostasis—since, according to what also Žižek himself says, the demonstration of the constitution of the subject is a mode of *critique* of the subject as a substantial entity. The "full realisation" of the *subject*, if we agree that it is tantamount to its "full *constitution*", is not there in the thought of any "poststructuralist" *anyway*; the concept of "fullness" itself coinciding with the *illusion of hypostatisation*, ever since Kant exposed as an illusion the hypostatisation of the "idea" or "regulative principle" of the "systematic" or "in conformity with aims [zweckmäßigen] unity".[55] *The subject is either considered as "full" to start with, that is, it is hypostatised, or else it is considered as being constituted, that is, the critique of hypostatisation, and consequently of "fullness", has already been put into effect.*

One can discern two complementary to each other misleading gestures in Žižek's approach. We could say that the first one is simply the "upshot" of a confusion that is already present in Laclau and Mouffe and to which I referred above at length. When Žižek equates the (*impossible*, according to himself) "full realisation of identity in the symbolic field" with the conversion of the subject to hypostasis, he is actually taking to extremes the line of thought that substitutes the *real* object with the object *of knowledge*. As we have seen, in Laclau and Mouffe, the system of differences, either on the level of language or on that of society, aims at the *constitution of the object*, and fails in completing the constitution process due to the existence of antagonism. In their case, the substitution mainly consists in a confusion between cognitive determination (i.e. a primarily subjective entity) and determination as (real) causality/necessity; a confusion aggravated by the authors' insistence on stressing the *material* character of "discourse", which includes the dimension of antagonism. Žižek is content with considering that what he calls "symbolic", which corresponds to Laclau and Mouffe's "syntagmatic" dimension, also includes real relations anyway, and that in its (impossible) full realisation ends up being a substance, i.e. an object in the primary sense.

The second misleading gesture on Žižek's part consists in the following. Hitherto, in critical thought since Kant, the refutation or the avoidance of hypostatisation came about as a result of the *critique*—that is, of the exposure—of the hypostatising illusion. It is important to note here that it is not a matter of an illusion in the simple sense of a lie, a fraud or an error, but

---

54. Immanuel Kant, *Prolegomena zu einer jeden künftigen Metaphysik, die als Wissenschaft wird auftreten können*, Stuttgardt: Philipp Reclam jun., 1989 (first edition: 1783), pp. 105-111 - English translation (Paul Carus): *Prolegomena to any future metaphysics that can qualify as a science*, Chicago and La Salle, Illinois: Open Court Publishing Company, 1902, pp. 99-104.

55. Kant, *Kritik der reinen Vernunft*, p. 598 ff. – English translation: p. 399 ff.

of what Kant calls "unavoidable illusions" of reason,[56] one of which is the "psychological paralogism", that is, the hypostatised subject. In Žižek, the avoidance of hypostatisation, that is, of the conversion of the subject to a hypostasis, comes about with the subversion/hindering of the full realisation of a "symbolic" but at the same time real process by the—in Žižek's terms—Lacanian "real", by "pure antagonism", that is, ultimately, by a variation of the (once again in Žižek's terms) Hegelian Lord/Bondsman dialectic: by the impossibility of completion inherent in the subject's identity.

The above approach by Žižek may have two consequences. In one case, we are led to an utter impossibility of practicing critique. Since the impossibility of the completion of the subject's identity and consequently of its conversion into hypostasis is there anyway due to the intervention of the "real", there is no point in any sort of critique. But there is also the case that Žižek may mean that critique consists in *becoming aware* of the inherent impossibility of identity completion, in the sense of "pure antagonism". And it seems that this is actually what he means, at least at some points.

Together with Laclau and Mouffe's theory he also "modifies" Althusser's theory of ideology, on which the former is partly based. So he claims that, during the process of ideological "interpellation", the ideological illusion consists not in the *misrecognition* of class antagonism or of the relations of production, as Althusser would say,[57] but *on the contrary*, in the "proletarian's" belief that the cause for the non-completion of his identity as a human being is the external, the real antagonistic other, that is, the "capitalist"—and not the "internal impossibility" of which the real antagonist is just a "projection".[58]

Here of course we have not a simple modification of Althusser's position but a departure from it of several light years, and in two most obvious ways. Firstly, Althusser is not in the least interested in the Hegelian-humanist thesis of the full realisation or non-realisation of the subject's identity. On the contrary, he had most severely criticised precisely this approach to Marxism, and his concern with ideology had this very critique as its starting point.[59] And secondly, perhaps more importantly, Althusser's hair would stand on end if he found out (he died in 1990, the year that Laclau's book with Žižek's text was published) that someone using his theory, even through Laclau and Mouffe's "filtre", even simply *referring* to it, ends up with the view that it's all in the mind, really.

---

56. Kant, *op.cit.*, pp. 339-340 – English translation: pp. 232-233.

57. Louis Althusser, *Positions*, Paris: Éditions sociales, 1976, pp. 133-134 – English translation: Louis Althusser, *Lenin and philosophy and other essays* (translated by Ben Brewster), London: NLB, 1971, pp. 169-170.

58. Laclau, *op. cit.*, pp. 251-252.

59. Louis Althusser, *Pour Marx*, Paris: Éditions la découverte, 1986, pp. 225-258 – English translation (Ben Brewster): *For Marx*, Harmondsworth: Penguin Books, 1969, pp. 219-247. See also Doxiadis, *Subjectivity and power*, pp. 36-38.

I am certainly not interested either in salvaging some Althusserian orthodoxy or in supporting Althusser's obviously economistic approach, summed up in the formulation that what is "misrecognised" in ideological "recognition" is "in the last resort, the reproduction of the relations of production and of the relations deriving from them".[60] I am nonetheless interested in the way in which Žižek conceives of the notion of *critique*.

If he does mean that critique consists in the realisation of the inherent impossibility of identity completion, then we cannot help bringing to mind Engels' well-known thesis on freedom being based on knowledge of necessity.[61] Here of course necessity's place is taken by something equivalent to its opposite, i.e. by indeterminacy—if we take into account that Žižek bases his conception of "pure antagonism" on the equivalent of Laclau and Mouffe's "paradigmatic" dimension, which, as we have seen, is the dimension of indeterminacy. But how far can we accept as "indeterminacy" something inherently within us that cannot be removed no matter how we may be aware of it? In other words, an objection that could be raised both against Engels's initial thesis and its Žižekian variation is this: if we accept that practicing critique is a crucial component of the actual freedom of thought, is it truly freedom of thought and truly critique to become aware of something that can in no way be changed? To rephrase the question in terms of hypostatisation and of the *critique* of hypostatisation: even if we accept that Žižek's scheme consists in the *subversion* of the process whereby the subject would become hypostasis, is it not hypostatisation to consider something non-material to be unchangeable by thought, therefore independent of it, *hence in this (primary) sense as objective?*

A possible answer might be that Žižek, once again in correspondence with Laclau and Mouffe, includes even "pure antagonism" in "materiality". But this case should rather be excluded, since there would then be no sense in the basic modification he effects on Laclau and Mouffe, which is the *internalisation* of antagonism. (In any case, considering *everything* as material entities leaves no space for critique of hypostatisation, for quite apparent reasons, which I will elucidate later.)

I suppose that the answer given by Žižek would focus on pointing out the *negative* nature of "pure antagonism", together with what this entails, according to his own reading of Lacan: the subject as "'the empty space of the structure'", or as "the point of failure of subjectivation",[62] the *impossibility* of the full realisation of the subject's identity, the (Lacanian) real as *impossible*, etc. Therefore, Žižek might say, the reproach that something (non-material) is considered as given, unchangeable, independent of thought,

---

60. See above, fn. 57, and *ibid.*, p. 46 ff.

61. Karl Marx and Friedrich Engels, *Collected works, Volume 25*, London: Lawrence & Wishart, 1987, pp. 105-106.

62. Laclau, *op. cit.*, pp. 251 and 254.

objective, hypostatical, does not stand, simply because that "something" *does not exist, it is not, it is non-Being*, and thus there is no danger of it being considered as hypostasis.

However, the way in which Žižek theorises "negation" *is not itself negative*. I believe that some reference to how he conceives of the Hegelian Lord/Bondsman dialectic will clarify what I mean by this. Interpreting this dialectic in accordance with the concept of "antagonism" in Laclau and Mouffe, he claims that there are two possible readings. The first one, with which he disagrees, views the positivity of each side merely as the negation of the other. The Bondsman is the negation of the Lord and vice versa. "In this case, the antagonistic relationship is in a way symmetrical: each position is only its negative relation to the other (the Lord prevents the Bondsman from achieving full identity with himself and *vice versa*)." According to his reading, however, "the other itself (The Lord, let's say) is, in his positivity, in his fascinating presence, just the positivation of our own—Bondsman's—negative relationship towards ourselves, the positive embodiment of our own self-blockage. The point is that here, the relationship is no longer symmetrical: we cannot say that the Bondsman is also in the same way just the positivation of the negative relationship of the Lord."[63]

My own reading of Žižek now: *negation is subordinated to identity*. The fact that it determines it, that it does not allow it to be completed, that it is its limit, does not in the least detract from the fact that negation *presupposes identity and is included within it*. So however non-completed, liminal, negatively determined, void, this non-identity of the "Lacanian subject", which exists before or after subjectivation, and which remains unscathed by critique and thus independent of thought, cannot but be some form of hypostatisation.

More important though is the specific character that hypostatisation assumes in this case. We have seen that Žižek actually builds his own theory on Laclau and Mouffe's conceptualisation around antagonism. In order to characterise his intervention, I employed at the start the admittedly aphoristic formulation: "he Hegelianises whatever catches his fancy"—perhaps a somewhat unfair formulation in this particular instance, not because he does not Hegelianise, but because Hegelianism is already there in Laclau and Mouffe. It is there in half—the other half is completed by Žižek. I will presently explain what I mean.

We have seen that the main direction of Laclau and Mouffe's whole theoretical elaboration, which at the same time differentiates them from the rest of the "poststructuralists", consists in the radicalisation of the concept of "equivalence", in such a way that the system of *differences* is considered as the stabilising element, while equivalence, which *supports antagonism*, constitutes its *subversion*. In this theoretical movement, we could say that one

---

63. *Ibid.*, p. 253.

observes the first stage of Hegelian reductionism: differences are reduced to opposition. Žižek carries out the second stage: he subordinates opposition to identity.

Žižek often embellishes his texts with jokes. In his first book published in English, *The sublime object of ideology* (1989), one year before Laclau's book that includes his own text as an appendix, he quotes an admittedly very good one: Someone visits an art gallery in Moscow, where he sees a painting carrying the title: "Lenin in Warsaw". The painting shows Lenin's wife in bed with a young member of Komsomol. The bewildered visitor asks the curator: "But where is Lenin?" And he replies, "Lenin is in Warsaw."[64]

I have purposely neglected so far to mention the title of Žižek's text that is included in Laclau's book as an appendix: "Beyond discourse-analysis". The term "discourse-analysis" does not even once appear in Žižek's text. Not even the word "discourse", apart from two or three times mainly towards the beginning of the text, purely incidentally and in the form of an adjective ("discursive"). I suppose that if one were to ask Žižek: "But where is discourse-analysis?", he would answer, in full accordance with the nice joke: "But my text is *beyond* discourse-analysis."

Joking apart, this doubtlessly paradoxical and perhaps for a theoretical text unprecedented disjunction between title and content is probably not accidental. There are two possible explanations, which may both apply, since they complement each other. First, Žižek may indeed believe that with his text as well as his approach in general he *transcends* discourse analysis, in the sense that he disconnects himself—carrying Laclau and Mouffe along with him—from the "poststucturalist" viewpoint. The equation, or in any case the connection, between what Žižek calls "poststructuralism" and discourse analysis is of course not altogether inappropriate, but why couldn't he have picked a more unequivocal title, say, "Beyond poststructuralism"? Let us note furthermore that Laclau, as one can read on the book's backcover, was at the time when Žižek's text was published Director of a graduate programme carrying the title "Ideology and Discourse Analysis", and it would therefore be rather difficult for him to accept his own disconnection, and not merely for official reasons. So we come to a second possible explanation.

There is an extremely important "poststructuralist" thinker, perhaps the most characteristic exponent of "poststructuralism", from whom we may presume that Žižek would not wish to dissociate himself completely. I am referring to Jacques Derrida. I believe that, however serious the differences one may find between Žižek and Derrida, there is something basic that connects them.

Derrida's name is as absent from Žižek's "Beyond discourse-analysis" text as discourse analysis itself. At some particularly crucial point however, Derrida's presence is strongly felt precisely for his being absent. This is at

---

64. Slavoj Žižek, *The sublime object of ideology*, London: Verso, 1989, p. 159.

the point where Žižek, having invoked the Hegelian Lord/Bondsman dialectic so as to internalise Laclau and Mouffe's concept of "antagonism", and attempting to justify this philosophical choice, says the following:

> "This reference to Hegel might seem strange: isn't Hegel the 'absolute idealist' *par excellence*, the philosopher reducing all antagonism to a subordinate moment of the self-mediating identity? But perhaps such a reading of Hegel is itself victim of the 'metaphysics of presence': perhaps another reading is possible where the reference to Hegel enables us to distinguish the pure antagonism from the antagonistic fight in reality. What is at stake in pure antagonism is no longer the fact that—as in an antagonistic fight with the external adversary—all the positivity, all the consistency of our position lies in the negation of the adversary's position and *vice versa*; what is at stake is the fact that the negativity of the other which is preventing me from achieving my full identity with myself is just an externalization of my own auto-negativity, of my self-hindering."[65]

I cannot resist here the temptation of wordplay: Derrida's *absence* here is made manifest by way of the term "metaphysics of *presence*". Perhaps the whole of Derrida's philosophy could be summed up in the formulation that it is a *critique of the "metaphysics of presence"*.[66] So he may well not mention him by name, but Žižek at this particular point could be considered purely Derridean.

I have said that this is a "particularly crucial" point. It is the point where Žižek "apologises", so to speak, for his Hegelianism, as to two vital issues: first, as to the *idealism* of Hegelianism, and second, as to the Hegelian subordination/reduction of antagonism, that is, of opposition, to ("self-mediating") identity. Moreover, there is a way in which the former is directly connected to the latter: the subordination of antagonism to identity is presented as the *concrete expression* of Hegelian idealism.

In a text by Foucault, one finds a similar apostrophe with reference to Hegel; "similar" as to its *rhetorical form*. Semantically, it is in a *more or less inverse* direction. I will cite the extract, because both the rhetorical similarity and the semantic inversion are quite impressive.

> "And yet, how is it that we fail to recognize Hegel as the philosopher of the greatest differences and Leibniz as the thinker of the smallest differences? In actuality, dialectics does not liberate the different; it guarantees, on the contrary, that it can always be recaptured. The dialectical sovereignty of the same consists in permitting the different to exist, but always under the rule of the negative, as an instance of non-being. It may appear as the successful subversion of the Other, but contradiction secretly assists in the salvation of the identical."[67]

---

65. Laclau, *op. cit.*, pp. 252-253.

66. See, for example, Jacques Derrida, *De la grammatologie*, Paris: Éditions de Minuit, 1967, pp. 71-72 – English translation (Gayatri Chakravorty Spivak): *Of grammatology*, Baltimore, Maryland, and London: Johns Hopkins University Press, 1976, p. 49.

67. Michel Foucault («Theatrum philosophicum», 1970), *Dits et écrits: 1954-1988, II*, Paris: Gallimard, 1994, p. 90 – English translation (Donald F. Bouchard and Sherry Simon): Michel Foucault, *Language, counter-memory, practice: Selected essays and interviews*, Oxford: Basil Blackwell, 1977, pp. 184-185 (translation slightly modified).

Both Foucault and Žižek begin their apostrophe with a rhetorical question concerning a "commonly accepted" view regarding Hegel, in order to differentiate themselves from it afterwards. The inversion of course rests in the fact that in Foucault Hegel is presented as only *apparently* dissociated from Leibniz's classical idealism, and as *ultimately* that post-Kantian philosopher who contributes to the "salvation" of identity, while in Žižek this reading—by Foucault, but once again with no name being mentioned—is presented as superficial.

I have said however that there is a *more or less* inverse (semantic) direction. It is of some importance to understand here the *asymmetry* of theoretical correlations and differentiations, because in the realm of theory one does not pick "sides" as one-dimensionally as in politics or in football. I believe that in the case of Žižek, a leading "successor", so to speak, of Laclau and Mouffe, one finds issues intersected and tested, but at the same time disguised and concealed in a misleading fashion, which are important questions of post-war theoretical discourse generally speaking, and which concern the thematic of the present text: discourse analysis and its theoretical/philosophical grounding.

Žižek's reading of Hegel is indeed the inverse of that carried out by Foucault, in that the former refers to the German philosopher positively while the latter does so negatively. On the other hand, the asymmetry of the inversion arises from the fact that Žižek *does not explicitly deny Hegel's idealism, neither the fact that he subordinates antagonism to identity*. Quite the contrary, the very notion that the real opponent, that is, the real other as antagonist, is but the *externalisation* of the "*auto-negativity*" and the "*self-hindering*" that are responsible for the non-completion of identity is precisely the *justification* of the Hegelian notion of the reduction of antagonism to the "*self-mediating*" identity, as Žižek himself puts it a few lines above.

How then does Žižek differ from the, according to him, "commonly accepted" reception of Hegel? In other words, what precisely is the reading of Hegel that "is victim" to the "metaphysics of presence", and from which Žižek consequently wishes to dissociate himself? Excluding the improbable, but also depending on some other evidence to which I will refer further on, I believe that what mainly bothers Žižek at this point is the negative use of the characterisation "idealist", more precisely, the characterisation "*absolute* idealist", in the sense that the adjective "absolute" usually adds a negative semantic charge. Perhaps he would have no particular problem with a *moderate* idealism, and in any case what seems mainly to bother him is the *critique carried out on the basis of the distinction idealism/materialism*.

Up until and including the period when the text published in Laclau's book was written (1987), Žižek's country, Slovenia, was a nation of actually existing socialism. Mistrust towards critique based on the above distinction was consequently a totally to be expected and perfectly justifiable resistance against an antiquated, retrogressive, dogmatic intellectual policing, identified with the mental bureaucracy of those countries' regimes. However, what matters here is that Žižek is not opposed to some classical Marxist *eco-*

nomistic sort of materialism, but to the view that on one hand characterises Hegel as an idealist, which is something clear as daylight and which in itself I suppose that even Žižek would not deny, and on the other—and this is more important—adopts a critical standpoint against the (idealist-Hegelian) subordination of antagonism (and opposition) to identity. And for this reason, even though he has (negatively) referred just above to the *Marxist* reading of the Lord/Bondsman dialectic,[68] he does not, in order to denote the view from which he dissociates himself, employ the term "dogmatism" or "vulgar materialism" or "economism", but rather the Derridean term "metaphysics of presence".

---

68. Laclau, *op. cit.*, p. 252.

Chapter 4
Derrida and the concept of "presence"

Is there indeed a connection, in Derrida himself, of the "metaphysics of presence" with *some sort* of opposition to *some sort* of materialism, or with some sort of opposition to the *distinction* idealism/materialism? It is true that the concept of "presence" in Derrida has been connected with his own version of the critique of the *subject*: of the subject as *present* to its own self, either as "consciousness" or as "transcendental signified".[69] On the other hand though, the specific choice of the term "presence" cannot mark *only* this path of critique. The famous Derridean "deconstruction", which aims precisely at the "*de-construction of the transcendental signified*", is directed first and foremost not against the subject, but against what Derrida calls "*logocentrism*" —which he actually considers as "matrix of idealism"[70]- and the "*metaphysics of presence*".[71]

I quote a lengthy extract from a discussion of Derrida with Jean-Louis Houdebine and Guy Scarpetta in 1971, because I believe it is quite revealing precisely for the way it addresses this issue:

---

69. See, for example, Jacques Derrida, *Positions* (translated by Alan Bass), London: Athlone, 1981, pp. 21-22.

70. *Ibid.*, p. 51.

71. See above, fn. 66.

"If I have not very often used the word 'matter', it is not, as you know, because of some idealist or spiritualist kind of reservation. It is that in the logic of the phase of overturning this concept has been too often reinvested with 'logocentric' values, values associated with those of thing, reality, presence in general, sensible presence, for example, substantial plenitude, content, referent, etc. Realism or sensualism—'empiricism'—are modifications of logocentrism. (I have often insisted on the fact that 'writing' or the 'text' are not reducible *either* to the sensible or visible presence of the graphic or the 'literal'.) In short, the signifier 'matter' appears to me problematical only at the moment when its reinscription cannot avoid making of it a new fundamental principle which, by means of theoretical regression, would be reconstituted into a 'transcendental signified'. It is not only idealism in the narrow sense that falls back upon the transcendental signified. The latter can always come to reassure a metaphysical materialism. It then becomes an ultimate referent, according to the classical logic implied by the value of referent, or it becomes an 'objective reality' absolutely anterior to any work of the mark, the semantic content of a form of presence which guarantees the movement of the text in general from the outside."[72]

What matters here is that Derrida—in line with the largest part of his philosophical practice—elaborates philosophical questions by constantly involving linguistic/semiological concepts. In this particular case, this allows us to discern something which is fundamental in his approach. In the first place, the close connection, which in his view exists in what he calls "metaphysical materialism" and which appears here as a variation of the "metaphysics of presence", between on one hand "presence in general" and its various specifications ("thing", "reality", "sensible presence", "objective reality"), and on the other hand the *linguistic term "referent"*. And in the second place, his conviction that in "metaphysical materialism" the "transcendental *signified*", which idealism "in the narrow sense" falls back upon, acquires the form of an "ultimate *referent*".

So since Derrida himself approaches the problem with a basically linguistic conceptualisation, it would be worth our while to linger on this (as we also did in Laclau and Mouffe's case). Derrida seems here to believe that the problem of "metaphysical materialism" in relation to language manifests itself as to the importance or "value" attributed to the referent. In contending that in the "materialism" from which he dissociates himself the "transcendental signified" is equated with the referent, he is implying that the latter is idealised and then hypostatised, i.e. considered as objectively existing. As a linguistic term, however, the referent is indeed considered, by definition, to be objectively existing, that is, as existing outside and independently of language, but it is in no sense idealised. Again by definition, since it is radically distinguished from the ideational aspect of language, that is, from the signified.[73] Derrida would be right to consider that nevertheless the referent is idealised, in a view about language that would maintain the text is determined by some pre-existing "ultimate" referent. But there is no such view

---

72. *Ibid.*, pp. 64-65.

73. See especially the distinction made by Benveniste, in his critique of the concept of the arbitrariness of the sign in Saussure – see above.

in linguistics. Referents, as long as they are external objects, are indeed considered as existing before language, but not as determining it—once again by definition. How could they, given that the principle of the arbitrariness of the sign means the *non-existence* of a cause-effect relation between referent and sign?[74]

So to what sense of "matter" is Derrida opposed? Is he bothered perhaps by the (linguistic) concept of referent itself as something existing outside language, outside the text, and which is independent of it? I believe in fact that in the critique of the "metaphysics of presence", which is Derrida's central critical target and which is here revealed as "metaphysical materialism", we can discern the foundations of both Žižek's latent or "moderate" idealism and Laclau and Mouffe's peculiar hypostatisation of "discourse". Before I proceed, however, I should once more point out that one has to deal with complex and asymmetrical correlations, the fuller significance of which will emerge only if we also take into account some most important differentiations and divergences.

From the "values associated with those of thing, reality, presence in general, sensible presence, for example, substantial plenitude, content", which Derrida lines up together with the referent as values that were connected to "'logocentric' values", and which therefore form manifestations of the "matter" of "metaphysical materialism", the only one having any sufficiently definite meaning is "sensible presence". So we could presume that he opposes a quite conventional notion of matter as that which is perceivable by the senses. Perhaps more revealing is the distance he keeps, a few pages further down in the same discussion, from the following "determination" of "matter" provided by Houdebine, with a reference to Lenin: "...[matter] is fundamentally determined, as a philosophical concept, by its '"unique" property', as Lenin says, 'of *being an objective reality*, of existing outside our consciousness'".[75] That is, he also keeps his distance from the notion of matter as having the exclusive (I presume that this is here the meaning of '"unique"') property of objective existence.

Let us now see Derrida's *positive* relation to the concept of "matter". During the discussion with Houdebine and Scarpetta, both they and Derrida himself bring up the notion of *absolute exteriority* (or "*irreducible heterogeneity*") as roughly synonymous with that of matter.[76] Even though in these same pages Derrida questions the possibility of existence of the "*concept*" of absolute exteriority, as we will see further down, exteriority is indeed a crucial notion in his thought. So our first reaction would be to say that Žižek wrongly invokes the critique of the "metaphysics of presence" in order to justify the *internalisation* of the Hegelian Lord/Bondsman dialectic, given that the former is based on exteriority.

---

74. I refer to Benveniste's same critique.

75. *Ibid.*, pp. 73-75.

76. *Ibid.*, pp. 60-64.

The essential issue, however, does not lie in whether we have to do with exteriority in the case of Derrida and interiority in the case of Žižek, but in whether in either case we have to do with materialism or idealism; in whether, that is, as I maintained above, the deeper philosophical background to the Derridean critique of the "metaphysics of presence" does indeed provide a theoretical alibi to Žižek's idealism, or whether I unjustly reproach Derrida for (crypto-) idealism, maybe Žižek too, and—why not?—Hegel as well, in the sense that it might be assumed, in this latter case, that the critique of the "metaphysics of presence" would serve as a basis for a *materialist reading* of Hegel, similar to the reading suggested by Žižek.

So the basic question is to what extent we could hold that the way in which Derrida elaborates the concept of exteriority provides the foundations for a philosophical materialism. Regardless therefore of whether Žižek is "justified" or not in using Derrida as an alibi for the internalisation he effects, our concern is to investigate Derridean "exteriority" having in mind the above question.

First of all, exteriority as to what? As we saw just above, Derrida keeps his distance from the "Leninist" thesis that a fundamental (and exclusive) property of matter is *its objective existence outside consciousness*. On the other hand though, the critique of the "logocentrism" (or "phonocentrism") of the Western conception of language and the linguistic sign, which is the central specification of the critique of the "metaphysics of presence", at least in the first period of Derrida's work, aims mainly to demonstrate *the exteriority of the signifier in relation to consciousness*. I quote an extract from a discussion of Derrida with Julia Kristeva in 1968, which is included in the same volume:

> "*Phonē*, in effect, is the signifying substance *given to consciousness* as that which is most intimately tied to the thought of the signified concept. From this point of view, the voice is consciousness itself. When I speak, not only am I conscious of being present for what I think, but I am conscious also of keeping as close as possible to my thought, or to the 'concept', a signifier that does not fall into the world, a signifier that I hear as soon as I emit it, that seems to depend upon my pure and free spontaneity, requiring the use of no instrument, no accessory, no force taken from the world. Not only do the signifier and the signified seem to unite, but also, in this confusion, the signifier seems to erase itself or to become transparent, in order to allow the concept to present itself as what it is, referring to nothing other than its presence. The exteriority of the signifier seems reduced. Naturally this experience is a lure, but a lure whose necessity has organized an entire structure, or an entire epoch; and on the grounds of this epoch a semiology has been constituted whose concepts and fundamental presuppositions are quite discernible from Plato to Husserl, passing through Aristotle, Rousseau, Hegel, etc."[77]

77.*Ibid*, p. 22. Elsewhere Derrida also connects the "experience" of the voice/consciousness identification with the Cartesian cogito - Derrida, *De la grammatologie*, pp. 146-147 – English translation: pp. 97-98.

Here of course the crucial phrase is: "The exteriority of the signifier seems reduced." Immediately after this, Derrida specifies the critique of the "reduction of the exteriority of the signifier" by criticising Saussure for "'psychologism'", in so far as the latter considers the linguistic sign as a "'a two-sided *psychic* entity'", and consequently includes semiology in "general psychology".[78]

How convincing is the division: on one hand, "interiority = psychicality", and on the other, "exteriority = materiality"? Saussure himself has already undermined this division, since, in those same paragraphs where he talks about the linguistic sign as a "two-sided psychological entity", he says: "The sound-image is sensory, and if I happen to call it 'material', it is only in that sense, and by way of opposing it to the other term of the association, the concept, which is generally more abstract."[79] But "that sense only", *being sensory*, is obviously sufficient in this particular case. Something may be internal, in the sense of having been internalised by means of the senses, and at the same time material: since Saussure *distinguishes it from the concept*, he cannot but accept its materiality, even if "only" in the sense of being sensory. Besides, the very notion of being sensory also warrants *its external origin*. Given all these, we should rather accept that, according to the approach that he himself follows, the fact that he employs the term "psychological entity" to include also the sound-image, i.e. the signifier, together with the fact that he characterises the latter as "the psychological imprint of the sound",[80] consists in a misuse of the word "psychological". The essence of the Saussurian conception of the signifier is materialist.

To be sure, Derrida refers to the "experience of the voice" as a *lure* of Western thought, which has to do the proximity of the voice to consciousness etc. In so far as something like that is true, that is, in so far as there is in fact a tendency in Western thought to experience the voice as something transparent, dematerialised, and to confuse it with thought itself, we cannot but agree with Derrida's critique—"phonocentrism", in this sense, leads to the hypostatisation of thought: the voice as thought is first idealised, and then objectivised, that is, considered as existing independently of thought itself.

Derrida's "alternative" to phono-logo-centrism is quite well-known, and it is about time to concern ourselves with it: writing as *différance*.[81] Derrida constructs the "neographism" *différance* (instead of *différence*), so as to remind us that he uses a noun that corresponds *at once* to both senses of the

---

78. Derrida, *Positions*, pp. 22-23. Saussure, *op. cit.*, pp. 66 and 15-16.

79. *Ibid.*, p. 66.

80. *Ibid.*, p. 66.

81. I retain untranslated the Derridean French term *différance*, following the wise choice of at least one English translator.

verb *différer* – which means "to differ" but also "to defer": that is, it is a noun meaning *at once* "difference" but also "deference".[82]

He retains, in other words, the fundamental Saussurian principle that meaning in language is produced in a system of elements differing from each other, that is, signs, and that in this sense there is no stable relationship between signifier and signified, that this relationship is constantly being determined by its relations with other signs. He "radicalises" however this principle, by claiming that in this way the production of meaning is constantly (and indefinitely) *deferred*. It is within the framework of this logic that he substitutes the phonocentric, in at least one of its dimensions, concept of the linguistic *sign* with its "grammatological" equivalent: *gram*. Whereas in the Saussurian *sign*, according to its phonocentric reception, consciousness, being identified with the voice, is presented to itself as what it is, on the basis of a lure of a self-presence that has no need of an exterior instrument or accessory, the Derridean *gram*, as an element at once *differing* and *deferring*, is a *trace* of pre-existing or external signifying systems — better still: systems of writing — and in this sense, by subverting the presence/absence distinction, it undermines every presence: either of consciousness to itself, or of some "present" signified or referent, which the signifier or sign respectively is considered as simply *re*-presenting.[83]

It is important to stress that the conceptualisation of Derridean *différance*, even though it is significantly differentiated from the "classical" Saussurian approach, has as at least one of its fundamental starting points the notion of *difference* that is crucial in that approach, and, what is more, in its most subversive sense, which in fact, as we have seen, he "radicalises" further. To go back for a moment to Laclau and Mouffe and to their close but problematic relation with the poststructuralists that we mentioned: as to this point at least, it is odd indeed how they manage to refer positively to Derrida,[84] and at the same time to classify difference among the "conservative" or "stabilising" components of language and society (see above). But I will come back to this.

So we could say that the concept of writing as *différance* is the way in which Derrida specifies *exteriority*. (And in this he most evidently differs from Laclau and Mouffe, who, as we have seen, line up difference with interiority, considering language and society as — unsuccessfully, because of *antagonism* — *closed* systems of *differences*.) Perhaps more than the "neographism" *différance*, what should here concern us is the first part of the concept: the term *writing* (*écriture*). Why does Derrida choose the word "writing" to specify *différance*? An answer of course would be that he wishes to distinguish *différance* from the concept of *speech*, which entails, potentially at least, elements of phonocentrism. And we could possibly accept that something similar applies, even if to a lesser extent, to the concept of *discourse* (*discours*).

---

82. See Derrida, *De la grammatologie*, p. 97 – English translation: pp. 66-67.

83. See Derrida, *Positions*, pp. 25-29.

84. Laclau and Mouffe, *op.cit.*, pp. 111-112.

Since however he ultimately treats even speech itself in terms of *différance*,[85] why does he not simply choose the word *language* (*langage*), which includes speech but also writing? Why does he not talk (or write) about *language* as *différance*?

I suppose that an answer to this would be that in the concept of writing *there is more emphasis on exteriority*. With reference to the above extract from the discussion with Kristeva, a concrete manifestation of writing's exteriority is the inevitable use of *external instruments*: indeed, in order to write you need pen and paper, or a computer. But how important is this "sensualist", in some sense, conception of exteriority for Derrida's thought? In another extract we cited, this time from the discussion with Houdebine and Scarpetta, he has said (in parenthesis): "(I have often insisted on the fact that 'writing' or the 'text' are not reducible *either* to the sensible or visible presence of the graphic or the 'literal'.)"

It is well-known that Derrida devoted a bulky portion of his first texts, especially in *Of Grammatology*, to demonstrate an axiological priority enjoyed by speech as opposed to writing in the whole history of Western thought, an axiological priority that also forms the basis, or the main characteristic, of Western culture's phono-logo-centrism. His central argument has to do with the false, in his view, conception of *writing as representation of speech* that has prevailed in Western thought. From within his extremely elaborate reading of philosophical and linguistic texts, we can all the same discern two crucial aims of his reasoning that refer to a rather simple cultural *event*: *First*, to point out the *hellenocentric* character of the Western conception of writing, which falsely, in his view, tends to equate writing in general with the system of writing that prevailed with the establishment of the phonetic alphabet by the ancient Greeks. *Second*, to demonstrate that not even "so-called", as he calls it, phonetic writing is truly phonetic, i.e. that not even the systems of writing based on a phonetic alphabet form a representation of speech.

Let us assume that both the above assertions by Derrida are correct. In such a case, the question that is raised is the following: if we accept that writing indeed, either as writing in general or as "so-called" phonetic writing, is not a representation of speech, then what is there remaining from the concept of writing that would justify the existence of the term? Derrida could be content with the term *différance* to describe the non-phonocentric properties of language or signifying systems. Why does he insist on the term "writing", against all its conventional significations?

I quote an extract from a text by Derrida on Freud, in which he refers in a quite characteristic and revealing fashion to how he conceives of "writing":

> "We have already defined elsewhere the fundamental property of writing, in a difficult sense of the word, as *spacing*: diastem and time becoming space; an unfolding as well, on an original site, of meanings which irreversible, linear consecution, moving from point of presence to point of presence, could only tend to repress, and (to a certain extent) could only fail to repress. In particular in

---

85. See Derrida, *op. cit.*, p. 27.

so-called phonetic writing. The latter's complicity with logos (or the time of logic), which is dominated by the principle of noncontradiction, the cornerstone of all metaphysics of presence, is profound. Now in every silent or not wholly phonic spacing out of meaning, concatenations are possible which no longer obey the linearity of logical time, the time of consciousness or pre-consciousness, the time of 'verbal representations'. The border between the non-phonetic space of writing (even 'phonetic' writing) and the space of the stage (*scène*) of dreams is uncertain."[86]

We are here presented with a quite fascinating image of "writing" as liberated from the linear sequence of time, comparable indeed with the imaginative spatiality and noetic unfolding of dreams. At the same time, however, what we witness being systematised is a classification of "negative" and "positive" elements, on the basis of which Derrida, on one hand, practices his critique of what he calls "metaphysics of presence", and on the other, counterproposes, in place of the latter and the logo-phonocentrism that goes with it, his own, "difficult" sense of spacing and writing.

So on the "negative" side, that is, on the side of the "*metaphysics of presence*", we have: time, irreversibility, linearity, moving from point of presence to point of presence, so-called phonetic writing, logos, time of logic, of consciousness, of pre-consciousness and "verbal representations", the principle of noncontradiction. While on the "positive" side, which is to say on the side of "*writing*": spacing, becoming space, unfolding of meanings, silent or not purely phonic spacing of meaning, non-phonetic space of writing (even "phonetic" writing), the space of the stage of dreams.

As to the "metaphysics of presence" side, perhaps we can grasp the specificity of Derrida's approach if we stay a while on the first three terms: time, irreversibility, linearity. Derrida lines up together the second and third terms, as though he considers them as common properties of the first one, and as though one property presupposes and/or necessitates the other. On the other hand, we know that, while irreversibility forms a fundamental property of time *itself*, linearity does not concern time itself but *its representation*, and, what is more, a certain *form* of its representation: its *graphic*, and more specifically its *geometric* representation. Ultimately, that is, what Derrida calls "*linear* consecution" does not have to do with time itself, but with a *graphic and spatial representation* of time. Which is to say that the time that Derrida wants to dispense with by way of "writing" and "spacing" is *already written and spaced* – representationally, of course. It is just that we have to do with a conventional graphic and spatial representation of time, from which it is perfectly justifiable that Derrida would wish to depart, and to counterpropose in its place a more radical graphicality and spatiality.[87]

---

86. Jacques Derrida, *L'écriture et la différence*, Paris: Seuil, 1967, p. 321 – English translation (Alan Bass): *Writing and difference*, London: Routledge and Kegan Paul, 1978, p. 217 (translation slightly modified).

87. On this, see also Derrida, *De la grammatologie*, pp. 105-106 – English translation: p. 72.

The problem, however, is that, by joining the fundamental property of irreversibility with the conventional representation of time, he seems as though he wishes to dispense also with time itself.

More accurately, to avoid being considered to reproach Derrida for paradox: the phrase in which irreversibility, linearity, but also the next "negative" element, "moving from point of presence to point of presence", appear in common goes as follows: "irreversible, linear consecution, moving from point of presence to point of presence". I believe that at this point *linearity*, which, as we have seen, forms a property of representation, *intrudes* between *irreversibility* and *moving from point of presence to point of presence*, which do not belong to representation and which *are roughly synonymous*. That is, the term "linear" is used so as to attribute a representational character to something that is signified both as "irreversibility" and as "moving from point of presence to point of presence", and which is actually *not* representation. It is the object on the basis of which representation is *defined*, as *re*-presentation, as *presenting anew*; in other words, *presence* itself: that which representation presents anew. Presence as a general condition is indeed "moving from point of presence to point of presence", there is no *static* presence, not even in what Derrida calls "metaphysics of presence". At the same time, "moving from point of presence to point of presence" is a way of describing the irreversible—which is to say the *temporal*—property of presence. Someone or something that has moved from point A to point B was present before at A and is present now at B, and this is irreversible in the sense that someone or something cannot be present at both points at once. And the equivalent applies to time itself: the present moment, when some other moment is now present, has passed irretrievably.

This Derrida calls linearity, he equates it with the "time of logic", and I suppose that this is mainly to what he refers with the "principle of noncontradiction", which forms "the cornerstone of all metaphysics of presence". I repeat that if it were *only* a matter of a critique of the phonocentric hypostatisation of the "voice-as-consciousness", one would not hesitate to agree with his critique. Derrida's target though here seems much broader: by representationalising and "logicising" what he calls "presence", thereby transforming it into a "*metaphysics* of presence", he tends towards displacing critical thought's centre of gravity *from the critique of representation to the critique of presence*; in other words, from the critique of representation *itself* to the critique of its *object*; which is something that amounts to the re-introduction of critical philosophy into the *philosophy of representation*, concurrently with its withdrawal from the *philosophy of the object* of representation. In accordance with the terms in which the issue has been posed since Kantian critical philosophy, we would suggest that in this sense Derrida's intervention, perhaps in a way more effective than other relevant contemporary approaches (as to the range of his influence), marks the return of critical thought to the *philosophy of the infinite* and its withdrawal from the *philosophy of finitude*.

I am aware that we are now entering very "deep waters", and for this reason I will approach the issue by first making a remark of a more "historical" sort, so that the reader may have a picture of what kind of theoretical stakes I have in mind. I have maintained elsewhere[88] that perhaps Foucault's most subversive contribution to contemporary critical thought was the demonstration of a radical discontinuity in modern thought and knowledge, which dates around the turn of the eighteenth to the nineteenth century. This is focused on the infinite/finitude question, which in the realm of philosophy is manifested with a corresponding discontinuity between Cartesian and Kantian philosophy. Foucault's critical target was Hegelianism and phenomenology in their several variations, including existentialism, which rested on the *denial* of this discontinuity and on the establishment of a continuous course in philosophical development since Descartes.[89] I believe that a more important manifestation of the radical differentiation between Foucault and Derrida than their row over the interpretation of an excerpt from Descartes's *Meditations*[90] has to do with the fact the latter's work forms an attempt not merely at the *unification* of the philosophy of finitude with the philosophy of the infinite (which unification as a rule results at the expense of the former anyway[91]), but at a *complete restoration* and *predominance* of the latter as to the scope of critique itself – that is, as to *what constitutes the very target of critique*.

In the critical philosophy of finitude, the central target of critique is the hypostatised infinite, which is to say the infinite considered as objectively existing, on the basis of the axiomatic principle that the only objectively existing entities are fundamentally finite – which means finite by themselves and not determined as finite by some infinite entity. We could in fact consider as a materialist version of the critical philosophy of finitude the philosophy that is based on the axiomatic acceptance that two *fundamental and exclusive* properties of material entities are *fundamental finitude and objective*

---

88. Doxiadis, "Foucault and ideology", pp. 11-42.

89. See Kyrkos Doxiadis, "Foucault and the three-headed king: State, ideology and theory as targets of critique", *Economy and Society*, Volume 26, Number 4, November 1997, pp. 518-545.

90. Derrida, *L'écriture et la différence*, pp. 51-97 –English translation: pp. 31-63-, Foucault, *Dits et écrits: 1954-1988, II*, pp. 245-268 and 281-295 –English translation (Jonathan Murphy and Jean Khalfa): Michel Foucault, *History of madness*, London and New York: Routledge, 2006, pp. 550-590-, and Jacques Derrida, *Résistances de la psychanalyse*, Paris: Galilée, pp. 89-146 – English translation (Peggy Kamuf, Pascale-Anne Brault and Michael Naas): *Resistances of psychoanalysis*, Stanford, California: Stanford University Press, 1998, pp. 70-118.

91. See, for example, in Hegel's *Philosophy of right*: "The actual Idea is mind, which, sundering itself into the two ideal spheres of its concept, family and civil society, enters upon its finite phase, but it does so only in order to rise above its ideality and become explicit as infinite actual mind." - Georg Wilhelm Friedrich Hegel, *Grundlinien der Philosophie des Rechts*, Frankfurt: Suhrkamp, 1982, p. 410 – English translation (T.M. Knox): *Philosophy of Right*, New York: Oxford University Press, 1967, p. 162.

existence - which is to say that *all* material entities and *only these* are fundamentally finite and objectively existing. In this way, there arises a possibility for a *materialist* critique of the hypostatised infinite *from the viewpoint of (fundamental) finitude*. The (materialist) critique of the hypostatised infinite coincides with the critique of *representation as ideology*.[92]

Let us return to Derrida. How can the *object* of representation be a target of critique, either as material entities or as (fundamentally) finite entities or as objective entities (meaning it is not necessarily specified whether these coincide)? The relation of thought to material or (fundamentally) finite or objective reality can only be experimental or technological or, more generally, usage-like, it cannot be critical. In the natural sciences critique has no reason of existence other than as (indigenous) critique of the *discourse* of the natural sciences and of its (technological or otherwise) *applications*. Even in the critique of a socio-economic system, say of capitalism, critique is not addressed towards machines, money or consumer goods themselves, but towards the subjects positively related to it (towards capitalists, towards those that subtract surplus-value), as well as towards the discourses, representations and ideologies that legitimise and sustain it. (Let us also here remind ourselves of the subtitle of Marx's *Capital*.)

The object of representation may form a target of critique as long as the *concept* of representation is criticised. Caution: not representation in some of its concrete manifestations, ideological or otherwise, in which case we would merely have to do with critique of representation and hence there would be no withdrawal from the philosophy of finitude, but as long as the *concept of representation itself* is criticised. More specifically, as long as the target of critique is the *conceptual foundation* of representation, which is the *concept of the object* of representation, that is, the *concept of presence*. What I mean to say is that Derrida, by way of the "representationalisation" of presence to which I referred above, aims at the subversive critique of the *concept* of representation. Quite simply, if one rejects the *concept* of presence, then also the *concept* of *re*-presentation, that is, of *re*-presenting, has no reason for existence.

While explicating above the "representationalisation" of presence, I said Derrida joins the—representational—property of *linearity* with "moving from point of presence to point of presence" and with its roughly synonymous *irreversible—i.e. temporal—property of presence*. As to the former, the response to this joining-confusing effected by Derrida is that there is not necessarily anything linear about moving from point of presence to point of presence. The linear relationship between two points also entails a *continuity* between them, hence the fundamentally representational character of linearity.[93] On the contrary, there may be a movement from point to

---

92. See above, fns. 88 and 89. I will be at length concerned with this below.

93. See Kyrkos Doxiadis, "On the relation of representation to reality" (in Greek), in: Gerassimos Kouzelis and Pantelis Bassakos (eds), *Light – image – reality (topika xi)*, Athens: Nissos, 2006, pp. 87-95.

point with these being *discontinuous*. Besides, one could maintain that it is precisely the conception of movement as *moving between points connected with linear continuity* that renders insoluble the famous Zeno's paradox: the notion of an *infinitely* decreasing (but never annihilated) distance between Achilles and the tortoise is conceivable only *on the basis of a linear, i.e. representational, continuity*. The infinite does not exist objectively, that is, in the *object* of representation or in *presence, not even as infinitely small*. While it does exist of course in representation; but even there in its purely subjective, i.e. in its conceptual dimension. Let us also remind ourselves of the well-known impossibility of the material representation of a (geometric) point. The infinite, whether as infinitely great or as infinitely small, exists only as a concept; *as hypothesis and not as hypostasis*.

Likewise, irreversibility has no necessary connection to linearity. In a linear, i.e. representational relationship between points, one may *intelligibly* go back and forth as many times as one wishes, or even be, *also intelligibly*, at two or more points simultaneously. Irreversibility does not have to do with the "time of logic", nor with the "principle of noncontradiction". It is the most basic specification of the fundamental property of material entities, i.e. of fundamental finitude. "Irreversibility" here means *irreversible finitude*: that is, the condition of something being finite, of having limits, in an *irreversible* manner. This is why irreversible finitude coincides with *temporality*. The fact that something or someone cannot be present at two points at once has to do neither with the logical principle of noncontradiction nor with the *metaphysics* of presence, but with presence *itself*, which is to say with materiality, and consequently with its fundamental, irreversible in this case, finitude: in other words, *with temporality as a fundamental condition of existence of material entities, and not as linear or representational continuity*. On the contrary, fundamental finitude, moreover (fundamental) *irreversible* finitude, which is to say (fundamental) temporality, ensures *radical discontinuity* between material entities: "I am finite", that is, "I have limits", means, among other things: "I have limits *that separate me* from something else, *that prevent me* from being united or *continuous* with it". If we define here *temporality* as *irreversible* finitude, we could also define *spatiality* as finitude *in general*. Spatiality is not necessarily irreversible. Someone or something may move from one point to another. However, as *fundamental* spatiality, that is, as spatiality pertaining to material entities, it neither is linear nor abolishes discontinuity. The movement of material entities is strewn with obstacles.

Chapter 5
Language, writing, representation

Let us return to Derrida's writing as *différance*. According to what we have said so far, as a *critical* concept, as a concept aiming at the critique of some other concept, we could say that *it is what remains from the concept of representation after the critique, that is to say the removal, of the concept of presence.* In other words, it is representation relieved from the *linearity* of "classical" representation, but also, perhaps more importantly, from the *object* of representation: it is representation without a presence to represent. What is left is the question of why he chooses the term "writing". Once again, regarding this matter, Derrida's aim is critical, and once again his position is related to his particular attitude towards representation. As it is well-known, and as we have seen above, Derrida's basic critical stance in relation to writing is summed up in his thesis that *writing does not consist in a representation of speech*, and that this is so even with "so-called", as he calls it, phonetic writing.

So does then Derrida mean that there is *no correspondence whatever* between "so-called" phonetic writing and speech? It would be blatantly paradoxical and Derrida obviously does not claim such a thing. But he seems to be implying that, to the extent that there does exist some relation of correspondence between speech and writing, priority should be given not to the former but to the latter: "It [the spacing of *différance*] is also the becoming-space of the spoken chain—which has been called temporal or linear; a becoming-space which makes possible both writing and every correspondence between speech and writing, every passage from one to the other."[94]

Therefore there is correspondence, but it is not a correspondence whereby writing would form a re-presentation of the "presence" that is speech, but rather a correspondence based on the spacing of *différance*, a spacing that is peculiar to writing but that also leads to the becoming-space of speech and hence to the possibility of correspondence between the two.

In the above extract we notice a specific manifestation of Derrida's tendency to join linearity, which is to say continuity, with temporality, and, in contrast, discontinuity with spatiality. As I have already suggested, (linear) continuity and discontinuity do not have to do with temporality or spatiality but with whether it is a matter of representation or of fundamentally finite, that is material, entities. Derrida himself seems to accept that speech *by itself* is not *necessarily* linear (and "temporal"), but that it "has been called" so. However, he considers as necessary the intervention of writing (as *différance*) so that speech may be "spaced"—that is, according to his view, so that speech can dispense with its linearity.

Compared to speech, however, writing is more linear and continuous. If, in accordance with what I maintained above, we get rid of the coincidence between temporality and linearity, we can readily grasp the *discontinuity of speech*. I am obviously referring to the countless *pauses* that accompany oral discourse, and that attest to the *awkwardness* of the human brain during the operation of speech, the human brain being itself fundamentally finite, with a finite memory and finite capacities of linguistic expression. Discontinuities of course are also brought about by the other, multiple and most frequent, dysfunctions of speech: syntactic errors, incoherences, needless repetitions, slips of the tongue of all sorts, insofar as in language we are concerned with *conceptual* continuity and not with the "purely natural" continuity of a sound (whose existence is highly doubtful anyway, for reasons I explained above, referring to the temporality and spatiality of material entities generally speaking).

There are many, including myself, and, from what I have heard, Derrida himself, who quite often when speaking to some large audience have a written text in front of them, from which they read. It is one of the several occasions of "passage from one to the other" between writing and speech to which Derrida is referring in the above extract. I believe it is a quite revealing case of this relation. If the spacing of *différance* consists in the characteristic of discontinuity shared in common by writing and "spaced" speech, we certainly have no such thing here. On the contrary, the *feeling of security* provided by the written text to someone delivering a speech or a lecture has to with the *ensuring of continuity* provided by writing to speech.

---

94. Derrida, *Positions*, p. 27.

One does not have to sympathise with the axiological priority given to speech by Western culture according to Derrida in order to accept that phonetic writing is a representation of speech. It is no accident that Derrida's main target in *Of Grammatology*, as to this particular issue, is Rousseau, who indeed, within the framework of his naturalistic romanticism, promotes a beautification of the "naturalness" of speech as against the "artificiality" and "complementarity" of writing.[95] But this is not the problem, neither is it of course a matter of "*simple*" representation. Simple representation does not exist. Representation is something highly complex, *creative*, and most importantly *active*. If we accept Foucault's relevant analyses,[96] the main characteristic of the way in which representation operates is the fact that it *classifies* and *orders* the object that it represents. What else does phonetic writing do other than *ordering* speech, putting it *in order, tidying it up*, arranging it in a *continuous sequence*?

Let us attempt to clarify some fundamental concepts. If writing is a *representation* and speech the *object* of this representation, does this mean that speech is an objective entity? Of course not, obviously here, in the case of the object *of representation*, as in the case of the object *of knowledge*, we have to do with a *non-primary* sense of "object".

So let us take things from the start. If we define representation as taxonomic or ordering discourse, as discourse that classifies or orders, then there arises the question of defining the general term, i.e. "discourse". Discourse cannot be defined as something separate from language, and this is apparent even in the case of Laclau and Mouffe, who tend, as we have seen, to attribute to discourse an altogether objectified character: they do the same with language. *To begin with*, we will here remain on a linguistic approach to discourse, taking into account mainly Benveniste's intervention on this particular issue, which marks the passage, in the field of linguistics "*per se*", from a semiological to a so to speak "*post*-semiological" problematic, and which has to do with a *displacement of emphasis* from language as a more or less autonomous system *to the relation of language to referents*.[97] So we opt for a "definition" of discourse that does not separate discourse from language, it merely marks this *epistemic displacement of emphasis*, and we say that *discourse is language in relation to referents*.

---

95. See Derrida, *De la grammatologie*, p. 145 ff. – English translation: p. 97 ff.

96. See Michel Foucault, *Les mots et les choses: Une archéologie des sciences humaines*, Paris: Gallimard, 1966, especially p. 220 –English translation: Michel Foucault, *The order of things: An archaeology of the human sciences*, London: Tavistock, 1974, p. 208-, and above, fn. 93.

97. See especially Émile Benveniste, *Problèmes de linguistique générale, 2*, Paris: Gallimard, 1974, pp. 43-66. This emphasis on the relation to referents I believe is Benveniste's basic *positive* contribution from the viewpoint of discourse analysis. On the other hand, as it has already been seen, I insist that to consider the relation between signifier and signified as a relation of necessity is misleading and perhaps responsible for several manifestations of the virtual abolition of the distinction between objectivity and subjectivity that we are dealing with here.

So coming back to the above definition of representation: representation is language in a *taxonomic or ordering* relation to referents. Thus phonetic writing is a language that orders referents, i.e., in this case, speech. Let us be scrupulously precise and explanatory: The letter *a* is a (linguistic) sign, of which:

- the signifier is *the visual image* of the letter as it is imprinted on our brain when we see it on paper or on the computer screen (as well as afterwards, for as long as we remember it),
- the signified is *the concept of the phoneme* that we know it symbolises, and
- the referent is *the phoneme itself* that it symbolises.

The last one requires special caution. The "phoneme itself" is not a pure sound, in which case we would have a purely objective/material element, but by itself *a (linguistic) sign*: on a different level though, on the level *of speech as language*. So let us move right away onto that level, to see what happens there in terms of "discourse" and "representation", and then we will return to writing. In speech as language, and in the case of the phoneme that is the referent of the letter *a*:

- the signifier is the *sound-image* of the phoneme as it is imprinted on our brain after we hear it,
- the signified is *potentially the corresponding part of the concept* that we will form when the whole word that includes the phoneme is heard, and
- the referent, on this level, on the level of the phoneme, does not exist – in speech as language referents appear from the level *of the word* onwards.

So in speech as language, from the level of the word onwards, as long as there are referents, by definition we will also have *discourse* – consequently we *might* also have *representation*: it will depend on each case, that is, on the extent to which the relation of speech as language to referents is taxonomic/ordering or not. There is no general way of *classifying discourses into taxonomic/ordering and non-taxonomic/non-ordering*, and this is simply because non-taxonomic/non-ordering discourses cannot be classified, since their referents cannot either.

Two things should be noted here. The first is that, since referents appear from the level of the word onwards, *the referentiality of speech is also a way of separating (spoken) words*. In this sense, the extent to which there is continuity between words or not will depend on the continuity of the referents, which, on the other hand, *if it exists, is brought by (speech as) language itself*—ultimately, that is, on the extent to which we have to do *with taxonomic/ordering discourse, i.e. with representation, or not*. There is no self-contradictory circularity here, since we have a *two-way* relationship—between signs and referents—*anyhow*. We merely have one more indication of both the *externality* and the *instability* of the continuity of speech (since it depends on a relation with unstable and largely external referents), two characteristics that are not to be found in (phonetic) writing.

The second thing we should note is that the fact that speech *may not* be taxonomic or ordering, i.e. representational, is what renders it more primary in comparison to phonetic writing. *Not axiologically* more primary, *structurally* more primary. The fact that speech *may not* be in a taxonomic or ordering relation to referents is a consequence of the fact that as a system of communication, as a system of *social* production of meaning, it does not form a representation of some *other* communication system (as it happens in the case of phonetic writing), but is more directly related to the *individual dimension* of communication, *without evading its (anyhow inescapable, by definition) sociality*. And by "individual dimension" I am not referring to anything "transcendental" or having to do with "consciousness", but rather to something material, in fact definitely so: to the human body, and more specifically to the human brain and to the nervous system of the human organism. The arrangement of the sound-images as signifiers is but a way of "putting in order", of "ordering", the function of the human brain that is responsible for the production of meaning. In this sense, speech as language is more primary than phonetic writing, because, even when it has no representational relation to referents, *it forms the "zero degree" of representation*: it forms *a "representation", i.e. an ordering, of itself, and at the same time a precondition for any other (external) representation*.

Nor do I here maintain that there is any exclusiveness of speech as to the function of *primary* language in the above sense. Language could be defined as any *actual ability to form concepts (or to produce meaning)*. We could consider as *primary* language, in the sense of *not necessarily representational language*, certainly the language of the deaf and dumb, perhaps some forms of *non-phonetic* writing, and—why not?—the languages of the various arts, precisely to the extent that art is not necessarily representational.

We now go back to why Derrida insists on the term and the concept of writing. I believe that, from the whole of this highly elaborate part of his work, the most enlightening answer is related on one hand to a concept on which he actually *grounds* writing and *différance* and on the other hand to the way he interprets a certain controversial passage from Saussure to which I have already referred. The concept is *trace*, and the passage is where Saussure, by way of a misuse according to my interpretation of the term "psychological", characterises the signifier as "the psychological imprint of the sound", while he at the same time accepts its material and sensory character.[98]

Derrida too seems to disagree with the use of the term "psychological imprint" for the signifier, but for more or less opposite reasons. He particularly insists on the importance of the distinction between the sound itself and its "imprint", and he interprets this distinction in his own, thoroughly Husserlian-phenomenological fashion. He believes there is an "absolutely decisive heterogeneity", a "radical dissimilarity", between the "appearing sound [*le son apparaissant*]" and the "appearing of the sound [*l'appar-*

---

98. Saussure, *op. cit.*, p. 66.

aître du son]", and he claims that Saussure's "sound-image" or "signifier" is the structure of the latter, which he equates with "what Husserl would name the *hylè/morphè* structure".[99] He is eventually led to a completely abstractive conception of the signifier, to what he calls *trace*, in accordance with which the latter "potentially" pre-exists not only meaning but also every sensory element, abolishing at the same time a whole range of "conventional" distinctions:

> "*The trace is in fact the absolute origin of sense in general. Which amounts to saying once again that there is no absolute origin of sense in general. The trace is the* différance which opens appearance [*l'apparaître*] and signification. Articulating the living upon the nonliving in general, origin of all repetition, origin of ideality, the trace is not more ideal than real, not more intelligible than sensible, not more a transparent signification than an opaque energy and *no concept of metaphysics can describe it*. And as it is *a fortiori* anterior to the distinction between regions of sensibility, anterior to sound as much as to light, is there a sense in establishing a 'natural' hierarchy between the sound-imprint, for example, and the visual (graphic) imprint? The graphic image is not seen; and the acoustic image is not heard. The difference between the full unities of the voice remains unheard. And, the difference in the body of the inscription is also invisible."[100]

One could hardly resist the temptation to say that here we have the substitution of the "transcendental signified"—a constantly and irrevocably professed target of Derrida's critique—with the "transcendental signifier". It would not be arbitrary to infer something like this. The transcendentality of the "trace"-signifier is something *explicitly* established by Derrida in a twofold manner. First, by repeated direct references to Husserl's transcendental phenomenology, concerning mainly the treatment of the "trace" as the "grammatological" equivalent of (phenomenological) "transcendental experience".[101] And second, complementing the first, by the systematic disparagement of the sciences that deal with the study of the function of the brain in relation to the sensory aspects of language: "...the essence of the *phonè* cannot be read directly and primarily in the text of a mundane science, of a psycho-physio-phonetics."[102]

Derrida's "ambiguous" relation to phenomenology is quite well-known. He himself, in those same pages where he is heavily relying on the phenomenological approach regarding both how he interprets Saussure and his—unequivocal, even if indirect—treatment of the "trace" as a transcendental signifier, goes to great length to render this "ambiguity" quite appar-

---

99. Derrida, *op. cit.*, p. 93 – English translation: pp. 63-64.

100. *Ibid.*, p. 95 – English translation: p. 65.

101. *Ibid.*, especially pp. 90-91 – English translation: pp. 61-62.

102. *Ibid.*, p. 95 – English translation: pp. 64-65. It is no accident of course that in order to effect this "transcendentalisation" of the signifier he is mainly relying on the linguistics of Hjelmslev (*ibid.*, especially pp. 83-91 – English translation: pp. 57-62), whose conceptualisation has played a decisive role in what I have elsewhere called "primacy of the signifier" in semiological thought - Louis Hjelmslev, *Prolegomena to a theory of language* (translated by Francis J. Whitfield), Madison, Wisconsin: University of Wisconsin Press, 1961, and Barthes, *op. cit.*, my Afterword, p. 349 ff.

ent: "... *a thought of the trace can no more break with a transcendental phenomenology than be reduced to it.* Here as elsewhere, to pose the problem in terms of choice, to oblige or to believe oneself obliged to answer it by a *yes* or *no*, to conceive of appurtenance as an allegiance or nonappurtenance as plain speaking, is to confuse very different levels, paths, and styles. In the deconstruction of the arche, one does not make a choice."[103]

Derrida obviously has every right to point out the self-evident fact that if one is positively related to some elements of a theoretical approach this does not mean that one totally or even for the most part identifies with it. In this case, however, Derrida's relation to phenomenology is posited in quite specific terms. He *accepts the concept of "transcendental experience", provided this is exempted from the tutelage of the "theme of presence".*[104] It would not be overly schematic to suggest that the concept of the "trace", in a manner analogous with what holds for the conceptualisation of "writing" and *différance* in relation to representation upon which it is directly based, *is but what remains from "transcendental experience" once what Derrida calls "presence" has been removed from it.* And what is more, in this movement of "de-presentation" or "non-presentation" of experience in general and more particularly "transcendental experience", some elements of which, according to Derrida himself, are already there in Husserl,[105] Derrida may well "deconstruct" the "arche" or whatever else. As for phenomenology, not only does he not deconstruct it but he actually promotes further its contribution to the history of modern thought *in the same direction.*

Husserl, in the second part of the Introduction to his *Cartesian meditations* (1929), which is entitled "The necessity of a radical new beginning of philosophy",[106] posits this necessity in relation to the "brilliant development" having taken place during the three centuries that have lapsed since Descartes's *Meditations* in the positive sciences, which "are now feeling themselves greatly hampered by obscurities in their foundations". Transcendental phenomenology should aim at a repetition in contemporary terms of the radical break effected by Descartes, consisting in "a radical turn: from naïve Objectivism to transcendental subjectivism".[107]

The method of transcendental phenomenology consists first and foremost in the "*transcendental-phenomenological reduction*", or in the (Cartesian or phenomenological) "*epoché*", that is, in the "parenthesising" of the objective

---

103. Derrida, *op. cit.*, p. 91 – English translation: p. 62.

104. *Ibid.*, pp. 90-91 – English translation: pp. 61-62.

105. *Ibid.*, p. 91 – English translation: p. 62.

106. Edmund Husserl, *Cartesianische Meditationen: Eine Einleitung in die Phänomenologie*, Hamburg: Felix Meiner, 1977, pp. 5-8 – English translation (Dorion Cairns): *Cartesian meditations: An introduction to phenomenology*, The Hague: Martinus Nijhoff, 1977, pp. 4-6.

107. *Ibid.*, p. 6 – English translation: p. 4

world, the natural world, whatever is accessible through the senses: in not taking for granted either its existence or the validity of the (positive) sciences that approach it, in order to investigate *beforehand* the possibility of a solid subjective basis for any scientific knowledge of the objective world, on a level completely independent of it, and uninfluenced by the "objectivist" prejudices caused by sensory experience.

One of Husserl's main concerns, throughout the largest part of the *Cartesian meditations*, is the insistent effort to include in the natural/objective world, which should be "parenthesised", the psychical reality of the subject. Perhaps most revealing is a paragraph in which he explicates the transcendental-phenomenological method:

> "It would be much too great a mistake, if one said that to follow this line of research is nothing else than to make *psychological descriptions* based on purely internal experience, experience of one's own conscious life, and that naturally, to keep such descriptions pure, one must disregard everything psychophysical. A great mistake, because a *purely descriptive psychology of consciousness* (though its true method has become understandable and available only by virtue of the new phenomenology) is *not itself transcendental phenomenology* as we have defined the latter, in terms of the transcendental phenomenological reduction. To be sure, pure psychology of consciousness is a *precise parallel* to transcendental phenomenology of consciousness. Nevertheless the two must at first be kept strictly separate, since failure to distinguish them, which is characteristic of *transcendental psychologism*, makes a genuine philosophy impossible. We have here one of those seemingly trivial nuances that make a decisive difference between right and wrong paths of philosophy. It must be continually borne in mind that all transcendental-phenomenological research is inseparable from undeviating observance of the transcendental reduction, which must not be confounded with the abstractive restricting of anthropological research to purely psychic life. Accordingly the difference between a sense of a psychological, and that of a transcendental-phenomenological, exploration of consciousness is immeasurably profound, though the contents to be described on the one hand and on the other can correspond. In the one case we have data belonging to the world, which is presupposed as existing – that is to say, data taken as psychic components of a man. In the other case the parallel data, with their like contents, are not taken in this manner, because the whole world, when one is in the phenomenological attitude, is not accepted as actuality, but only as an actuality-phenomenon."[108]

He has already said above about psychology that it is included, together with biology and "anthropology", in the "objective or positive" sciences, and that the psychical life with which it is concerned, even as *"purely internal experience"*, belongs to the "objective" world that the phenomenological "epoché" prevents us from accepting as existing.[109] Given all these, the *"infinite realm"* of "transcendental experience" opened up by the phenomenological "epoché"[110] is radically separated from the object of psychology – a science that presumably Husserl had in mind in the Introduction when refer-

---

108. *Ibid.*, pp. 33-34 – English translation: pp. 31-32.

109. *Ibid.*, p. 27 – English translation: p. 25.

110. *Ibid.*, p. 29 – English translation: p. 27.

ring to the development of the positive sciences that lead to the "necessity of a radical new beginning of philosophy". Descartes's fatal error, according to Husserl, was that, while he was at the "gateway" of genuine transcendental philosophy, he had transformed the "philosophizing Ego" into a "*substantia cogitans* [thinking substance], a separate human '*mens sive animus* [mind or soul]'"[111]- thereby leaving open the possibility for the subsequent psychologistic confusion in which the psychological and transcendental ego are identified. A main concern of the method of the transcendental-phenomenological reduction therefore, according to Husserl, should be to establish a field, that of "transcendental experience", where I as transcendental thinking subject "remain untouched in my existential status [Seinsgeltung], regardless of whether or not the world exists"[112] and in which "world", as we have seen, psychical life is also included.

The critique of "phonologism" and of the (intricately connected) "metaphysics of presence" inherent in Western thought generally speaking but also in Husserl himself is carried out by Derrida in the same direction *of further deepening and refining phenomenological reduction or "epoché"*. Derrida does with linguistics and the "phonocentrism" of the linguistic sign something equivalent to what Husserl had done with psychology and "psychologism". He attempts to establish a field, I will not say of thought, nor of existence, nor of subjectivity, because, as we have seen and as we will see, all such and some other categories imply distinctions which are abolished or undermined by the movement of *différance*, so let us say the field of *différance* or of the *trace* itself, which will remain "untouched". "Untouched" by what or as to what? Once again, we cannot say "by the world" or "as to the world's existence or non-existence", because the world as well presupposes a distinction between "*in* the world" and "in 'another world'", which is also undermined by the "trace" and *différance*.[113] What we have with Derrida is *différance* as a *radicalised field of transcendental experience, "untouched" by any sort of "presence"*: specifically, by "presence" as it is introduced by linguistics, a science that, like "psychology" for Husserl, is dangerously close to subjectivity, and consequently in a position to threaten its transcendentality. In a triple "defensive" gesture of transcendental-phenomenological reduction, Derrida abolishes the three forms of "presence" introduced by the linguistic problematic: *signifying substance, speaking subject, referred object*.

In his book on Husserl, *Speech and phenomena* (1967), Derrida writes:

"Does not Husserl contradict [rhetorical question – the question mark is lost because of the excerpt's intercession] what he has asserted about the independence of the intention and fulfilling intuition when he writes,

> 'What its meaning [*Bedeutung* – that of the word 'I'] is at the moment can be gleaned only from the living utterance and from the intuitive circumstances that surround it. If we read this word without knowing who wrote it, it is per-

---

111. *Ibid.*, pp. 25-26 – English translation: pp. 24-25.

112. *Ibid.*, p. 26 – English translation: p. 25.

113. Derrida, *op. cit.*, p. 95 – English translation: p. 65.

haps not meaningless (*bedeutungslos*) but is at least estranged from its normal meaning (*Bedeutung*)."¹¹⁴

Husserl's premises should sanction our saying exactly the contrary. Just as I need not perceive in order to understand a statement about perception, so there is no need to intuit the object *I* in order to understand the word *I*. The possibility of this nonintuition constitutes the *Bedeutung* as such, the *normal Bedeutung* as such. When the word *I* appears, the ideality of its *Bedeutung*, in as much as it is distinct from its 'object', puts us in what Husserl describes as an abnormal situation - just as if *I* were written by someone unknown. This alone enables us to account for the fact that we understand the word *I* not only when its 'author' is unknown but when he is quite fictitious. And when he is dead. The ideality of the *Bedeutung* here has by virtue of its structure the value of a testament. And just as the import of a statement about perception did not depend on there being actual or even possible perception, so also the signifying function of the *I* does not depend on the life of the speaking subject. Whether or not perception accompanies the statement about perception, whether or not life as self-presence accompanies the uttering of the *I*, is quite indifferent with regard to the functioning of meaning. My death is structurally necessary to the pronouncing of the *I*. That I am also 'alive' and certain about it figures as something that comes over and above the appearance of the meaning. And this structure is operative, it retains its original efficiency, even when I say 'I am alive' at the very moment when, if such a thing is possible, I have a full and actual intuition of it. The *Bedeutung* 'I am' or 'I am alive' or 'my living presence is' is what it is, has the ideal identity proper to all *Bedeutung*, only if it is not impaired by falsity, that is, if I can be dead at the moment when it is functioning. No doubt it will be different from the *Bedeutung* 'I am dead', but not necessarily from the *fact* that 'I am dead'. The statement 'I am alive' is accompanied by my being dead, and its possibility requires the possibility that I be dead; and conversely. This is not an extraordinary tale by Poe but the ordinary story of language. Earlier we reached the 'I am mortal' from the 'I am'; here we understand the 'I am' out of the 'I am dead'. The anonymity of the written *I*, the impropriety of the *I am writing*, is, contrary to what Husserl says, the 'normal situation'. The autonomy of meaning with regard to intuitive cognition, what Husserl established and we earlier called the freedom or 'candor' [*franc-parler*] of language, has its norm in writing and in the relationship with death."¹¹⁵

---

114. Edmund Husserl, *Logische Untersuchungen, Zweiter Band, I. Teil*, Halle a.d. S.: Max Niemeyer, 1913, p. 82 – English translation (J. N. Findlay): *Logical investigations, Volume I*, London and New York: Routledge, 2001, pp. 218-219.

115. Jacques Derrida, *La voix et le phénomène: Introduction au problème du signe dans la phénoménologie de Husserl*, Paris: Presses Universitaires de France, 1967, pp. 107-108 – English translation (David B. Allison): *Speech and phenomena and other essays on Husserl's theory of signs*, Evanston, Illinois: Northwestern University Press, 1973, pp. 95-97.

And at some point in *Of Grammatology* he writes: "All graphemes are of a testamentary essence. And the original absence of the subject of writing is also the absence of the thing or the referent."[116]

In the long extract one notices that he is trying to rescue the essence of Husserl's contribution as to the autonomy of meaning from the contradictions into which, according to Derrida, he himself falls when he makes meaning dependent on the "living utterance" and its "intuitive circumstances", by using precisely the Husserlian method of transcendental-phenomenological reduction. As an example or prototype of the latter, he brings out the autonomy of linguistic understanding from perceived referents. And in an analogous fashion—not without justification—he infers that the *living presence of the speaking subject* should be excluded from the field of meaning precisely insofar as we have to do with the field of *transcendental experience*, which it is the aim of the phenomenological "epoché" to establish as such. Indeed, what is the speaking subject *as living presence* if not the *perceived referred object* of the word *I*? In this sense we can also understand the equivalence he points out in the second, short extract between the ("original") absence of the subject and the absence of the thing or the referent. Things and present subjects, in common with perception, have to be included in the phenomenological "epoché", if the method based on the latter is not to contradict itself. When at the end of his book on Husserl, Derrida (*reprovingly*) says: "phenomenology [...] is always phenomenology of perception",[117] he is unequivocally even though implicitly suggesting that phenomenology has hitherto not managed to remain consistent in its method of phenomenological reduction. And at the end of the penultimate chapter, when he says: "*Phenomenological reduction is a scene, a theater stage*",[118] he should doubtlessly include himself amongst its protagonists.

---

116. Derrida, *De la grammatologie*, pp. 100-101 – English translation: p. 69.

117. Derrida, *La voix et le phénomène*, p. 117 – English translation: p. 104.

118. *Ibid.*, p. 96 – English translation: p. 86.

Chapter 6
Subjectivity and finitude

We now come to another important issue arising in the above two extracts: to the correlation between, on one hand, the privileged place Derrida bestows on writing as against speech, and on the other, death and the "testament": "All graphemes are of a testamentary essence." I believe that here is perhaps the most revealing point as to the "preference" Derrida shows towards "writing". I will not be concerned with something that has been said regarding Derrida's relationship to Judaism. This might warrant someone to suggest I am trying to attribute Derrida's philosophical positions to religious prejudice. Nor will I pay any particular attention to the fact that at the age of electronic writing, the notion of a "testamentary" essence of "all" graphemes may seem somewhat strange (a point not altogether irrelevant, if we take into account the fact that Derrida himself has maintained that the emphasis he gives to writing is not unrelated, even though "very secondarily", to "the current upheavals in the forms of communication, the new structures [...] that massively and systematically reduce the role of speech, of phonetic writing, and of the book"[119]). An incomparably more important issue in the correlation between writing and death-testament is Derrida's therein implicit attitude as to subjectivity on one hand and finitude on the other.

---

119. Derrida, *Positions*, p. 13.

Let us start with the former. Of course the theme of the connection between writing and permanence that transcends human life is far from novel: "scripta manent" and what have you. The thing is that Derrida claims this holds not only for writing "in the narrow sense", but also for *language in general, including speech*. And it is in this sense that he thinks writing as *différance* pre-exists and is a precondition for speech. Derrida may well claim that what he says –about language and death- "is not an extraordinary tale by Poe", the fact remains however that the crucial passage from the specific "extraordinary tale" by Poe ("The facts in the case of M. Valdemar") is cited as a motto at the beginning of his book on Husserl (whence the above long extract).[120] It is quite obvious that he has been inspired by this tale, that he considers it to be a revealing allegory for what happens in language – for the "ordinary story of language". To summarise it in one sentence, Poe's story is about the case of a man who has just died and says: "...now – *I am dead*".[121]

Here of course we should be rigorously fair, and first of all take into account Derrida's critical scope as to using Poe's "allegory" – and more generally as to the correlation between "writing" and death. His aim is to "deconstruct" the transcendental subject of Husserl's phenomenology, as well as of every philosophy based on the concept of consciousness. As he very characteristically puts it: "This movement of difference is not something that happens to a transcendental subject; it produces a subject."[122] In this sense, when he maintains that a precondition for being able to say "I am alive" is being able to be dead, he is not being paradoxical, he is criticising "living presence" in the sense of a transcendentally autonomous and self-existent consciousness. The point, however, is that the way he practices this critique, which as we have seen mainly consists in putting to work "in the extreme" the method of phenomenological reduction, leads to the following philosophical/theoretical result: *to the removal of language, and ultimately of the field of subjectivity in general, from human life*, not *only* in the *phenomenological* sense of the *transcendental* experience of the *"present to itself" subject*, but *also* in the *materialist* sense of the *biologically given and spatio-temporally determined* experience of the human *organism*, of the human *body*.

This latter sense has of course nothing to do with what Derrida would call "metaphysical materialism" and Husserl "naïve Objectivism", but with something that—in these terms, i.e. in terms of *life* and *body*—appeared *after* Derrida's texts under consideration, where he elaborates the concept of writing as *différance*, and that belongs to what we call *non-economistic materialism*. I am referring here to the Foucauldian conceptualisation of *bio-politics*

---

120. See Derrida, *La voix et le phénomène*, p. between title and first p. of main text (with no number) – English translation: p. 1.
121. Edgar Allan Poe, *Selected writings: Poems, tales, essays and reviews*, Harmondsworth: Penguin Books, 1967, p. 357.
122. Derrida, *op. cit.*, p. 92 – English translation: p. 82.

and the *political technology of the body*—concepts that could hardly be deemed as standing for any of the above mentioned "naïve" or "metaphysical" theoretical schemes.

The irony is that precisely this (non-economistic) materialist conceptualisation by Foucault has been read by two American students of his work as a further development in the phenomenological tradition of Husserl and Merleau-Ponty[123]—something that had as a rather grotesque consequence more or less the overturning of things as to the generally prevailing reception of each of the two French thinkers' philosophical position: Derrida being considered as a poststructuralist critic of phenomenology, and Foucault as a poststructuralist phenomenologist. While in fact Derrida is the "poststructuralist" phenomenologist, and the critic of phenomenology, from a viewpoint not simply "poststructuralist" generally speaking but more specifically (non-economistic) materialist, is Foucault.

Elsewhere (see also above) I have quite extensively referred to how Foucault, mainly in *The Order of Things*, demolished phenomenology's basic thesis about the continuity between Cartesian and Kantian philosophy, by demonstrating the radical significance of *finitude* in Kantian and post-Kantian thought, in fields of knowledge not just purely philosophical but more generally epistemic.[124] We are thus led to the latter of the above issues that emerge with the correlation between "writing" and death, i.e. to where *Derrida* stands as to the question of finitude.

It would be worthwhile to start with one of his much more recent formulations—from a 1991 lecture published in 1992 and again in 1996—where he directly expresses his *disagreement* precisely on the issue of the Kantian, the Heideggerian and the Foucauldian notion of finitude, more specifically as to the problem of the *fundamental* (or "originary") *or not* character of (Kantian) finitude, a problem of crucial importance as to the discontinuity or continuity, respectively, between pre-Kantian and Kantian philosophy, since everybody agrees of course that *non-fundamental* (or "derived") finitude, that is, finitude determined in relation to the infinite, was there in pre-Kantian thought too:

> "It is true that if originary finitude obviously makes us think of Kant, it would be unable to do so alone, that is—to summarize an enormous venture in a word, in a name—without the active interpretation of the Heideggerian repe-

---

123. Hubert L. Dreyfus and Paul Rabinow, *Michel Foucault: Beyond structuralism and hermeneutics*, Brighton: Harvester, 1982, especially pp. 44-52, 97-98, 111-112, 165-167 and 206. See also Doxiadis, "Foucault and the three-headed king", p. 525 ff.

124. Doxiadis, "Foucault and ideology", p. 23 ff. Foucault had already since 1961 pointed out the importance of finitude in Kant – see Michel Foucault, *Introduction to Kant's Anthropology* (translated by Roberto Nigro and Kate Briggs), Los Angeles, California: Semiotext(e), 2008. And in *The Birth of the Clinic*, a work of 1963—which Derrida mentions in his critique to which we will refer just below— he had already made the connection between finitude and the human body; Michel Foucault, *Naissance de la clinique*, Paris: Presses Universitaires de France, 1993, pp. 201-203 - English translation (A.M. Sheridan): *The Birth of the Clinic: An Archaeology of Medical Perception*, London: Tavistock, 1973, pp. 197-199.

tition and all its repercussions, particularly, since this is our topic today, in the discourse of French philosophy and psychoanalysis, and especially, Lacanian psychoanalysis; and when I say Lacanian, I am also referring to all the debates *with* Lacan during the past few decades. This would have perhaps deserved some mention here on the part of Foucault, especially when he speaks of originary finitude. For Kantian finitude is precisely not "originary", as is, on the contrary, the one to which the Heideggerian interpretation leads. Finitude in Kant's sense is instead derived [...]. But let us leave all this aside, since it would, as we say, take us a bit too far afield."[125]

Let us go back to *Speech and Phenomena*. In that book's last pages, Derrida goes "a bit too far afield", and is directly concerned with the issue of finitude and its relation to the infinite, not with direct reference to Heidegger, but with direct references to Husserl, to Kant, and to Hegel:

> "That Husserl always thought of infinity as an Idea in the Kantian sense, as the indefiniteness of an '*ad infinitum*', leads one to believe that he never *derived* difference from the fullness of a *parousia*, from the full presence of a positive infinite, that he never believed in the accomplishment of an 'absolute knowledge', as the self-adjacent presence of an infinite concept in Logos."[126]

But here too Derrida "corrects" Husserl, together with Kant, by re-establishing the phenomenological continuity in the history of philosophy—a continuity from which, on this particular matter, Husserl, following Kant as to the notion of a *non-"positive"*, that is to say, of a *hypothetical* infinite, of an infinite in the sense of *indefiniteness* or of *non-finitude*, tended to diverge.[127] To effect this (double) "correction", Derrida invokes Hegelianism: Hegelianism, "within the schema of a metaphysics of presence which relentlessly exhausts itself in trying to make difference derivative", "seems to be more radical" than phenomenology,[128] because, according to Derrida, given precisely this whole schema that also totally includes phenomenology, it becomes necessary to think the "*positive*" infinite *from within*. Finitude therefore appears not with the "derived" pre-Kantian sense of the non-infinite, but also certainly not in the sense of an "originary" or fundamental finitude that according to Foucault one finds in Kant (with which Foucault's interpretation as we have seen Derrida disagrees—or does he perhaps here agree, since he mentions the non-positive, that is, in this case, non-fundamental

---

125. Derrida, *Résistances de la psychanalyse*, p. 136 – English translation: p. 109. On pointing out the importance of the Heideggerian concept of finitude in Lacanian psychoanalysis, see also Doxiadis, *Subjectivity and power*, p. 127 ff.

126. Derrida, *La voix et le phénomène*, p. 114 – English translation: p. 101.

127. In relation to this, see also one of Derrida's older (1962) texts about Husserl – Jacques Derrida, «Introduction», in: Edmund Husserl, *L'origine de la géométrie* (translated by Jacques Derrida), Paris: Presses Universitaires de France, 1962, especially pp. 28-29, fn. 1 – English translation: Jacques Derrida, *Edmund Husserl's Origin of geometry: An introduction* (translated by John P. Leavey), Lincoln, Nebraska, and London: University of Nebraska Press, 1989, pp. 44-45, fn. 37.

128. Derrida, *La voix et le phénomène*, p. 114 – English translation: p. 101.

character of the Kantian *infinite?*). Finitude here appears in a *Hegelian* fashion. In particular, it is at this point where perhaps more acutely than anywhere else the most profoundly Hegelian character of *différance* comes into view:

> "...the positive infinite must be thought through (which is possible only if it thinks *itself*) in order that the indefiniteness of *differance* appear *as such*. Hegel's critique of Kant would no doubt also hold against Husserl. But this appearing of the Ideal as an infinite *différance* can only be produced within a relationship with death in general. Only a relation to my-death could make the infinite *différance* of presence appear. By the same token, compared to the ideality of the positive infinite, this relation to my-death becomes an accident of empirical finitude. The appearing of the infinite *différance* is itself finite. Consequently, *differance*, which does not occur outside this relation, becomes the finitude of life as an essential relation with oneself and one's death. *The infinite* differance *is finite.* It can therefore no longer be conceived within the opposition of finiteness and infinity, absence and presence, negation and affirmation."[129]

Let us start from the last sentence. The Hegelian unity of negation and affirmation, which here but also more generally in Derrida's thought is given shape in the concept of *différance*, becomes a basis for the critique of the "metaphysics of presence" (abolition of absence and presence opposition), but at the same time the foundation upon which the finitude and infinity distinction will be undermined. Why do I say "*distinction*" and not "*opposition*" regarding this latter pair of concepts? Because to judge whether there is a relation of opposition between them it is not enough to have the privative affix *in-* of the second word. As Derrida himself acknowledges in that text about Foucault, there is fundamental (or "originary") finitude and non-fundamental (or "derived") finitude. And as he recognises in this text about Husserl, there is fundamental (or "positive") infinite and non-fundamental infinite (or infinity as "indefiniteness"). The question of which finitude and which infinite we are dealing with is of decisive importance as to whether we have to do with a relation of opposition or with something else. Moreover, the four possibly resulting combinations cannot be taken into account at random; each one of these is dependent on—and in turn defines—some specific philosophical choice.

In this sense, at least one of the four possible combinations should be excluded: one cannot accept at once the fundamental infinite *and* fundamental finitude. Using an outrageously outmoded division, I will say: In the former case one is an idealist, in the sense that he believes in God or in some substitute for him, in some infinite, absolute, hypostatised, considered-as-objectively-existing, idea. In the latter case, we have to do with what I have called in this text "materialist version of the critical philosophy of finitude", which consists, among other things, in the axiomatic admission of two fundamental *but also exclusive* properties of material entities: that they are

---

129. *Ibid.*, p. 114 – English translation: pp. 101-102.

fundamentally finite *but also hypostatical, i.e. objectively existing*. So it is not a matter of an opposition or antithesis, but rather a matter of an *antinomy* in the sense of the *Kantian* dialectic.[130] It is a matter of two positions or theses that are incompatible with each other. The incompatibility of the two theses may perhaps be best demonstrated with an allusion to Luther's *partly analogous* argument in his renowned dispute with Erasmus regarding free will. If one accepts the objective existence of an omniscient and omnipotent (that is, *infinite*) being, it means one accepts that everything is determined by it; consequently there is no room for accepting the freedom of the will of finite entities, in this case, of human beings.[131] By partial analogy, we can here say, nor is there room for accepting the thesis that finite entities are *by themselves* finite, that is, *fundamentally* finite.

This is obviously not Derrida's view. Even though he keeps his distance from the Hegelian term *Aufhebung*,[132] Derrida seems to accept the Hegelian scheme of *antithesis* (not antinomy) and at the same time *unity* between (fundamental) infinity and (fundamental) finitude—in the (Hegelian) sense of *contradiction* (*Wiederspruch*)—which consists in the *infinitely alternating determination* (*Wechselbestimmung*) between the two.[133] On the other hand, he has to purge Hegelianism, together with phenomenology, of the "metaphysics of presence", which amounts to the transcendence of the hypostaticality or the positivity of the infinite *but also of finitude*.[134] The role of this double transcendence is assumed by *différance*, which, as "infinite *différance* of presence", it "*de-presents it*". As to the positive infinite, *différance* is what comes after (Hegelian) "absolute knowledge" (*absolute Wissen - savoir absolut*), that is, according to Derrida, after the "closure" of the history of metaphysics which *has taken place*,[135] thereby setting forth itself as infinity in the sense of indefiniteness. As to fundamental finitude, *différance* is "*relation to death*".

---

130. Kant, *Kritik der reinen Vernunft*, pp. 399-512 – English translation: pp. 249-334.

131. Erasmus and Luther, *Discourse on free will* (translated by Ernst F. Winter), London and New York: Continuum, 2005, pp. 83-120.

132. See Derrida, *De la grammatologie*, p. 104 – English translation: p. 71. The German word *Aufhebung* has the dual meaning of *elevation* and *cancellation*.

133. See Georg Wilhelm Friedrich Hegel, *Wissenschaft der Logik*, I, Frankfurt: Suhrkamp, 1969, pp. 151 ff. and 166 ff. – English translation (A.V. Miller): *Hegel's Science of Logic*, Amherst, New York: Humanity Books, 1969, pp. 138 ff. and 150 ff.

134. One of the multiple versions of the Greek word *ousia*, which is in turn one of the avatars of *parousia (presence)*, according to Derrida, is *hypostasis (substance)* - Derrida, *L'écriture et la différence*, p. 411 – English translation: pp. 279-280.

135. See Georg Wilhelm Friedrich Hegel, *Phänomenologie der Geistes*, Frankfurt: Suhrkamp, 1970, p. 575 ff. –English translation (A.V. Miller): *Hegel's Phenomenology of Spirit*, Oxford: Oxford University Press, 1977, p. 479 ff.-, and Derrida, *La voix et le phénomène*, p. 115 – English translation: p. 102.

So the "expurgation" of Hegelianism (and hence of phenomenology) from the metaphysics of presence comes as a movement of transcendence effected by *différance*, in which we can discern the following structural constituents or "stages":

- Maintaining *in essence* the Hegelian schema of "*contradiction*" between the positive infinite and fundamental finitude.
- Substituting the positive infinite with *différance*, consequently "de-presenting" the former.
- Setting forth the "contradiction" between infinite *différance* and fundamental finitude, thereby "de-presenting" the latter.

In the "conventional" Hegelian contradiction between the positive infinite and fundamentally finite entities, the latter's finitude is in essence abolished by way of their idealisation taking place within this relationship of contradiction. In this sense, Hegelianism, even as a post-Kantian philosophy that takes fundamental finitude into account, inevitably restores the (pre-Kantian) metaphysics of the infinite: An only to be expected outcome of the infinite-finitude unity/antithesis "on equal terms", i.e. in the fundamental version of both, is the predominance of the former. This is mainly what Hegelian hypostatisation consists in: the various other sides of the Absolute Spirit's contradictions are but "formerly" fundamentally finite entities that have been idealised, while retaining on the other hand their hypostaticality: History, Humanity, Nation, People, State.

The Derridean movement of *différance*, in so far as it engages in a relation of "contradiction" with fundamentally finite entities as "relation to death", does not abolish the latter's finitude while maintaining their hypostaticality and restoring in this (post-Kantian) fashion the (pre-Kantian) metaphysics of the infinite, but it effects on contemporary thought a conceptual outcome more "radically Hegelian" than "conventional" Hegelianism: In essence it abolishes the *distinction*—neither the *antinomy* nor the *antithesis*: the *distinction*—between *fundamental finitude* on one hand and the *non-fundamental infinite* on the other. This distinction is not a relation of opposition or antithesis because we do not have to do with homogenous quantities. And it does not constitute an antinomy, since one can without contradicting oneself believe at once in the former, as a fundamental property of *objectively existing, i.e. hypostatical* material entities, and in the *subjective, i.e. hypothetical existence* of the latter. The philosophical conviction of the coexistence of fundamental finitude and the non-fundamental infinite but at the same time of the *radical distinction between them*, as it has already become apparent and as it will more extensively be demonstrated further on, forms the basis for the "materialist version of the critical philosophy of finitude" and consequently for the critique of hypostatisation.

But how does *différance* abolish this distinction? Non-fundamentally infinite *différance* engages in a relation of "contradiction" with fundamentally finite entities as "relation to death".[136] Of course the association of finitude with the relation to death is already there in Heidegger,[137] and a discussion about whether in his case too we have to do with similar conceptual results would indeed take us a bit too far afield. What is certain is that in Foucault, whom as we have seen Derrida reproaches for being based on Heidegger without mentioning him, (fundamental) finitude is not confined to death, death constitutes but *one* of its forms.[138] Death as a biological fact is not the property of finitude *itself*, but rather *one of the limits, one of the ends (fins) that it describes*. If death has some special importance as a limit, it is of course because it constitutes the *ultimate* limit of life. But we can in no sense identify death with finitude in general, neither with limits in general. In human beings, a limit is also the fact that they cannot fly (without the assistance of some machine). Even as ultimate limit of life, death is not the *opposite* of life, it is merely its end, its inevitable conclusion. In Derrida, the concept of *"relation* to death" in essence abolishes the concept of fundamental finitude as *existence of concrete (fundamental) limits*, and transforms it into the *idea of antithesis to life and to existence in general*. It is only to be expected that the "contradiction" between infinite *différance* and finitude as "relation to death" substitutes the fundamental finitude/non-fundamental infinite distinction with the perpetual Hegelian play of existence/non-existence, affirmation/negation, identity/non-identity. Within this conceptual/philosophical framework and with this meaning of finitude and death, language-as-writing-as-*différance* easily becomes conceivable upon the prototype of testament or of a M. Valdemar who though being dead insists on speaking and declaring his death.

On the basis of what I have already said, I believe it is evident that the distinction between the non-fundamental infinite and fundamental finitude is *equivalent* to the distinction between subjectivity and objectivity; since on one hand the latter terms of the distinctions constitute *fundamental and exclusive properties* of material entities, and on the other hand and as a consequence, the non-fundamental, *i.e. the hypothetical* infinite, as well as *non-fun-*

---

136. In the case of Derrida, I insist on using quotation marks for "contradiction", because it is of course not a Derridean but rather a "conventionally" Hegelian term (see above, fn. 133). Derrida, once again more "radically Hegelian", merely uses "is" or "becomes". Elsewhere, in similar cases, he uses *erasure (sous rature)* – a method also "radically Hegelian" but also phenomenological; see, for example, Derrida, *De la grammatologie*, pp. 65 and 89 –English translation: pp. 44 and 60-, and Husserl, *Cartesian meditations*, p. 25, fns 1 and 2.

137. See Martin Heidegger, *Kant und das Problem der Metaphysik*, Frankfurt: Vittorio Klostermann, 1998, p. 242 – English translation (Richard Taft): *Kant and the problem of metaphysics*, Bloomington and Indianapolis, Indiana: Indiana University Press, 1990, p. 165.

138. See especially Foucault, *Les mots et les choses*, pp. 323-329 – English translation: pp. 312-318.

damentally finite entities, i.e. entities determined as finite in relation to some (hypothetical in this case) infinite, constitute the *exclusive form of existence* of subjective entities, that is, of ideas, of concepts, of products of thought. The virtual abolition of the former distinction by Derrida is therefore *equivalent* to the abolition of the latter.

Language and discourse form a privileged field where the significance of this distinction emerges. Language as *the actual ability to form concepts* and discourse as *language in relation to referents* constitute in common the framework of a problematic where subjectivity as production of meaning is incessantly interwoven with the two *objective aspects* of language: *its material conditions and its referentiality*. As we have seen above, Derrida *transcendentalises the signifier*, thereby he radically downgrades the significance of the former, since, as we have also seen, material conditions first and foremost emerge in the *materiality of the signifier*. Moreover, he fundamentally undermines the *initially* material, that is, the *initially primarily* objective character of referentiality, when he equates the "transcendental signified" with the "ultimate referent".

However, apart from downgrading the objective *aspects*, we could say that Derrida's approach *also* undermines *the primarily subjective* character of language (and consequently of discourse). It is no accident that when he refers to *signifieds* he almost exclusively uses the derogatory term "*transcendental signified*". If "transcendental" here meant the opposite of the empirical, as it does at least at some points of Kantian theory,[139] then we would have a pleonasm, since signifieds are the non-empirical—and in this sense transcendental—element of language *par excellence*. But he uses the singular: he substitutes signifieds *in general* with the *one* "transcendental" signified, thereby implying that any conception whatever of subjectivity as a distinct realm of existence inevitably leads to the acceptance of a *centre*, which, depending on each case, acquires "different forms or names": God, *archē*, subject etc.[140] In other words, he seems to be implying that *any acceptance whatever of subjectivity in its specificity is equivalent to its hypostatisation*.

Particularly revealing as to this is the fact that he considers "unhappy" Saussure's use of the term "concept" when explaining what it is he is substituting with the linguistic term "signified". What does Derrida find bothersome in the term "concept"? Is it perhaps the fact that it implies precisely the *non-reducible* element of the realm of subjectivity? Since how else could we conceive of the subject if not as "that which forms concepts" and hence how else of subjectivity if not as "the realm of the formation of concepts"? It is moreover indicative that instead of the "concept" he prefers the term

---

139. See Howard Caygill, *A Kant Dictionary*, Oxford: Blackwell, 1995, pp. 399-400.

140. On the concept of the "transcendental signified" as "centre", see Derrida, *L'écriture et la différence*, pp. 410-411 – English translation: pp. 279-280.

"ideality of the sense" ("idéalité du sens")[141] – something that abolishes in a most effectively surreptitious manner the *inherent plurality and multiplicity of the conceptual realm*.

Let us now come to a crucial matter concerning (once again) the reading of Saussure, the materiality of the signifier, the concept of difference, as well as the latter's "transformation" by Derridean *différance*. "Before" the use of the double sense of the verb *différer*, and the consequent connection of "difference" to "deferment" (of meaning), a particular reading of the concept of difference in Saussure by Derrida has taken place, which predetermines to a significant extent its transformation into *différance*. The relevant "key-phrase" in Saussure is: "…in language there are only differences *without positive terms*".[142]

It is indeed a misinterpretable formulation. There are at least two possible readings. The first one *opposes* difference to positivity, thereby equating the former to negativity. The phrase would thus be "translated" as follows: "In language there are only differences, that is, only terms negative to each other." According to this line of reasoning, the fact that the letter *b* differs from *a* is reduced to the fact that it is *non-a*, the fact that *c* differs from both is reduced to the fact that it is *non-a* and *non-b*, and so forth. It seems that it is this reading that Gilles Deleuze has in mind in his book *Difference and repetition*, and this is why he blames Saussure for reducing difference to negativity.[143] Apparently the same reading is shared by Derrida – from a radically different viewpoint of course, in so far as his version allows for a Hegelian interpretation of Saussure, in which everything is based on—and reduced to—the schema negativity/contradiction/antithesis/non-identity.

And it is true that Saussure himself is responsible for this equation, when he uses the terms "negative" and "differential" as if they were roughly synonymous.[144] However, this equation—which is unjustifiably arbitrary anyhow—is rendered quite unnecessary, once we take into account the way in which Saussure himself explains the meaning of difference. This way, in my view, leads us to a reading of the controversial formulation that *distinguishes* difference from positivity, *without however opposing* the one to the other, in the following specific sense: "In language there are only differences, that is, there are no terms that are not determined by differences with other terms." By "terms" Saussure is referring both to signifiers and signifieds. Nevertheless, I believe that this reading of Saussure allows first and foremost for the *non-reducible* character of the *materiality of the signifiers*. It is a materiality that *pre-exists* meaning, that to some extent *forms* relations of meaning, and that certainly cannot be reduced to them. The non-reducibility of differen-

---

141. Derrida, *De la grammatologie*, pp. 92-93 – English translation: p. 63; Saussure, *op. cit.*, pp. 66-67.

142. *Ibid*, p. 120.

143. Gilles Deleuze, *Difference and repetition* (translated by Paul Patton), London and New York: Continuum, 2004, p. 255.

144. Saussure, *op. cit.*, pp. 120-121.

ce to opposition or antithesis is the element that more than anything else demonstrates the specificity of language as against *conventional* signifying systems.

Perhaps the most revealing passage as to Derrida's—ultimately Cartesian—conception of language is when, towards the end of his interview with Kristeva,[145] he directly associates the advance of his own "deconstructive" approach with the "extension of mathematical notation, and in general the formalization of writing" (even though this "must be very slow and very prudent"), since "[e]verything that has always linked *logos* to *phonē* has been limited by mathematics, whose progress is in absolute solidarity with the practice of a nonphonetic inscription", and since "[a]bout these 'grammatological' principles and tasks there is no possible doubt".[146]

I believe that a confusion similar with the one between *difference* and *negativity* is that between the *arbitrariness* and the *conventionality* of the sign. Conventionality *removes* arbitrariness. The relationship between the mathematical symbol + and the arithmetic operation of addition is as much a relation of causality, i.e. of non-arbitrariness, as the relationship between a photograph and the object being photographed. It is just that in the former case we have to do with *social* causality, with a causality derived from the conventions of the mathematicians' community, and *in this sense* with "conventionality", while in the latter case we have to do with *natural* causality—a causality that can be explained by the natural-scientific field of optics, for example.

This does not mean that there is no conventionality, in the sense of social causality, in linguistic signifiers as well. But the element of convention, since it is an element of—be it social—*causality*, is what *diminishes* arbitrariness, it is not equivalent to it. It diminishes it, *but it does not eliminate it.* The fact that one may find in a dictionary seventeen different meanings for the same word, and that, inversely, in the same dictionary one may find more or less the same definition for an equal number of words, is a "simple" indication that arbitrariness in linguistic signifiers, far from being equivalent to convention—convention would end up with *one* definition/meaning for each word—or from merely being some "chance event" or some exceptional circumstance that can potentially be eliminated, constitutes a specific characteristic and inalienable element of any language.

In this sense, we could say that *arbitrariness* and *difference* together constitute the main guarantees for the non-reducibility of the linguistic signifiers' materiality. In differing but related fashions, both of them ensure the radical distinction of language from formal logic: difference warrants *the non*

---

145. Derrida, *Positions*, pp. 34-35.
146. *Ibid.*, p. 34.

-reduction of relations between symbols to the schema identity/non-identity,[147] while arbitrariness guarantees *the non-reduction of symbols-symbolised relations to a one-to-one correspondence.*

We could not deny of course that even mathematical symbols have some materiality. But this tends to be minimised as far as possible *as a matter of course*. I suppose that it would become extinct, together with the materiality of language, and following the destiny of the subjectivity-objectivity distinction, if some day Derrida's grammatological programme were to reach its consummation, and *différance*, despite of its creator's pessimistic admission, were to accomplish "the absolute reduction of the natural languages and nonmathematical notation".[148]

---

147. As an indicatory remark, we may bring here to mind the importance of *(binary) Boolean algebra* for both formal logic and computer science – see "George Boole", *Wikipedia*, 8 June 2008, http://en.wikipedia.org/wiki/George_Boole (9 June 2008), and "Claude Shannon", *Wikipedia*, 3 June 2008, http://en.wikipedia.org/wiki/Claude_Shannon (9 June 2008).

148. Derrida, *op. cit.*, p. 35. Let us be reminded here of Bertrand Russell's –half-serious/half-joking- apostrophe at the beginning of his well-known lecture on "Vagueness": "You all know that I invented a special language with a view to avoiding vagueness, but unfortunately it is unsuited for public occasions. I shall therefore, though regretfully, address you in English, and whatever vagueness is to be found in my words must be attributed to our ancestors for not having been predominantly interested in logic." - Rosanna Keefe and Peter Smith (eds), *Vagueness: A reader*, Cambridge, Massachusetts, and London: MIT Press, 1999, p. 61.

Part II
The Ontological Priority of the Material Component

Chapter 7
The materiality of language

By way of schematising, and moving on to a more positive treatment of the relevant problems, I would say that the basic difference of the present approach from the conceptualisation both of "discourse" in Laclau and Mouffe and of "writing" in Derrida lies in considering language—*and therefore discourse*—in all its forms (including phonetic writing as representation of "natural" language) as a privileged field where, *rather than being abolished*, the distinction between conceptuality/subjectivity on one hand and materiality/objectivity on the other *comes to the fore more lucidly*. And I believe that this is precisely because the cohabitation of these two realms of existence in this field is perhaps more intricate than anywhere else. In this sense, it would not be overly positivistic to suggest that I regard discourse analysis as a "privileged working space" for the study of this distinction.

At several points in the above pages, I tended to stress the non-reducibility both of the conceptual/subjective and of the material/objective component of language and discourse. I had pointed out the *primarily conceptual/subjective character* of language, in the sense that this is the *reason* for the existence of language, by definition; but I had also stressed in parallel the importance of *its material/objective aspects*, in the sense that these are the *conditions* of its existence: it would not exist without them. To systematise further this double emphasis, in a fashion that might perhaps be an indication that the coexistence of materialism and ethics is feasible, I would suggest that the conceptual component is marked by an *ethical* priority, as against an *ontological* priority that marks the material component.

Let us start with the latter. Approaching Poe's tale in a fashion somewhat more "pedestrian" than Derrida's, we could ask ourselves, where, mainly, does one meet with the supernatural element—be it under poetic license, but this is of no matter in this case—in the story of M. Valdemar? And the answer would be: in that it refutes the commonly accepted belief, based on scientific facts, that a necessary precondition for being able to say "I am dead" is to be alive. The ontological priority of material conditions here consists in that what counts is not the truth of the *concept* "I am dead", but the *material conditions of its production*; that is, that the nervous system, the respiratory system and the vocal cords of the specific individual function well enough for him/her to be capable of uttering this phrase—in other words, that the individual is alive. To take also an example from pedestrian contemporary everyday life, concerning the material conditions not of speech but of (phonetic) writing, one may well have formed thousands of wise concepts in one's text, and with one single oversight or computer failure (and if you have not loaded it into a USB stick), there goes the text together with the concepts (in case one does not remember them).

However, it is of at least equal importance that material conditions do not determine concepts merely negatively (as in the case of the normal function of—at least parts of—the human body in the first example and of the computer in the second one); that is to say, they do not merely form the "sine qua non" for the formation of concepts. Apart from something self-evident, that different communication media, and consequently different signifiers, contribute to the formation of different concepts, there is a more fundamental way in which signifiers influence the formation of concepts, and this directly derives from the signifiers' properties I mentioned above as that which ensures the *non-reducibility of their materiality*: that is, from *difference* and *arbitrariness*.

I believe that two key concepts of linguistics to which I have already referred, namely the terms *metonymy* and *metaphor*, are directly connected with the two above properties. It has been said that Saussure, Jakobson, and everyone who has followed them in this dual model, by way of an extreme and unabashed reductionism, ignore the wealth of the old rhetoric's tropes and reduce them to two. The essence of these terms does not lie in their use as rhetorical tropes, in such a case their use would certainly be reductionist and their analytical effectiveness rather poor; but in their *descriptive conceptual value*, on one hand as directly connected with the two above properties and on the other as constituting something much more fundamental than two rhetorical tropes, namely *the two dimensions of language: the "horizontal", also called "syntagmatic", and the "vertical", also called "paradigmatic"*.[149]

I have already clarified the direct connection of metonymy with difference, but I believe that the direct connection of metaphor *as well as* of metonymy with arbitrariness should also be clear: whether we have to do with arbitrariness between signifier and signified (Saussure before Benveniste's reading) or with arbitrariness between sign and referent (Saussure after Benveniste's reading), what matters is that anyhow we have to do with a property that characterises both the "vertical" or metaphoric and the "horizontal" or metonymic dimension. Moreover, these two terms, metaphor and metonymy, are the ones that bring to light in a most immediate fashion the latter of the two objective/material aspects of language that I mentioned earlier, namely *its referentiality*; as we have seen, both metaphor and metonymy describe relations not only between signs but also between signs and (*external*) referents, that is, also between signs and (*primary*) objects. These two terms are indeed what demonstrates most thoroughly the non-reducible character of the objectivity/materiality of language, and at the same time, as I will try to show, that which reveals how this component determines in a *positive* manner its subjective/conceptual component.

Before I proceed with the terms "metaphor" and "metonymy" themselves, however, I should say something more about how the two properties that are directly connected with them, namely arbitrariness and difference, relate to the non-reducibility of the objectivity/materiality of language. I have said some things regarding the distinction of language from formal logic. Once again though, a more *positive* connection is needed.

Let us start with *difference*. As we have axiomatically accepted, *fundamental* finitude is a fundamental property of all material entities (which is to say, of the only objectively existing entities). This means that material entities are *fundamentally* finite, that is, they are finite by themselves, they are not determined as finite by some infinite entity. This in turn entails the following. Between material (that is, fundamentally finite) entities there prevails a *radical discontinuity*. Since there is no supreme—that is, infinite—being with

---

149. Two things should be clarified here: First, even though above I distinguished "paradigm" as the signifier/signified relation from metaphor as relation between signs or between sign and referent, what I will say below about metaphor also holds for paradigm – in so far as both terms determine and coincide with the "vertical" dimension: since, for reasons I have explained (fn. 21), in order to refer to the "horizontal" dimension I have chosen the term "metonymy" rather than the term "syntagm", I also thought it worthwhile to choose the *corresponding* term "metaphor" for the "vertical" dimension. Second, it goes without saying that the use of the terms "vertical" and "horizontal dimension" is *purely metaphorical* (i.e. not literal – even though literal meanings are also metaphors: a more proper term for literal meaning would perhaps be "literal metaphor"). It is not a matter of dimensions in the geometric or linear sense. The metaphor in this case is based on the model of phonetic writing, where the (*absent*) signifieds or *other* (*absent*) signs (depending on the level of the analysis) are to be found "*below*" the letters or the words, while the (*present*) signifiers or the (*present*) signs (again depending on the level of the analysis) are to be found "*beside*" one another.

reference to which or because of which they are determined and/or exist, any *general continuity* between them is neither conceivable nor (in reality) feasible. In other words, the limits between (fundamentally) finite entities (that is, *their very property of being (fundamentally) finite*) are not limits of *continuity* but of *dis-continuity*. They are not limits in the sense of numbers being limits between them, in which case we know that from 2 we go to 3 and so forth *to the infinite*, but limits in the sense of *walls*: it is difficult or even impossible to transgress them, and quite often we do not know what lies behind them.

If there is to be difference, *not in the sense of non-identity but in the sense of non-reducible to identity alterity*, there has to be discontinuity. Staying on the "easy" example of numbers, we cannot accept as *difference* the fact that the "difference" between number 4 and number 7,291,277 is removed by two operations of division (of each number by itself).

Difference, as a *general condition of existence*, should be conceived as a *primary effect of the discontinuity between (fundamentally) finite, that is, material entities*. That two entities differ presupposes that, in principle at least, there are insurmountable or in any case difficultly surmountable limits. In other words, *the principle of difference between material beings is indissolubly linked with the property of their fundamental finitude and the radical discontinuity between them that the latter entails*.

In language, difference—*that is, discontinuity as well*—pertains to its material/objective elements, namely signifiers, in an *almost exclusive* fashion. According to how Saussure himself interprets his own formulation "in language there are only differences *without positive terms*", difference in language *differs from the differences there are between other material entities*, in the sense that *only this* exists.[150] We add: only this, as far as *the materiality of its (material) elements* is concerned. For example: a dog and a cat may have many differences, but before differences each of them has some characteristics that determine its materiality independently of its differences from the other: weight, shape, size, biological functions and anatomy, position in the animal kingdom etc. In language, the only thing that matters as to the materiality of phonemes or of letters or of words or of any other signifiers is that they differ among them. This is the only significant material element, but a *non-reducibly material* element.

We now come to *arbitrariness*. I have referred to how Benveniste criticises Saussure, by claiming that arbitrariness is not between signifier and signified but between sign and referent. I then disagreed with Benveniste's view that the signifier-signified relation is a relation of necessity and I explained that the relation in question is not *merely* a relation of arbitrariness in the sense of a *lack* of necessity or causality, but, more importantly (borrowing the terms from Laclau and Mouffe, although using them in a thoroughly different fashion), a relation of a "*split*" or of an "*impossible suture*" in

---

150. Saussure, *op. cit.*, p. 120.

the sense that we have to do with the relation that marks the distinction between two basic realms of existence: objectivity/materiality on one hand, subjectivity/conceptuality on the other.

What the above entails is that the *basic* relation of arbitrariness, in the (Saussurian) sense of *lack of causality*, is the relation between *signifier* and *referent*. It is quite simple: the *object* (i.e. the *referent*) "tree" does not cause the *sound* (and consequently the sound-image, i.e. the *signifier*) "tree". In this case we have to do with the relation between two *material/objective* elements. On the other hand, we know, or in any case we axiomatically accept, that a basic characteristic of material entities is the causality that pertains to the relations between them. Furthermore, we have to do with *objective* causality, in the same sense that material entities themselves are objective. We accept that causality exists independently of the *concept* of causality. To mention once more our favourite example with the earthquake, the same way we accept the objective existence of the shifting subsoil and the disruptions of equilibrium on the earth's surface, we also accept the cause-effect relation that links the former with the latter. The *scientific concept* of the earthquake also includes the *concept* of the above causal relation. Even when the former did not exist, and consequently neither did the latter, for example, when people used to believe in Enceladus, earthquakes did occur, and the cause was not Enceladus.

Apart from sharing with material entities themselves the property of objective existence though, causality possesses in common with them another of their fundamental properties, namely *fundamental finitude*. In a fundamentally finite universe that is made up of fundamentally finite, discontinuous-between-them-entities, a *general*, that is, *infinite* causality cannot exist. Moreover, one has to do with *fundamentally* finite causality, in the sense that, once again as with material entities themselves, there is no infinite being that determines it as finite. In other words, we have to do with *multiple*, fundamentally finite and therefore *discontinuous*-between-them *causalities*.

I believe that, *as a general principle, arbitrariness marks the fundamental finitude of causality between material entities*. That is, it is not a matter of a *complete non-existence* of causality, but rather of the *limits* of causality, i.e. of a *discontinuity* between *different causalities*. Arbitrariness, which *in this sense* could also be called *material indeterminacy*, is *the causal equivalent of difference*.

To return to language, as it should already be evident from what we have said so far, relations between *signs* and referents also include the relations between signs themselves: *each sign is the referent of some other sign* (the inverse though does *not* necessarily hold—if it did, it would amount to the abolition of the distinction between discourse and the non-discursive). *Referentiality is at once an internal and an external property of language (and discourse)*. At this stage of our approach, since we have for the time being set aside the relations between signifiers and signifieds, and since we are now concerned with arbitrariness as a relation between the material/objective elements of language (and discourse), as for the arbitrariness of *internal* referentiality, it goes without saying that this pertains to *the relations between signifiers*. Between the signifiers of different languages, arbitrariness is generalised and quite obvious. Less evident is the arbitrariness between the signifiers of the same language, given that most words derive from other ones. Of course the most evident arbitrariness—which is *also* responsible for the arbitrariness between different languages—prevails in the relations between signifiers and *external* referents. This particular arbitrariness, which is most apparent, which is indeed what Saussure had at least *mainly* in mind when he was talking about the arbitrariness of the linguistic sign, and which characterises all "natural" languages, in what precisely does it consist? Why is it self-evident that the object "tree" does not cause the sound (and the sound-image) "tree", neither the sound "arbre" nor the sound "Baum", and that consequently nor do these three sounds cause each other? Why is it considered as self-explanatory that the object "tree" causes some other material object, e.g. the object "wooden table", but not the linguistic sound (of whatever language) that corresponds to it (to the object "tree")?

The answer is related to the fact that, as we said just above, within the same language arbitrariness is largely reduced – that is, with the fact that between signifiers of the same language there are *to a large extent relations of causality*. In other words, the *limitation*, that is, the *finitude* of causality, which as we have said is what arbitrariness basically is, in the case of the relation between signifier and (external) referent consists in that we have to do *with different systems of causality, and consequently with discontinuous-between-them causalities*. If we stay on the example with the tree: The *object* "tree" may be involved, as a *cause of the wooden table*, in the causality system of the production of material goods, for example; and as an *effect of the seed*, in the causality system of the reproduction of the plant kingdom. It remains however *outside*, either as cause or as effect, *the causality systems of the languages that refer to it*.

The object "tree", as *at once cause and effect of (at least) two different causality systems*, serves as an example of how there can be a continuity between such different, and consequently initially discontinuous between them, material systems. The examples of course are countless. The specificity of language consists in that, even though (*partly*) a material system of causalities itself, *as a material system* it establishes no continuity with the different material systems of causalities to which it relates. I believe that this is where the essence of the arbitrariness between signifiers and (external) referents lies.

Having investigated the two basic properties of language that ensure the non-reducibility of its materiality, namely difference and arbitrariness, we can now formulate our basic thesis on subjectivity in language, that is, on signifieds: *The signifieds, or concepts, are what fills in the gaps of the discontinuity brought about by the fundamental finitude of the material/objective elements of language: namely, as to the relations between signifiers, by the property of difference, and as to the relations between signifiers and (external) referents, by the property of arbitrariness*. The fact that they fill in the gaps of discontinuity *does not necessarily mean* that they abolish discontinuity and establish continuity;

they certainly do this *in some cases*, but not always. Below we will examine when and how. More generally, let us say that the filling in of the gaps constitutes a "proof" for the existence of subjectivity in language. In the following sense: language, as a *systematically discontinuous system*, both in the internal relations of its material elements (difference) and in the relations of causality with other material systems (arbitrariness), could not do what it does, it would have no reason of existence, if the realm of subjectivity was not inherent in it, in the form of signifieds or concepts. The "proof" in this case could not but be hypothetical, since we have to do with the realm of hypotheticality itself, accepting that "hypothesis" means "formation of concepts" (while "hypostasis" marks objective existence).

In an alternative formulation, we could say that, just as discontinuity *itself*, in the dual form of the properties of difference and arbitrariness, ensures the non-reducibility of language's objectivity/hypostaticality/materiality, so the *gaps* of the (dual) discontinuity ensure the non-reducibility of its subjectivity/hypotheticality/conceptuality.

We may now come to how the terms "metaphor" and "metonymy", being directly linked with arbitrariness and difference, and consequently with the objectivity/materiality of language (and discourse), also demonstrate how the latter determines its subjectivity/conceptuality. Having explained above that arbitrariness is the *causal equivalent* of difference, I believe that, from an ontological viewpoint and since we are here still concerned with the question of the ontological priority, the fundamental term here is *difference*. I will thus try to show how the conceptualisation of metaphor and metonymy may lead to a *thought on difference*, which does not allow for the reductionism that permeates both Hegelianism and formal logic, and that consists in reducing difference to opposition or antithesis and in treating the latter as the other side of identity. To formulate the issue in one sentence, I believe that the conceptualisation of metaphor and metonymy can effect *a non-reductionist connection between identity, opposition and difference*.

Before I proceed to investigate this issue, I have to interject an important clarification. The "determination" of conceptuality by materiality, which consists in the former *being caused* by the latter, since the former is as we said just above hypothetical by definition, cannot but be itself hypothetical. Hypotheses, that is, theories, also exist in the natural sciences of course, as well as *in ontology when it refers to material entities themselves*. The difference though is that, in those cases, hypotheses refer to causalities that we accept, even if axiomatically, they exist objectively; that is, as I said above with the example of the earthquake, that they exist independently of the concepts referring to them. Causality here *remains* hypothetical also on the level of the "object" in quotation marks, since the effect part of the cause-effect relation, i.e. subjectivity itself, is by definition a *non-primary* object. The same holds for the inverse case, when subjectivity/conceptuality occupies the position of cause and objectivity/materiality that of effect: for example, when we form concepts, i.e. make hypotheses or construct theories, about how subjectivity influences matter *by way of action*. In other words, to put it bluntly: I believe that whatever I say in this text, as to what happens both in subjectivity and in the relation between subjectivity and objectivity, *would not exist if I did not say it and if the theories I am based on in order to say it did not exist either*. And this not according to some principle of the type: "everything is relative" or "all things are constructions", but because I believe that *everything directly related to concepts and subjectivity should in principle be considered as primarily free and self-determinable*.

A justifiable question of course would be the expected: how then does theory in the area of philosophy and of the broader field of the human sciences differ from fictional literature? An answer we could give is that *the incessant — explicit or implicit — empirical referent as well as the constant empirical-scientific background of this theory is historical facts and historical science respectively*. Without of course implying that history and historiography do not involve *innumerable* questions of relations of subjectivity and objectivity, I believe nonetheless that in those cases there is the *objective* component of *already accomplished facts* -in precisely the sense of *material* facts or events: even the existence of some recorded evidence is a *material* fact-, which also determines to a large extent the way in which theory is practiced; *when* it does so, in so far as we once more have to do with a *hypothetical* determination, which amounts to saying *when* theory *does* differ from fiction.

The issue at hand now is how a thought on difference inspired by Saussurian linguistics and particularly by the conceptualisation of metaphor and metonymy could lead to a non-reductionist connection between identity, opposition and difference. Very schematically and on a first level of analysis, metaphor encompasses the concepts of identity and opposition, while metonymy the concept of difference.

According to linguistics-semiology, metaphor means *similarity-comparability-substitution-disjunction*, and metonymy means *contiguity-combination-conjunction*.[151]

Let us start with the former. This nexus of four alternative terms that describe what metaphor means creates the conceptual leeway for the *non-effaceable distinction* between identity and opposition. That is, for a distinction that makes it plain that neither is opposition a covert form of identity nor can in any other fashion one concept be reduced to the other. Why is this so? Because both identity and opposition, within this conceptual nexus of the four terms, acquire a *functional autonomy as concepts*, precisely because the significance of each is allowed to be demonstrated, in its *complexity*, its *flexibility* and its *practical usability*. Somewhat more specifically, but *rather schematically and without this being unqualified in its practical application*, when it is a matter of identity, the terms similarity-comparability-substitution *are more "in play"*, and when of opposition, the terms disjunction-substitution-comparability; let us say in these orders of priority.

---

151. See above, fn. 18.

Now the distinction between these two groups of terms, between similarity-comparability-substitution-disjunction (i.e. metaphor) on one hand and contiguity-combination-conjunction (i.e. metonymy) on the other, ensures the non-reducible relation between opposition and difference. It is clear that we have to do with two separate conceptual complexes, in which each one of these two concepts acquires its functional autonomy in a way even clearer than in the case of identity and opposition, since in this case it is a matter of two separate groups of terms anyway. *Nevertheless*, the non-Hegelian approach treats opposition as a special kind of difference. This, in the metaphor/metonymy conceptualisation, is provided for by the fact that quite often some conceptual-symbolic relationship can be considered *either* as metaphor *or* as metonymy.

Let me take as an example a question I have repeatedly put in my undergraduate course *Communication and Power*: leader of New Democracy/leader of PASOK. There is *opposition* (disjunction-substitution-comparability: leaders of the two large *rival* Greek political parties), so we have to do with metaphor, but there is also *difference that is not opposition* (conjunction-combination-contiguity: they *coexist* in the same political system), so we have to do with metonymy.

Perhaps we could say in correspondence to the above that, in cases where metaphor implies opposition, this metaphor is a special kind of metonymy. Besides, the most close interweaving existing anyhow between the two terms is already apparent, in so far as we hold that if metaphor is to exist there should "first" be metonymy.

Let us stay on the example with the two large Greek political parties. First of all, to avoid being reproached that, after all my obsession with the distinction between subjectivity and objectivity, I myself bring back the confusion of the Laclau and Mouffe's sort by dealing with real political parties in linguistic terms, I hasten to make clear that, in saying here "New Democracy/PASOK", I mean the *signs* of those real political parties: *their names*, as well as the *discursive formations* that are endorsed and marked by these names. These are signs and discursive formations inherent in contemporary Greek political discourse, in the discourse that *refers* to contemporary Greek political life (in the narrow sense of the activity of political parties and governments), that is *enounced* within it and that is therefore *formed* by its material components (socio-economic interests, influences and dependences, financial strength, control over state apparatus, already existing electoral strength), but that also in turn to a vast degree *forms* it by constituting acting subjects and by articulating the practices of which it consists.

Our insistence (here as well) on the distinction between subjectivity/conceptuality on one hand and objectivity/materiality on the other, and consequently on the specificity of discourse in relation to its material conditions and to non-discursive practices, consists in pointing out that relations of opposition and difference *as relations of metaphor and metonymy* are *discursive* relations and *not real (objective)* relations, without however this implying that there is not a *most close interdependence* between the former and the latter. The fact that there is nevertheless a distinction and mutually relative autonomy between them entails that whatever we say about the non-reducibility between identity, opposition and difference, which will first of all concern discursive relations, would hold *even more* with objective relations, given the *additional indeterminacy* brought about by this distinction and mutually relative autonomy.

Let us start with metaphor and opposition. The "three-sided" opposition existing between them guarantees that we have to do with a complex relation, which cannot be reduced to negation, or to the other side of identity. The relation is one of opposition in *concrete* ways:

- *Disjunction:* Beside the words (the signs) "(currently) governing party", there should be *either* one name *or* the other, we cannot have both. The disjunction in this case marks the "harshest" form of opposition both in political discourse and in the corresponding practices. It is a matter of those terms of the political system that ensure that as a rule after every electoral battle one party will be the victor and the other the vanquished. Disjunction is the linguistic equivalent to what more or less correctly in contemporary political discourse is called *bipolarism*.

- *Substitution:* After the next elections, it is *possible* that one name will *substitute* the other beside the title of "governing party". Substitution here lessens the intensity of the opposition, in the sense that whichever party wins the elections will be called to govern the same country and in the same constitutional-institutional framework with that of its predecessor. On the other hand, the very concept of substitution maintains a quite safe distance between opposition and identity: "substitution" means that *now someone else* is in the same position. To the extent that the programmes of the two parties are indeed opposite (which is obviously highly questionable), they do not identify with each other simply by the fact that either one may form a government's programme.

- *Comparability:* Particularly as to comparability, it emerges perhaps more distinctly than in the other two forms of opposition in what sense is opposition a special kind of difference: if the parties bearing the names "New Democracy" and "PASOK" are to be *opposite* to each other, it goes without saying that they should *differ*—besides, "comparing" means observing similarities and differences. Since we are on the level of discursive relations, comparison here concerns first and foremost the programmes but also the multitude of other ways in which the discourse of the political parties is enounced, and by extension their corresponding or *non*-corresponding practices.

Let us now go to metonymy and difference. To start with, while in metaphor comparison is inevitable because it may lead either to identity/similarity or to opposition as a special kind of difference, in metonymy difference is considered as *given from the very beginning*. But we have to do with a "three-sided" difference, which renders unfeasible its subordination to opposition or its reduction to the other side of identity. Once again the significance of the "different kinds of difference" consists in the *concretisation* of being different:

- *Conjunction:* The discourses of New Democracy and PASOK are *conjunct* to each other in that they define in common and in a dominant fashion the practice of public political dialogue. Any view expressed on a major Greek political issue cannot avoid taking into account the positions of *both* the ruling party *and* the opposition.

- *Combination:* Both in parliament and outside, the discourses of the two parties *combine* in the sense that one party promotes governmental policies while the other criticises them. The combination consists in that the two discursive practices are the two absolutely necessary and complementary terms of the "parliamentary game".

- Finally, *contiguity:* The semiology of the spatial arrangement of parliamentary benches demonstrates the ideological position by which parties define themselves in terms of the Right-Left axis. Therefore, the fact that they are *immediately contiguous* (no other party lies between, notwithstanding some rather peculiar cases – Politiki Anixi, LAOS) is an indication that, at least as far as their self-definition is concerned, the two large parties meet at more or less the centre of the ideologico-political spectrum.

I set forth the above examples, obviously not as a model for the analysis of political discourse, let alone of its referents. As to the latter, perhaps at this point the occasion arises to clarify something that should have already become evident: Discourse analysis does not aspire to constitute *by itself* a method for the analysis of non-discursive practices. At best, it demonstrates how discourse *might* influence and form non-discursive realities and practices, and how in turn it is constituted in those (further down we will of course refer to the "burning" issue of the *distinction* between *discursive* and *non-discursive practices*).

But even as to political (or any other) discourse itself, it is blatantly apparent that a methodology based *only or mainly* on the conceptualisation of metaphor and metonymy would be most insufficient. And not merely because as description of relations of meaning, despite the quadruple and triple alternative signification of the two basic concepts respectively, it is actually of a quite limited range, but for one additional reason as well: I gave the above examples so as to explain how the concepts of metaphor and metonymy demonstrate the *materiality of signs and discourse* in a way that does not allow for their reduction to the pair *identity/opposition,* neither to *formal-logical relations.* In this sense, without this meaning to say that the conceptualisation of metaphor and metonymy is *entirely* useless as a tool for the analysis of *representational* discourse, the logic that it defines is *more or less the inverse* of the taxonomic logic of the latter.

On the other hand, even though we do not have to do with a self-contained analytic tool, the *multiplicity*, the *discontinuity* and the *asymmetry* that characterise relations between signs and between discursive formations and that emerge by way of the conceptualisation of metaphor and metonymy, pertain to a correspondingly multiple and asymmetric more general *logic*, i.e. *conceptual correlation*, that is effectively congruous both with the (of crucial importance, as will be made evident further down) *non-representational footholds* of representational discourse—there is no *purely* representational (i.e. *purely* taxonomic) discourse—and with the likewise multiple and discontinuous form pertaining to the *referents* of (political or otherwise) discourse, i.e. to (political or otherwise) practice. Something which is not the case with a bipolar logic of the sort, for example: "liberalism/socialism *or* populism/modernisation and their exponents", which would hand over to a purely descriptive analysis of "conjuncture" whatever it could not fit into some of its bipolar schemes, either on the level of discourse or on that of practice.

As I believe I have shown when referring to Laclau and Mouffe's work, even in highly complex and articulate attempts to analyse political phenomena, in so far as they reduce—be it after an especially sophisticated conceptual elaboration—all differences to the identity/opposition schema (or equivalence/antagonism or any other of its versions or variations), they are indeed inadequate when we have to do with cases that cannot be included in it. Laclau and Mouffe, somewhere rather close to the beginning of their theoretical approach, criticise economistic Marxism on the basis that it leaves outside its theoretical/interpretative scheme whatever cannot be reduced to the "base" and to the class system deriving from it.[152] They do something rather similar though with the logic of "equivalence". What happens with social movements if they do not comply with it? Do they simply remain included within the existing "system of differences", which means, if we "translate" Laclau and Mouffe's terminology, within the dominant sociopolitical regime?[153]

We have already pointed out Laclau and Mouffe's quite striking and in some sense provocative differentiation from the rest of the "poststructuralists" as to the question of the approach to "difference"; a differentiation all the more striking with the case of Derrida, the thinker who apparently more than anyone else radicalised difference by way of its conversion into *différance*. Apparently though: to close the circle of correlations, in a similar sense to which I believe that Laclau and Mouffe laid the foundations for Žižek's flagrant Hegelian idealism (see above), I also think that something equivalent was done by Derrida as to the conservative transformation of difference by Laclau and Mouffe. With the generalisation of discourse (or of writing, in Derrida's terms)—in relation to which generalisation Laclau and

---

152. Laclau and Mouffe, *op. cit.*, p. 48.

153. Even though she is a theorist not dissociated from some sort of Hegelianism, see Judith Butler's related critique - Butler, Laclau and Žižek, *op. cit.*, pp. 162-169.

Mouffe expressly refer to him[154] — the conceptual preconditions for the approach of both discourse itself and the non-discursive on the basis of either formal logic or of Hegelian contradiction have already been laid.

In the passage from Derrida cited by Laclau and Mouffe, we read: "...This was the moment when language invaded the universal problematic, the moment when, in the absence of a center or origin, everything became discourse, provided we can agree on this word, that is to say, a system in which the central signified, the original or transcendental signified, is never absolutely present outside a system of differences. The absence of the transcendental signified extends the domain and the play of signification infinitely."[155] I think it is quite obvious that the (otherwise self-evident) interjection: "provided we can agree on this word", implies that in his own work he prefers the term "writing". Laclau and Mouffe insist on the word "discourse", and this is what allows them to refer positively to the way in which Foucault uses this term.[156] With one important differentiation.

They explicitly criticise Foucault for the distinction between *discursive practices* and *non-discursive practices*. According to them, all practices are discursive practices.[157] So while the common use of the *term* "discourse" at first glance associates them more with Foucault, in essence they are definitely closer to Derrida in that they accept *the generalising character of discourse — or of writing, regardless, in this case*. That is, I believe that, while the distinction between generalised (according to Laclau and Mouffe) "discourse" and (Derridean) "writing" is certainly there but it is of lesser importance compared to their fundamental accord that there is nothing *outside* discourse or *outside* writing or the text,[158] the disaccord of both the ones and the other with Foucault on this particular issue is of paramount importance and has to do with our central topics: the conception of materiality and the subjectivity-objectivity distinction.

As we saw at the beginning, Laclau and Mouffe stress the material existence of discourse, being opposed to the view that promotes its mental character. The thing is, though, that the importance of the materiality of discourse, as well as of materiality in general, emerges only in relation to *what is not material in it, which thereby differentiates it from what lies outside it*. The approach that says: "Everything is discourse, and discourse is *only* (or *mainly*) material (and not mental)", far from constituting some radical version of a post-Marxist materialism, it on quite the contrary diminishes to the point of extinction the *critical effectivity of the category "matter"*.

---

154. Laclau and Mouffe, *op. cit.*, pp. 111-112.

155. Derrida, *L'écriture et la différence*, p. 411 – English translation: p. 280.

156. Laclau and Mouffe, *op. cit.*, pp. 105-106.

157. *Ibid.*, p. 107.

158. See Derrida, *De la grammatologie*, p. 227 ff. – English translation: p. 158 ff.

Chapter 8
Discourse and the non-discursive

In the preceding pages, I was following two different but constantly interlinked theoretical trajectories. One was to demonstrate the stalemates arising from the various forms of the abolition of the distinction between subjectivity and objectivity into which a vast portion of the "post-Althusserian" and more generally "post-structuralist" problematic has led itself, choosing, I think not in the least arbitrarily, as their main representatives, Laclau and Derrida respectively. The other was to try and "salvage", so to speak, some concepts which I nonetheless consider important to a materialist grounding for discourse analysis, from Saussure's linguistic-semiological problematic, on the interpretation of which both the above theoretical approaches have largely been based, certainly each in its own different way, and certainly both offering an interpretation different from mine.

It has been many years ago since I referred to the particularity of Michel Foucault's work, regarding on one hand his proximity to and on the other his differentiation from both Althusserian Marxism and structuralism.[159] His relation to Althusserian Marxism had concerned me mainly regarding the question of *ideology*—that is, Foucault's relation to the term "ideology" in general. This has since repeatedly concerned me;[160] and I suppose it will keep on concerning me. His relation to structuralism I had approached mainly with reference to a *thematic* of structuralism, namely the thematic of narrative and the media, which in my view could be approached on the basis

---

159. Kyrkos Doxiadis, "Foucault, ideology, communication" (in Greek), *Review of Social Research*, 71, 1988, pp. 18-43.

160. Doxiadis, *Subjectivity and power*, Doxiadis, "Foucault and the three-headed king", Doxiadis, "Foucault and ideology".

of some Foucauldian terms, without being particularly occupied with matters of *methodology and its philosophical presuppositions*.

Therefore two matters remain in abeyance, which concern the way in which Foucault differentiates himself from the two above theoretical trends, and which share, as we will see, a common philosophical background. The first one concerns Foucault's relation to Marxism as a *materialist philosophy of social relations and practices*, and the second one his relation to Saussurian linguistics as a *materialist methodological approach to language and representation*.

Starting with the investigation of the first relationship, it would not be excessively arbitrary to suggest that a large part of his work, at least in one of its dimensions, puts to work Marxist philosophy of social history in a *non-economistic but certainly materialist direction*, both from a viewpoint of thematics—investigating how concrete power mechanisms led to the formation of the first capitalist relations of production[161]—and from a conceptual viewpoint, utilising the conceptualisation of *social classes* to explain the asymmetric diffusion of sexual discourses and practices in modern Western societies.[162] The non-economistic (*but materialist*) approach consists: first, as to thematics, mainly in the emphasis given to the human *body*, as a central locus but also means for the exercise of power in general and not merely as a bearer of productive capacity; and second, methodologically, in the importance attributed to *space* in the analytical descriptions of how power is exercised, as against the economistic logic of the *time* of capitalist accumulation and development and of the succession of the various modes of production.[163]

Foucault's relation to Marxism is an issue about which much has been written and said. I have repeatedly dealt with this topic, and as to this I can do nothing but refer to my older relevant texts.[164] Putting it in one sentence, in my older writings I was focusing mainly on Foucault's differentiation from the Hegelianism that characterised most Marxist trends, as well as from the economism that was also characteristic of Marxism, including Althusserianism. The *new* element in my current approach is the question of materialism.

---

161. See, for example, Michel Foucault, *Discipline and punish: The birth of the prison* (translated by Alan Sheridan), Harmondsworth: Penguin Books, 1979 (French edition: 1975), but also Foucault, "La vérité et les formes juridiques", *Dits et écrits 1954-1988, II*, especially pp. 570-623.

162. See especially Michel Foucault, *The History of sexuality, Volume 1: An introduction* (translated by Robert Hurley), London: Allen Lane, 1979 (French edition: 1976), pp. 119-129.

163. See, for example, Foucault, *Dits et écrits 1954-1988, III*, pp. 28-40 – English translation: Michel Foucault, *Power/knowledge: Selected interviews and other writings 1972-1977* (translated by Colin Gordon, Leo Marshall, John Mepham and Kate Soper), Brighton: Harvester, 1980, pp. 63-77. On this, see also Kyrkos Doxiadis, *Nationalism, ideology, mass media* (in Greek), Athens: Plethron, 1995, pp. 11-43.

164. See above, fns 159 and 160.

My view on this question could first of all be summed up in the following aphoristic formulation: *Foucault is profoundly materialist without declaring it*. I believe that the fact that Foucault's materialism is "undeclared" is for reasons similar to those for which, as I have maintained, he has explicitly dissociated himself from the term "ideology".[165] Materialism as a philosophical stance, since the nineteenth century has been identified with "official" Marxism, and consequently with economic reductionism, in one or other of its multiple versions, from Lukács's Hegelian class reductionism to Althusser's structural economism.

Let us say that the avoidance of declaring his materialism was "necessary" within a certain discursive regime (I am employing a term of his own[166]), which indeed tended to identify materialism with the "official" Marxism from which Foucault took pains to differentiate himself. The cost of course was that this was one of the factors that led to him constantly being included, by that same dominant discursive regime, amongst the most preeminent names of "postmodernism"—given that the latter is indeed characterised, among other things, by the fact that it does not care one bit about the question of materialism (and idealism). A somewhat more extreme misinterpretation, which is also partly due to Foucault's denial of presenting himself as a materialist, was Dreyfus and Rabinow's ranking him among the phenomenologists to which I referred above. Foucault's concern with the body, during the period in which he was occupied with the study of disciplinary mechanisms and of sexuality, insofar as it did not promote itself as a materialist problematic, was "easily" interpretable as some variation of the phenomenology of perception of the Merleau-Ponty sort.[167]

Obviously the problem of Foucault's materialism is not a matter of a simple declaration. I am of course not implying that if Foucault had simply declared himself to be a materialist when concerned with the body and surveillance mechanisms all the above misinterpretations would have been avoided. Furthermore, the fact that Foucault had not declared himself as a materialist may be related to something more profound, and not merely to his wish that his name is not connected with "official" Marxism.

There is some additional irony in the fact that Dreyfus and Rabinow convert him into a phenomenologist. I referred above to the fact that phenomenology was a main target of Foucault's critique, at least during the first period of his thought. So if we accept that, on the level of *generally declaring* himself as "materialist", the basic reason for his denial was to avoid being identified with "official" Marxism, on the level of *concretely formulating* his materialism his denial to clarify his position was probably due to his insistence on completely dissociating himself from the phenomenologists. I will presently explain what I mean by this.

---

165. *Ibid.*, p. 25.

166. Foucault, *Dits et écrits 1954-1988, III*, pp. 143-144 – English translation: Foucault, *Power/knowledge*, pp. 112-113.

167. See above, fn. 123.

It has already become apparent from my hitherto theoretical analysis—and I intend of course to show this more extensively below—that Foucault's non-economistic materialism acquires its concrete form in what I have called above a "materialist version of the critical philosophy of finitude". On the other hand, the philosophy of finitude has largely been identified with phenomenology, as is evident in some of the above references to Husserl, and as is also shown by Foucault's own analyses in *The order of things*.[168] The truth is that in this particular issue phenomenology undermines itself. Taking into account both Derrida's "correction" of Husserl that we saw above and the phenomenologists' own writings, it is quite evident that, in this continental-European philosophical trend, prevailing since the beginning of the twentieth century, *fundamental* finitude ultimately concedes its privileged place to some version of the (fundamental, that is, hypostatised) infinite.[169]

---

168. Foucault, *Les mots et les choses*, especially pp. 329-346 – English translation: pp. 318-335.
169. Quite schematically, I would say that this "concession" on the part of phenomenology is concretely discernible in mainly three philosophical manipulations:
(a) Consideration of philosophy, even if "in the form of an endless program", in accordance with the "concrete possibility of the Cartesian idea" of an "all-embracing science grounded on an absolute foundation", which ultimately, radically differentiating itself as to this issue from Cartesianism's natural-scientific orientation, aims at an "*all-embracing self-investigation*", a "universal self-knowledge" - Husserl, *op. cit.*, pp. 156 and 160-161 – English translation: pp. 152 and 156.
(b) Retention of "transcendental idealism" as the term that marks a systematic "explication of my ego as subject of every possible cognition", but with the simultaneous unequivocal rejection of the Kantian "possibility of a world of things in themselves", even "as a limiting concept" (Grenzbegriff) - *ibid.*, p. 88 – English translation: p. 86. Phenomenology's rejection of Kantian "things in themselves" is of decisive importance as to the undermining of Kantian philosophy's specificity in relation to Cartesianism, since, as Heidegger has shown, the distinction between "thing in itself" and "appearance" (Erscheinung) is conceivable only if it is seen as directly linked with the *finitude of human knowledge* (Endlichkeit der menschlichen Erkenntnis) and hence with the *finitude of human beings* (Endlichkeit des Menschen) - Heidegger, *op. cit.*, especially pp. 25-35 – English translation: pp. 17-23.
(c) Substitution of the Cartesian doublet God/Reason with the doublet World/Reason, by way of an acceptance of the inherent rationality of the world, and, at the same time, substitution of the Cartesian subject's metaphoro-metonymic relationship with God, which led to the former's potential omniscience-omnipotence (to this I will refer more extensively further on), with the human being's metaphoro-metonymic relationship with the world, which leads to a radical disparagement of the fundamental finitude of human beings, and to a consequent grounding for a Cartesian (philosophical) anthropology – see Maurice Merleau-Ponty, *Phénoménologie de la perception*, Paris: Gallimard, 1945, especially pp. 20-22 and 461-470 – English translation (Colin Smith): *Phenomenology of perception*, London and Henley: Routledge & Kegan Paul, 1962, pp. xix-xxi and 400-409.
It is quite indicative that Foucault in *The order of things* is not particularly concerned with precisely these aspects of phenomenology, thereby enhancing the misleading impression that the latter is but a further development of the Kantian "analytic of finitude" – see Foucault, *op. cit.*, especially pp. 336-337 – English translation: pp. 325-326.

The fact remains, however, that, as a philosophical *term*, finitude, once again within the framework of the discursive regime in which Foucault's work articulated itself, was indeed tied with phenomenology, and it would therefore be difficult if not impossible to formulate an explicit philosophical position that would on one hand present itself as materialist and on the other be based on the concept of (fundamental) finitude.

So the question is how, for all that, we could discern in Foucault's work some elements of a materialist philosophy based on finitude, in the sense that has been attributed to it in the present text: namely, of a philosophy based on the materialist axiom that fundamental finitude and objective existence are fundamental and exclusive properties of material entities.

At first glance, but also with reference to what I have said above about Foucault's relation to Marxist materialism, one would think that the period in which Foucault began to be concerned with discipline and with the body, i.e. the period between *The archaeology of knowledge* (1969) and *Discipline and punish* (1975), is the period of Foucault's big materialist turn: in the sense that he had hitherto remained in the epistemological field of the history of ideas, no doubt radically dissociating himself from the main trends prevailing in it, but nevertheless himself stressing that he remains on the level of discourse;[170] and that since that time, since around the early to mid seventies, being also largely driven by his activism around the problem of prisons in France, he began to be concerned with purely material issues, relating to the exercise of power beyond and to a large extent irrespectively of the realm of discourse and ideas. It has long been my view, and it still remains, that Foucault never ceased being concerned *mainly* with discourse, and hence with ideas, even when his thematic was directed towards sectors of social practice most evidently material and largely non-discursive. In addition, and to complement this view, I will here maintain that his (undeclared) materialism, in the (also undeclared) sense I mentioned above, emerges *mainly* in how he conceives of discourse itself on one hand and of discourse's relations to non-discursive practices on the other.[171]

I will start "backwards" with the latter, and specifically with the second part of the latter, since the former (that the emphasis was always on discourse) derives from it. I believe that the way in which Foucault conceives of the relation between discursive and non-discursive practices is of crucial significance, because on one hand it answers Laclau and Mouffe's critique as to the distinction between the two, and on the other, on a more general level and with regard to the question raised right from the start of the present text, it constitutes an indication of how one can hold a view on the relation

---

170. Michel Foucault, *L'archéologie du savoir*, Paris: Gallimard, 1969, p. 101 – English translation (A.M. Sheridan Smith): *The archaeology of knowledge*, London: Tavistock, 1972, p. 76.

171. A distinction most explicitly present in *ibid.*, pp. 212-215 – English translation: pp. 162-165.

between subjectivity and objectivity that does *not in the slightest* downgrade its complexity and intricacy, *without on the other hand tending to abolish it as a distinction*.

I will first of all agree with Beverley Brown and Mark Cousins, to whom Laclau and Mouffe refer in a footnote, that Foucault "makes no distribution of phenomena into two classes of being, Discourse and the Non-Discursive".[172] If we had to do with a *taxonomic type* of distinction, that is, with a distinction that would set some criteria according to which every element of existence could be considered *either* as discourse *or* as non-discursive, this would be anyhow far from Foucault's logic, since a central aim of his work was to criticise taxonomic thought and logic.[173] A question of course always left open in such cases is what *replaces* taxonomic thought and logic. The answer is directly given by the first part of the second issue raised above, i.e. by the way Foucault conceives of *discourse itself*. This way is such that it answers the second part too.

The way in which Foucault deals with discourse itself is *correspondingly non-taxonomic*. A *taxonomic* treatment of discourse would consist in an attempt to provide a *definition based on a one-to-one correspondence*, that is, to construct a stable conceptual framework, which would "automatically" provide the (*negative*) criteria for what is *not* discourse. If, for example, he were to say, "Discourse is any ensemble of linguistic symbols", and if, of course, we could agree on what is "linguistic symbols" (for example: words and, in written discourse, punctuation marks), then things would be quite simple. Whatever does not form an ensemble of linguistic symbols is not discourse. A taxonomic definition can by itself assign being and non-being into two more or less easily distinguishable categories. Whatever is discourse belongs to the first category, whatever is not to the second. Once again, since we have to do with taxonomy, the aim is to *establish continuity*. The *limits* set by the taxonomic definition are *limits of continuity between being and non-being*.

Before we proceed to how Foucault conceives of discourse itself (and thereby of its relation to the non-discursive), let me come back to my own "definition" of discourse that I provided above: "So we opt for a 'definition' of discourse that does not separate discourse from language, it merely marks this *epistemic displacement of emphasis*, and we say that *discourse is language in relation to referents*." I have used here quotation marks for the word "definition". It is certainly not a taxonomic definition, for two basic reasons.

One reason has to do with the "definition" of which it forms a derivative, so to speak, that is, with the "definition" of *language itself* that I provide a little further down: the "*actual ability to form concepts*". In this "definition"

---

172. Beverley Brown and Mark Cousins, "The linguistic fault: the case of Foucault's archaeology", in Mike Gane (ed.), *Towards a critique of Foucault*, London and New York: Routledge and Kegan Paul, 1986, p. 36, and Laclau and Mouffe, *op. cit.*, p. 145, fn. 13.

173. See especially Foucault, *Les mots et les choses*, pp. 60-261 – English translation: pp. 46-249.

we see "in play" three different concepts relating between them in such a fashion that precludes any establishment of continuity between being and non-being. The "formation of concepts", according to what we have said, is virtually coextensive with the realm of subjectivity in general. On the other hand, at the other end of the "definition", the concept "actual", which derives from the concept of *action*, refers to something that permeates both subjectivity and objectivity, even though it belongs *mainly* to the latter since it is something *mainly* material. And in the middle of the "definition", the concept "ability" perplexes matters even more as to the demarcation of limits of continuity, in so far as we have to do with the concept of *being able*, which we could *axiomatically* consider as something that calls into question any sort of limit, be it of continuity or of discontinuity.

Let us go now to the "definition" of discourse itself. There is first of all a syntactic unorthodoxy: "language *in relation*". "In relation" is an adverbial modifier, therefore, according to the rules of "orthodox" syntax, it could modify only a verb or a participle or an adjective or another adverb, and not a noun. But it is not a matter of error, quite often in language this irregularity takes place without it being considered as a mistake. "The above sentence", "the downstairs flat", "the person in the middle", "capital in general". In its generality, let us say that this syntactic unorthodoxy is one of the multitude of cases that demonstrate the *flexibility* of the logic of language and discourse (as against the inflexibility of formal logic), to which we have already referred above in relation to metaphor and metonymy and to which we will refer anew further down. In this case, the unorthodox use of the adverbial modifier "in relation" demonstrates first of all the intensely subjective character of the "definition" for an anyhow *mainly* subjective entity. If we had to "rectify" at any cost this syntactic unorthodoxy, we could say that here "in relation" modifies an *implied* participle: "language *considered* in relation to referents". Besides, the reasoning that led me to choose this particular "definition", as we have seen, directly involved the subjective element. The "epistemic displacement of emphasis" which is marked by this "definition" has to do with the *mainly* subjective realm of the formation of concepts in the relevant epistemological fields (linguistics, semiology etc.). Stressing the subjective element allows the "definition" from the start to avoid the (taxonomic) establishment of limits of continuity between *language* and *discourse*. Whether something is language or discourse will depend on the particular *consideration* (in relation...).

Let us now take into account the last part of the "definition": "in relation *to referents*". We could say that the closest verb corresponding to the noun *language* is the verb *to speak*. (I could certainly be reproached here by the Derrideans for a "phonocentric prejudice", but I believe I have adequately responded to this in my above treatment of the relevant matters.) We could also suppose that the corresponding verb for the noun *discourse* is *to say*. (Perhaps it is no accident that most Greek scholars translate *discourse* with *logos*, which directly derives from *legein* — *to say*.) What is the essential difference in meaning between the two verbs? Once again syntax proves to be quite illuminating. The verb *to speak* is *intransitive*, while the verb *to say* is *transitive*. So the corresponding verbs demonstrate two different considerations of language. *To speak*, being intransitive, i.e. being a verb that does not take a (direct) object, corresponds to language considered *by itself*, that is, *as speech*, that is, without objects, without referents. *To say*, being transitive, corresponds to language considered *as discourse*, that is, *in relation to objects/referents*.

Here is an incident frequently occurring today in everyday life. You call someone on the phone and they say, "I'll call you in a while because I'm *speaking* (or *talking*: the verb *to talk* is also intransitive) with such and such on my mobile." The possible indiscretion of the question, "And *what are you saying* (with such and such on your mobile)?", demonstrates the distance between the *two practices*; the *practice of speech* and the *practice of discourse*.[174] The *shared* concept of *practice* in this case makes it easier to understand that the distinction I pointed out above using the syntax terms *intransitive* and *transitive verb* is not as abstract as it may seem at first glance. Even the former of the two, speech, i.e. language considered by itself, severed from referents, can *as a practice* be something quite concrete, with extensive social significance and with most important material components.

To stay on the example with the telephone, what is more than obvious, especially in the age of the mobile phone, is the enormous importance of *speech time*. As we are constantly being reminded by the advertisements, *what you say* is of absolutely no importance, as long as you are able to *speak* for as long as you wish, paying little. Another such example is time of speech in parliament, which is distributed among the speakers according to the regulations of the parliament, regardless of what they have to say. Some more subjective examples, though not necessarily less important. We often confront garrulous people without paying the slightest attention to what they say, we simply find them bothersome on account of their speaking so much. The student can't wait for the class to end, and is not listening at all to what the teacher is saying, just concerned that he/she is still speaking. We hear someone speaking in an entirely unknown language and consequently have no idea as to what they are saying. And a more positive example: we hear a song in a language that we also do not know, but we hear the speech of the lyrics with pleasure without knowing what they say, because we happen to like the singer's voice.

It would of course be wrong to assume that the above examples do not even have to do with language or practice of speech since we take into account only signifiers and not signifieds. In every example, signifieds are there and are definitely taken into account, even though in their generality. We know it is not merely a matter of dealing with some noise, and this is of definitive significance. With the mobile phone, as it is once more mani-

---

174. I deliberately use here the term "*practice* of speech" and not "speech *act*", one of the reasons being to avoid confusion with the term used in J.L. Austin and John R. Searle's *speech-act theory*, since the concept of speech act in that theory also implicates *reference*, thereby being clearly distinguished from speech *as language by itself*, i.e. *without referents*, as I mean it here. See Searle, *op. cit.*, especially pp. 72-96.

festly clear from advertising, an enormous part is played by the consumer's wish for *communication*, i.e. for exchange of *meaning*. In parliament, as well as in all institutions of public speech, what is supposed to matter in democracies is the equal rights as to *freedom of expression*, which means expression of *ideas*. We become irritated with a garrulous person, and we consequently *avoid listening to him/her*, which means we disparage his/her *thought*. Something similar happens with the hasty student and the teacher. We are annoyed with *not understanding*, and thus with not grasping the *concepts* of an unknown language. Finally, the *emotion* conveyed by a voice we enjoy hearing even though it sings in an unknown language betrays the seductive presence of the inaccessible *meaning* of the words.

So we are dealing here with language in all respects, with practice of speech in its completeness, but not with practice of discourse. It is of no importance or we do not care or do not understand *what is being said* by the person who speaks. The *practice of discourse* has all the characteristics of the practice of speech *plus something more*: what the speaking person *says*.

For a better understanding of the essence of referentiality, let us stay a bit longer on the distinction between practice of speech and practice of discourse. Is it a distinction that is based merely on the particular "point of view" from which we happen to examine a specific instance of speech or discourse each time? In all the examples I gave above, it is quite clear that we *could*, from another viewpoint, be interested also *in what is being said* in each case, which means that we could also consider them as instances of practice of discourse. Can there be a case of some practice of speech, which, from whatever viewpoint we may approach it, could not be considered as practice of discourse? In other words, can there be a practice of speech, i.e.—to remind ourselves of the Saussurian terminology—a signifying practice, a practice of signifiers and signifieds, *without referents*?

In the tradition of analytic philosophy there is the famous *liar's paradox*. Someone (say A) utters the phrase: "I am now lying." The paradox consists in that the cases of the proposition's truth and untruth coincide while being mutually exclusive: If it is true that A is lying, then A is speaking truthfully (therefore A is not lying). If A is lying that A is lying, then once again A is speaking truthfully (therefore once again A is not lying).[175]

The paradox arises from the fact that it is an instance of practice of speech that is *absolutely self-referential*. The adverbial modifier "now" ensures that A (the speaking subject) is not merely referring to A's own speech, which could mean that A is referring to a phrase A uttered two or three seconds ago, but is referring to *A's own speech at the very moment A is uttering it*. A logically equivalent formulation of the proposition, which would consequently lead to the same paradox, would be: "This proposition is false."

---

175. For a systematic (analytic-philosophical) investigation of the liar's paradox, see Jon Barwise and John Etchemendy, *The Liar: An essay on truth and circularity*, New York and Oxford: Oxford University Press, 1987.

The impasse of absolute self-referentiality though does not emerge only in the case of the above most famous paradox. Let us take the opposite proposition: "This proposition is true (therefore it is not false)." Or even the—also logically equivalent—opposite of the initial version: "I am now speaking truthfully (therefore I am not lying)." How could one react to such a practice of speech? "Well done. Let me congratulate you for your honesty."

We could of course assume that, apart from themselves, the above propositions also have some other referents, such as propositions *in general* or speech *in general*, as well as, above all, the true/false distinction *in general*. But on this point we should agree with Searle, who defines *referring expression* as an expression that "serves to pick out or identify one 'object' or 'entity' or 'particular' apart from other objects".[176] If we accept Searle's definition, and it will become immediately apparent why and in what sense we accept it, the above generalities could not be considered as referents. So the above examples, as absolutely self-referential, and given the evident impasse to which absolute self-referentiality leads in both cases—to a paradox in the former case, to utter non-sense in the latter—are *non-referential*. They are instances of practice of speech without reference, that is, instances of a practice of speech that could not also be considered as practice of discourse, from whatever viewpoint it might be approached.

---

176. Searle, *op. cit.*, pp. 26-27.

Chapter 9
On referentiality

We thus have a *first component of referentiality*: If a practice of speech is to be referential, and therefore to be capable of being considered as also a practice of discourse, it should refer to something *other than itself*.

Let us now take another example, "This proposition is in English." Once again of course we have a proposition that is *at least primarily* self-referential. But here something else is also mentioned, which could be considered as adequately "particular", the English language, and not any other language. It could therefore be considered as a referent, and this proposition could be considered as not absolutely self-referential, therefore as also a practice of discourse, even if in a secondary sense.

However, it would not be overly sceptical if someone raised the following objection. In the previous examples too, we could consider as referents: propositions and not linguistic phenomena like punctuation, pronunciation, individual words etc., speech and not any other human activity, the true/false distinction and not any other distinction. "Particularity" is much too abstract to suffice as criterion for referentiality.

It is probably no accident that Searle uses the words "object" and "entity' as interchangeable, in this specific instance, with the word "particular". The word "entity" is also too abstract, but the word "object" not that much. Running the risk of being unfairly considered as playing with words, I maintain that the word "object" is not abstract, because, in its primary sense, is what abolishes or in any case undermines abstractness. I am referring of course to primary objectivity, about which we have axiomatically accepted, together with fundamental finitude, as forming a fundamental and exclusive property of material entities. This last bit, that it forms a property of material entities together with fundamental finitude, is what may account for the interchangeability of meaning between "object" and "particular" that we find in Searle's definition.

In discussing fundamental finitude, earlier we pointed out that one of its direct effects was the fundamental *discontinuity* existing between material entities. In this sense, material entities as primary objects are distinguished or "*apart*" from each other before language with its referentiality intervenes to distinguish them. This fact may also account for the multiformity of possible classifications of natural objects to be met with in different cultures.[177] In its primary form, reference does not separate one object from others in accordance with some pre-existing linguistic taxonomy that distinguishes the particular from the general on the basis of the genus/species distinction and of some rules of categorisation. It merely responds to the fact that material entities are anyhow separate, i.e. discontinuous, between them, without there being some supreme principle that would classify them according to their differences and similarities.[178] In this sense, the word that marks the primary referential function is not some noun, which always, in every language, presupposes some form of taxonomic categorisation, but the *demonstrative pronoun*: "this" or "that". The *primary referential function* is the *demonstrative* function. "Before" every linguistic classification and thereby naming, there is the question: "What is this?" This question is the *foundation* of referentiality. As a question, it has the following specificity. If it is to be posed, something is presupposed –"that" of which we are asking– that lies not merely outside itself (outside the question), but also *outside language and discourse in general*. Which amounts to saying that this question can *primarily* be posed only in the presence of some material object, accessible through the senses, be it indirectly, to which we can point.

So we have a *second component of referentiality* and consequently of the practice of discourse. *On a primary level*, reference *points* to something outside language and discourse, that is, to the world of material objects. It is in this sense that we can also understand the correspondence between *external* referents and *primary*, i.e. *material*, objects.

Thus the concept of "particular", which Searle uses in his definition of reference, should be seen not on the basis of the fundamental taxonomic genus/species distinction, but more or less in the sense of *concrete*, as the opposite of *abstract*. If we accept that abstraction is an *inherent* ability of the *intellect*, and is therefore coextensive with the actual ability to form concepts, that is, with language, constituting at the same time a precondition for any

---

177. See, for example, Claude Lévi-Strauss, *The savage mind*, London: Weidenfeld and Nicolson, 1972, pp. 135-216.
178. For an approach to related matters with reference to Wittgenstein –among others–, see A.W. Moore, *The infinite*, London and New York: Routledge, 1990, p. 187 ff.

taxonomy, its opposite, i.e. *concretisation*, consists in the *opening* of language towards its outside, towards the world of discontinuous material objects, in a *referential*, that is, *demonstrative* relation that pre-exists (on a primary level) any taxonomy and/or naming, and therefore any representation.

At this point, I believe we could invert Derrida's formulation, and suggest that one practice of *speech* without genuinely external referents is *(phonetic) writing*. In so far as, in disagreement with Derrida, we accept that (phonetic) writing is a representation of speech, we could at the same time accept that the former has no *genuinely external* referents. Represented speech directly depends on its graphic representation. Even though it initially has its materiality, there are countless cases where this materiality ceases to exist—when, for instance, the author of a certain text is dead or does not remember what he/she has written. Let us remind ourselves of the main theme of the film *Fahrenheit 451*. The people of the resistance learn whole books by heart, before the regime destroys them, in order to save the discourse, i.e. the speech, that these represent.

In this sense, the insistence on writing and the text on the part of Derrida and of all related theoretical approaches to discourse could definitely be said to involve some element of self-referentiality. Even though at first glance it may seem paradoxical, the attempt to disengage writing from the primacy of speech by calling into question the former's representational relation to the latter leads to restoring the predominance of speech through the back door, so to speak. This is speech no longer as the oral corporality of discourse, but in the sense of a signifying practice without genuinely external referents, which does nothing other than reproduce itself indefinitely. The emphasis on writing's autonomy from speech, far from adding externality to language, is on the contrary what prevents language from opening itself towards its genuine externality, which consists in its genuinely external referentiality, that is, what impedes the consideration of language in its written or oral or any other of its material or bodily manifestations, as *discourse*. The insistence on "writing" is not directed against "speech" but against "discourse".

Of course when pointing out that the "insistence on writing" disparages the concept of "discourse", I am referring to a certain philosophical choice. I do not mean that writing in general in all its manifestations is only self-referential or only practice of speech. To the extent that it is a representation of a practice of speech that is *also* a practice of discourse, it is itself a *practice of discourse*—insofar, of course, as we approach it as such, both on the level of its production, and on that of its reception, i.e. of reading. With this I quite simply mean to say that if one gives emphasis to discourse instead of writing, this does not mean one is concerned with things different from the ones concerning the Derrideans. It is with the same things that one is concerned—let us say with "texts"—only in a different manner.

Let us now take a formulation from Foucault's *Archaeology of knowledge*: "We know that logicians say that a proposition like 'The golden mountain is in California' cannot be verified because it has no referent: its negation is therefore neither more nor less true than its affirmation."[179] And then he explains that this is (also) something in which what he considers as "discourse" (to be exact, as "*statement(énoncé)*" which is "at first sight" the "constituent element", the "atom", the "elementary unit" of discourse, in the sense that discourse is constituted by statements[180]) differs from the "proposition" in the sense of logic. His "archaeological" approach accepts that even a fictional object—in a novel, for example—could be a referent.[181]

The issue here raised, however, requires some further investigation. First of all, in the sentence "The golden mountain is in California", it is understood that according to the logicians, there is no referent not of the sentence in general, but of the phrase "golden mountain".[182] The name "California" does have a referent, which is the specific geographical area forming one of the United States of America, well-known to all of us even if we have not visited it. If we are to be somewhat more pedantic, we could say that there may not be a referent of the phrase "golden mountain", but there certainly is a referent of the adjective "golden", every golden object, as well as of the noun "mountain", every mountain. So in a fairy-tale about the golden mountain, whether this is situated in California or anywhere else, the object "golden mountain" may be fictional and in this sense it would not exist if that particular fairy-tale did not exist, therefore in this sense it is not a primary object or a genuinely external referent, *but it is not a secondary object or a non-genuinely external referent as are (other) signifiers or some language or some other text or speech*. What I mean to say is this: I believe there is an intermediate realm of existence, in which we could include many sorts of fictional constructions, together with various kinds of objects *of knowledge* constituted by scientific fields, which intervene between discourse and the objective reality to which it refers. What is of interest in this intermediate realm is that there is a mutual relation of dependence between signs and referents as to the existence of both. In the example with the "golden mountain", this would not exist as an object if the fairy-tale about it did not, but neither would the fairy-tale (about the "golden mountain") exist if there were no golden objects and mountains. To take an example from the discourse of political economy, *surplus value* as an object *of knowledge* would not exist if the *theory* of surplus value did not, but neither would the latter exist if there were no *real* relations of production.

In no sense am I here equating fairy-tales and scientific fields like political economy. On the contrary, I first chose two examples of diametrically opposite discourses, so as to demonstrate right from the start the *generality*

---

179. Foucault, *L'archéologie du savoir*, p. 118 – English translation: p.89.

180. *Ibid.*, pp. 106-107 – English translation: p. 80.

181. *Ibid.*, pp. 118-119 – English translation: pp.89-90.

182. On the controversy regarding the "golden mountain" between Alexius Meinong and Bertrand Russell, see "Alexius Meinong's theory of objects: Critical judgments", *Ontologists of the 19th century*, 03/13/2008, http://www.formalontology.it/meinonga.htm (9 May 2008).

of this "intermediate realm". For a better understanding of the latter, we should of course first point out an evident *asymmetry* pertaining to what I mentioned above as "mutual relation of dependence". The asymmetry consists in the dependence of the *"intermediate realm"* upon *discourse itself* on one hand, while there is dependence of *discourse itself* upon *real objects* on the other. So if we were to describe the structure of the relations *objectivity* per se / *"intermediate realm"* / *discourse*, the description would not be rectilinear. There are the real (material) objects, and the discourse that refers to them could not exist without them. Discourse itself, however, does not refer to them *straightforwardly*. *By the very act of reference*, it creates an intermediate realm, which *corresponds* to the real objects without *identifying* with them. In terms of *form of existence*, this intermediate realm is discourse, and in this sense it belongs to the broader field of discourse. It is distinct, however, from discourse *per se* due to a closer *proximity* to real, i.e. to primary, objects. This intermediate realm could be called *referentiality* per se. So we have: *objectivity* per se / *referentiality* per se / *discourse* per se.[183] The awkward triple repetition of the phrase "*per se*" is but a way of being reminded of the crucially important fact of the asymmetric, discontinuous and polymorphous interweaving of these three realms of existence.

- Objectivity *per se*, where one finds *primary* objects, given that there are also the *intermediate* objects in referentiality *per se*, that is, the objects constructed by discourse, as well as the *secondary* objects in discourse *per se*, that is, signifiers as objects, and the *objective (i.e. material) conditions of enunciation* of discourse *(per se)*.

- Referentiality *per se*, where one finds the *intermediate* referents (= intermediate objects), given that there are also the *genuinely external* referents (= primary objects) in objectivity *per se*, as well as the *non-genuinely external* referents (= secondary objects) in discourse *per se*, that is, signifiers as referents.

- And finally, discourse *per se*, given that, as we have said, referentiality *per se* is also discourse, and given that discourse *is involved in a multitude of ways* with objectivity *per se*.

Let us stay a bit longer on the "intermediate realm", i.e. on referentiality *per se*. As quite often happens with all sorts of intermediate spaces and mediating factors, it can serve manifold uses as well as carry multiple dangers. The dangers in this particular intermediate space, as we have seen in Laclau and Mouffe's case but as we will also see further on, have to with the fact that, because of its proximity to both discourse *per se* and objectivity *per se*, it often leads to confusing the one with the other. The usefulness lies in that the conceptual establishment of referentiality *per se* facilitates the investigation of certain largely insoluble problems regarding the relation and distinction

---

183. For a somewhat corresponding –but not altogether similar- distinction in Foucault, see Foucault, *op. cit.*, p. 62 – English translation: pp. 45-46.

between subjectivity and objectivity. Schematising, we could say that the basic danger consists in the *hypostatisations* of each and every possible sort, while the usefulness consists in facilitating *their critical treatment*.

Let us go back to the sentence, "The golden mountain is in California". Probably the example was not randomly chosen by Foucault. We cannot fail to take into account a historical reality among the possible referents of this sentence, the gold rush to California that had taken place around the middle of the nineteenth century.[184] In which of the above three realms of existence would we include the gold rush? Doubtlessly in objectivity *per se*, largely at least, in the following sense. Of course we accept that there may have been subjective factors of an enormous degree behind that event, and insofar as this is true we should also accept that if those factors did not exist we might also not have had the event. However, an action, any action that does not strictly belong in the practice of discourse (or speech), has a material dimension autonomous from subjectivity (autonomous from subjectivity *in general* and not merely from the *actor's* subjectivity as it happens with the material dimension of the signifiers in the case of the practice of speech or discourse), therefore an *objective per se* dimension, which consists in its material *consequences*. It is a matter of the objectivity of the *already accomplished fact*. Let us repeat the "neutron bomb test", and let us consider the case of the world-devastating neutron bomb having fallen just before and the case of it having fallen just after the gold rush. The material condition of the California region after the bomb's falling would be radically different in the two cases. In the latter case it would also include all material creations and accompanying objects of the migrants and their offspring – together with their dead bodies and remains.

So the practice of discourse of the sentence "The golden mountain is in California", which itself belongs to *discourse per se*, has a *possible* referent, in the sense of a genuinely external referent, which one finds in *objectivity per se*, that is, which would certainly be there even if the sentence referring to it did not exist. I stress the word "possible", since the referential connection we make is based on conjecture. Therefore the relation of dependence or independence between the gold rush and the sentence is also based on conjecture. If *indeed* the connection is not random, we could assume that if the gold rush to California did not exist neither would the sentence.

Let us now take the referent "golden mountain". But before we go to this in itself, let us also examine "California" as a referent. Apart from the real region of California, which is a genuinely external referent, which exists even if no one is referring to it and which belongs to objectivity *per se*, and apart from the name "California", which as a sign belongs to discourse *per se*, there is also an "intermediate California". A California that is not the mere concept "south-western state of the USA", of which we could say that it is

---

184. Chinese gold diggers had named California itself "Gold Mountain" – see "Gold Mountain", *Wikipedia*, 5 May 2008, http://en.wikipedia.org/wiki/Gold_Mountain (9 May 2008).

included in the sign "California", but neither is it California in the purely objective-material components of the real geographical region. In this intermediate realm of referentiality *per se*, we could accept that there are more than one different "Californias". It is a matter of California as an *object of knowledge*, but according to the discourse we have in mind, we may have different Californias constituted as objects of knowledge. Thus, the California of the discourse of social geography is different from the California of the discourse of Hollywood films, for example. On the other hand, it goes without saying that these two Californias are not unrelated and that they have a lot in common, which commonness and relatedness largely emerge from the fact that *they are both determined "in the last instance" by the real California of objectivity per se*. The phrase "in the last instance" here is neither a nostalgic nor a sarcastic reference to Althusserian Marxism, I use it in quotation marks merely as a reminder of the asymmetric character of the relations of dependence between the three realms of existence. The California of social geography would not exist without the *discourse* of social geography, and the California of Hollywood films would not exist without the *discourse* of Hollywood films. But neither would the chapter of social geography referring to California nor Hollywood films about California exist if the *real* California did not. (About the latter it goes without saying that we take into account the hypothetical case of Hollywood being somewhere else, otherwise Hollywood films in general would of course not exist anyway if the real California did not.)

Let us now come to the California of the phrase that Foucault and the logicians use as an example. If we suppose the conjecture we made above that the gold rush is a genuinely external referent of this phrase is in fact valid, we could moreover assume that California as an *object of knowledge* in this sentence is constituted by a discourse *socio-historically coexisting and mutually determined* with the gold rush, which is the discourse of the migrant gold-diggers (which doubtlessly includes not only the discourse of the migrating individuals themselves but also the discourse *about* the gold rush, in that period's press, for example), before, during and after the migration/gold-rush process. California in that discourse is constituted as the "land of opportunity", of getting rich easily and fast, the land where sufficiently determined, skillful and dynamic people run no danger of not being generously rewarded for their merits. Perhaps this was an early version of the famous "American dream", which is still a dominant ideologeme in the USA and elsewhere.

So if we take into account *this* California, the California of the discourse of the gold rush, which is itself one of the "intermediate" Californias, in the sense that it belongs to the "intermediate" realm of referentiality *per se*, we can easily understand why the "golden mountain" too occupies a directly relevant place in this intermediate realm. Pointing out a simple metaphoric relation between "mountain" and "plenty" suffices to demonstrate a crystal-clear *metaphoro-metonymic* connection between "golden mountain" and "California": The "golden mountain" is *combined* with California (metonymy), since it is *there located*, but it is also *similar* to it, in so far as both the one and the other form variations of the "land of plenty and fortune". In this case, it is interesting that both the metaphoric and the metonymic part of the connection work both ways. Both the "golden mountain" and California could be either the sign or the referent in either the metaphoric or the metonymic connection. So the "golden mountain" and "California", as to the relations between them, are determined as belonging to the *intermediate* realm of referentiality *per se*, both by the fact that, as *referents* and *objects*, they correspond to some *genuinely external* referents and *primary* objects of objectivity *per se*—(real) gold and (real) mountains, gold rush, real California—and by the fact that the terms marking the two dimensions of language to which we referred at length above ensure that we *also* have to deal with *signs*, and that they consequently belong to the *broader field* of discourse.

The distinction between objectivity *per se* and referentiality *per se* should not lead to the false conclusion that we have to do with two entirely separate realms of existence and that the passage from one to the other is unfeasible. Especially in scientific discourse, the passage is definitely feasible; it is just that it follows *certain rules*. In the natural sciences, such rules have mainly to do with *experiment* and *observation*, while in historiographic research with the *various ways of verifying the reliability of existing documents*.

This is also the case of course with the distinction between discourse *per se* and referentiality *per se*. With that distinction, the passage from one to the other is also feasible, but somewhat differently. The passage mainly consists in the *different ways in which subjectivity is involved in the relation between the two levels*. Especially in narrative fiction (and not only there), where there is an equivalent distinction between the *level of discourse* and the *level of story*, we notice that quite often there is almost an identification between the subject-narrator, which belongs to the level of discourse (that is, to discourse *per se*, according to our own terminology), since it is the subject of its enunciation, and a subject-character, which lies on the level of the story (in referentiality *per se*), since it forms one of the narrative's referents.[185]

---

185. For a typology of narratives based on the distance between narrator and characters, see Tzvetan Todorov, *The poetics of prose* (translated by Richard Howard), Ithaca, New York: Cornell University Press, 1977, pp. 27-28.

Chapter 10
Archaeology of knowledge and discourse analysis

Let us now go back to Foucault's *Archaeology of knowledge* (1969). Perhaps a few words are in order as to the reception of this text in relation to Foucault's work generally speaking. It is probably the most *controversial* of his books. On one hand, it has been treated as a theoretical and methodological *distillation*, so to speak, of his previous work, and as such it has been considered important.[186] And on the other hand, it has been characterised, in comparison with his other books, as stringent, tedious, vaguely theorising, boring and rather pointless as a published text.[187] Some have even considered it as constituting a quite striking indication of the "failure" or "impasse" of his "archaeological method", and consequently as what (negatively) sparked off the passage to his "genealogical" period and his concern with power.[188]

---

186. See, for example, Gilles Deleuze, *Foucault* (translated by Seán Hand), London: Athlone, 1988, pp. 1-22.

187. See Alan Sheridan, *Michel Foucault: The will to truth*, London and New York: Tavistock, 1980, pp. 89-90.

188. See, for example, Dreyfus and Rabinow, *op. cit.*, pp. 79-100.

I have already pointed out elsewhere that the separation between Foucault's "archaeological" and "genealogical" period is overly simplifying and misleading.[189] There is surely an issue though, of how that particular text, *The archaeology of knowledge*, is posited within the context of his work generally speaking, as well as more broadly within the intellectual environment of that time.

One year after *The archaeology of knowledge*, in 1970, Roland Barthes's *S/Z* was published. A landmark in the semiological problematic,[190] it could perhaps be considered as possessing in common with Foucault's book the property of being a methodological text approaching a related field, which in its generality could be described with the terms *language, texts, discourse*. There is of course an important difference. Barthes's book contains his methodology together with its application. During the very analysis of Balzac's novella, Barthes simultaneously explains the elements constituting his methodological approach, which mainly consist of the five *codes* that he uses. Foucault, on the other hand, in *The archaeology of knowledge* explicates *a posteriori* his methodological approach in his previous books, mainly *The order of things* (1966).

The temporal and material distance between the application of the methodology itself and its theoretical elaboration, on one hand, provides Foucault with the privilege of "improvising" in relation to his older books, and, on the other, is an indication that it is not a methodological "programme" that Foucault had applied and will continue to apply, but rather a philosophical reflection on his work generally speaking. It focuses mainly on two aims. One aim, to which I will refer further down more extensively, is the aim of a *philosophical polemic*, related to the notorious question of the *subject*. The other aim is of more interest to us here, and consists in the philosophical investigation of the *general field* in which Foucault's hitherto studies were located, namely *discourse and/or knowledge*.

Discourse or knowledge? Why do I use here the conveniently vague but provocatively enigmatic "and/or"? Answering this question might in fact help us considerably to understand the essence of Foucault's "archaeological" approach.

One might first of all provide a "conjunctural" explanation for his preference of the latter term in the book's title as well as in naming his method: "archaeology of *knowledge*". Foucault's thought, since the *History of madness* (1961), had advanced as some sort of further development of that French intellectual current that has been called "historical epistemology",[191] and whose main representatives were Gaston Bachelard, Alexandre Koyré, Jean Cavaillès and Georges Canguilhem. There is thus some "epistemological inclination" in Foucault's thematics, which is specifically manifested in his

---

189. Doxiadis, "Foucault and ideology", pp. 33-35.

190. See above, fn. 20.

191. See Dominique Lecourt, *Marxism and epistemology: Bachelard, Canguilhem, Foucault* (translated by Ben Brewster), London: New Left Books, 1975.

being *mainly* concerned with what he calls *episteme*, that is, with what has already become or aims to become a science.¹⁹² However, it is also in *The archaeology of knowledge* that he explicitly states ethical discourse, the discourse of art, and even political discourse may have their archaeology too.¹⁹³ So where there is discourse there can be archaeology. We could therefore assume that the term *knowledge* (in French: *savoir*) oscillates between the narrower concept of *episteme* on one hand and the broader of *discourse (in general)* on the other.

Besides, to equate knowledge with the broader concept of discourse is not so arbitrary. It is a peculiar characteristic of Foucault's approach that he emphasises the *knowledge aspect* of *every* discourse, at the same time though broadening the sense of knowledge in such a way as to allow it to evade the restrictive status of science or even of *potential* science. Running the danger of appearing to interpret Foucault arbitrarily, I will give what could be considered as a "Foucauldian definition" of knowledge (savoir), which is parallel to the "definition" we have given for discourse: *the formation of concepts in relation to referents*. Once again as a *usable* definition, this designates on one hand the *emphasis on the referentiality* of discourse—and this is mainly what the stressing of its knowledge aspect consists in—and on the other discourse's disengagement from *signifiers* (according to the relevant "definitions": knowledge is equal to discourse minus signifiers). The latter surely has to do with a "tactical move" on Foucault's part, within the framework of his effort to dissociate himself from the semiological and structuralist problematic. The significance but also the cost of this "tactical move" will soon become apparent in my argument.

Let us stay though a little on the former, i.e. on the emphasis given to the referentiality of discourse. It is an emphasis that, in a "happy coincidence", so to speak, is also given in a text published the same year with *The archaeology of knowledge*, by one of the most important linguists after Saussure, namely Émile Benveniste.¹⁹⁴ Foucault's originality of course lies in the specific way in which he gives this emphasis, which consists precisely in broadening the sense of knowledge so as to be eventually coextensive with any sort of discourse.¹⁹⁵ One of the main advantages of this original connection of the referentiality of (any) discourse with knowledge is that in this way Foucault is capable of including in the scope of his critical analysis discursive fields that had hitherto remained immune to critique. By pointing

---

192. Foucault, *op. cit.*, pp. 248-251 – English translation: pp. 190-192.

193. *Ibid.*, pp. 251-255 – English translation: pp. 192-195.

194. See above, fn. 97.

195. In an obviously entirely different philosophical approach, and given that the equivalent French term is *connaissance* and not *savoir* as in the "archaeology of knowledge", Karl Mannheim with his "sociology of knowledge" broadens "knowledge" (*Wissen*) in a similarly radical fashion - Karl Mannheim, *Ideology and utopia: An introduction to the sociology of knowledge* (translated by Louis Wirth and Edward Shils), London: Routledge & Kegan Paul, 1936.

out the *knowledge* aspect of every discourse, Foucault deprives the institutionally recognised discourse of knowledge, namely science, of the privilege it possessed as exclusive bearer of knowledge, without on the other hand downgrading the importance of scientific discourse as to its practical effects. In the sense of knowledge as it operates in the "*archaeology* of knowledge", we already have the background to the theory of what Foucault was to designate later by the term "regime of truth".[196]

In a most revealing passage from *The archaeology of knowledge* under the title "Knowledge and ideology",[197] whose importance Foucault himself completely undermined by his later unjustifiable insistence on dissociating himself from the term "ideology",[198] what is most striking is the *positive* correlation effected between these two important dimensions of discourse. We could actually say that the positivity of the correlation is brought about by way of a dual and simultaneous conceptual *detachment but not complete disconnection*, on one hand of *knowledge* from *truth*, and on the other of *ideology* from *illusion*. By this double theoretical gesture, Foucault opens up an entire methodological field, in which any discourse may be investigated in terms of both *its rationality* and *its political effectivity*, without these two being mutually exclusive or antagonistic but without on the other hand being identified with or reduced to each other.

We should note, however, that the way in which knowledge and ideology are correlated, or in which rationality and political effectivity coexist, is not based on a *structural continuum*, constituted on the antithetical bipolarity truth/illusion, which would determine "degrees" of the one or the other direction according to how far each discourse or each statement stands from one or the other end. In the above terms, there lies a profound *asymmetry* that precludes any rectilinear correlation between them. The relation of rationality to truth is indeed *more or less* one of coincidence. Risking two more "usable definitions", which complement and correspond to the above "usable definitions" of discourse and knowledge, we could say that reason is the *correct* relation of language to referents, and truth is the *correct* relation of the formation of concepts to referents, where correctness each time is defined as obedience to some rules of discourse or knowledge pertaining also to the relation to referents, be it genuinely external referents, "intermediate" referents, or signifiers as referents (it goes without saying that in this last case the "correctness of the relation to referents" would be judged on the basis of some internal rules of discourse or language, as it happens with grammar as well as with formal logic).

The relation though of political effectivity to illusion is not even inevitable. A discourse may be characterised by great political effectivity, and at the same time owe this very political effectivity, i.e. its capacity to facilitate

---

196. Foucault, *Dits et écrits 1954-1988*, *III*, pp. 158-160 – English translation: Foucault, *Power/knowledge*, pp. 131-133.

197. Foucault, *L'archéologie du savoir*, pp. 240-243 – English translation: pp. 184-186.

198. See above.

the exercise of power, more to its rationality than to any sort of illusion. The examples are countless, mainly in the discourse of the natural sciences and its technological and other applications.

But there is also asymmetry in the relations between truth and illusion. The above "usable definition" of truth, with which Foucault would probably tend to agree,[199] does not allow for a general and unique criterion for truth or rationality. Different discourses, or "discursive *formations*", to use the directly relevant at this point term of Foucault,[200] have different rules of rationality and thereby different criteria for truth. So the truth/illusion distinction, which in its general and abstract form is a relation of antithesis or negation, in the analysis of concrete discourses it may merely point to the fact that we are dealing with a coexistence or combination of two or more different discourses, with different criteria and rules of rationality and truth. Ideological illusion, insofar as it exists, should not be seen as the opposite of truth or rationality, but more specifically as the *illusion of hypostatisation*, about which we have said some things already and with which we will be concerned again later.

One of the more easily understood examples we could take regarding the coexistence of discourses with different criteria of rationality and truth is the historical novel. Nobody would ever reproach the author of a historical novel for not remaining faithful to the truth of historical facts, since the latter concerns only one of the two main discourses implicated in the production of such a novel, namely the discourse of historiography. The discourse of fiction has other rules of rationality, such as, for example, in the field of the classical narrative, maintenance of some consistency in the plot. I suppose one might well conceive of an approach to the historical novel that would be based on the antithetical relationship fiction/real history, in which the former side would be equated to illusion and the latter to truth, and in which the schema would possibly acquire the form of a Hegelian contradiction. It is certain that such an approach would radically differ from an approach inspired by the Foucauldian archaeology of knowledge. The latter would first of all respect the fact that we have two different kinds of discourse with varying criteria of truth, and instead of approaching their relation on the basis of some antithetical pair like identity/opposition, truth/illusion etc., it would analyse it as an interweaving of discourses that are both similar and different, demonstrating a correlation of *similarity* and *difference*, in which the former *enhances rather than reduces* the latter. I will explain below what I mean by this.

Similarity in this instance consists, at least to start with, *only* in the fact that in both cases we have to do with discourse, and consequently with certain *common fundamental properties*. On the basis of what we have already said, we can actually outline *four fundamental properties* of *any* sort of discourse, and at the same time demonstrate how these bring to light the *differences*

---

199. See, for example, above, the reference in fn. 196.

200. *Ibid.*, pp. 44-54 – English translation: pp. 31-39.

between the discourses, remaining on the relatively simple example of the interweaving discourses of historiography and fiction in the case of the historical novel.

1. *Referentiality:* Having made the distinction between the genuinely external referents of the realm of objectivity *per se* and the intermediate realm of referentiality *per se*, it is easy to see how, in the historical novel, it is of special importance that historiographical discourse depends directly on the former, which is not the case with the discourse of fiction. Both discourses, however, meet in the intermediate realm, where the objects of historiographical *knowledge* directly influence the fictional referents, though not in a binding fashion. The historical knowledge of living conditions in Europe at the time of Napoleonic wars helps to constitute characters and adventures living and taking place therein, without predetermining the fortunes of the former or the specific outcome of the latter.

2. *Subjectivity:* The fact that historiographical discourse directly depends on objectivity *per se*, in the sense that it would not exist if the historical events and their objective consequences did not, does not mean that it is "less" subjective than the discourse of fiction. Here once again, as to the fundamental distinction between two realms of existence, it is not a matter of a distinction between two necessarily opposite to each other entities. In human affairs, on most occasions we have a coexistence of both, and when something is "very" objective this does not always mean it is "less" subjective, neither inversely. Historiographical discourse is subjective *in a fashion that is different* from the case of fiction. Respect towards the objective existence of historical facts is one of the rules obeyed by the historian as subject of historical discourse, who is thereby differentiated as to his/her constitution as subject from the subject-author of fiction. Apart from that though, there are other variables that differentiate the subject-historian from the subject-novelist and that do not directly relate to objectivity *per se*. They are variables having to do with the *conditions of enunciation* of each discourse, which, for reasons of methodological convenience, we could distinguish into *external* and *internal*.

    • The *external conditions of enunciation* in historiographical discourse largely concern the *scholarly institutions* within which it is produced. If, for example, we have a collective work of a research centre, or a school or university textbook etc. – in other words, conditions that determine both the *origin* and the *addressees* of historical discourse, and which thereby contribute to the constitution of the subjects of enunciation, as well as of those of reception. Equivalent but radically different are the external conditions of enunciation in fictional discourse, which have to do mainly with the *cultural framework*: "commercial" or "elite" publishing house, "reading public" to which it is addressed etc. The external conditions of enunciation also involve the question of the "author function", which in the case of the historian is radically different from that of the author of literary texts.[201] In the external conditions of enunciation we should also include *critical reception*, which once again is radically different in the two cases, since it is determined by the different institutions and mechanisms of reception (journals or magazines, newspapers, radio and television programmes, internet sites) of historical and fictional discourse respectively. Furthermore, differences in the external conditions also emerge in the heavy importance of sales numbers in novels, in comparison with history books that address a more "specialised" public.

- The *internal conditions of enunciation* in historiography concern the way the subject or subjects of historical science are involved in the discourse that they constitute and by which they are constituted in each case. Here once more the difference with fiction does not have to do with a relation of opposition, in which the science of history, in accordance with a scientistic Althusserian conception,[202] is a "discourse without a subject", while fiction, being an "ideological practice *par excellence*", abounds with subjectivity, but rather with the *different way* of the subjects' involvement in either case. The subjectivity of the historical researcher-writer enters into his/her discourse by way of elements like mode of writing, if, for example, he/she often intervenes by interpreting events or not, if his/her style is more narrational or more analytical, the use of primary sources and secondary bibliography, and his/her general ideological "positions". On the other hand, the question of subjectivity in fiction is posed right from the start in entirely different terms, which have mainly to do with the narrative mode, that is, how the subjectivities of the fictional characters are constituted in relation to the general subject of the narrative under consideration. I am here referring mainly to Tzvetan Todorov's well-known typology,[203] which distinguishes the types of narration into *omniscient, objective* and *subjective*.

In the analysis of the discourse of a historical novel, of course, what matters is how *a combination takes place* between thoroughly different external and internal conditions of enunciation of historiographical discourse on one hand and fictional discourse on the other. In this case, it goes without saying that the conditions of enunciation of fictional discourse

---

201. Foucault, *Dits et écrits 1954-1988, I*, pp. 789-821 – English translation: Foucault, *Language, counter-memory, practice*, pp. 113-138. See also Barthes, *op. cit.*, in my Afterword, p. 342, fn. 6.

202. Althusser, *Positions*, p. 123 – English translation: Althusser, *Lenin and philosophy and other essays*, p. 160.

203. See above, fn. 185.

predominate, insofar as we are dealing with the literary genre of the novel, and only indirectly with historical science. On the other hand though, the existence of hybrid cases, where in practice the very sharpness of the distinction between the two kinds of discourse is called into question, does not allow for an *a priori* or thoughtless classification. It may well be that the very analysis of the relations of combination as well as of predominance between the different conditions of enunciation of the two discourses might lead us to decide that a text at first glance presented as a historical novel ultimately should rather be considered as a historical study with some fictional elements, and of course the inverse could also be possible. The investigation of the ambiguity or polysemy of hybrid cases does not concern merely *subjectivity* but *all four fundamental properties* of any kind of discourse.

3. *Knowledge:* Since we have "defined" knowledge as "formation of concepts in relation to referents" and since we have already registered *referentiality* as a separate fundamental property, it follows that knowledge as a fundamental property of any discourse mainly concerns *concepts*. In order to understand the way in which concepts interweave but also differentiate in the case of the historical novel, we could take as an example a concept shared *on an entirely abstract first level* by both historiography and narrative fiction, namely the *concept of time*. Time as a concept in historiography enters in two very general ways, as *dating of events* and as *duration of conditions*. The first way mainly concerns the problem of the exact establishment of dates, while the second the question of distinguishing between short, middle and long duration, as well as all related complex problems of *periodisation* arising thereby. The question of duration also includes the issue of *different rates of development*, on one hand, rates of development of distinct *social formations,* e.g. "developed" and "developing" societies, and, on the other, rates of development of distinct *levels* in a social formation, e.g. "ideology" in relation to "political system". The concept of time in the fictional narrative obviously emerges in completely different terms. The basic distinction between *discourse time* and *story time*[204] could be said to hold also in the case of historiography anyway. There too we have the distinction between the time of writing and/or reading the historical study and the time the events or developments to which it refers took place. The difference though is that in the fictional narrative the discourse-time/story-time distinction is frequently involved directly in the subjectivity of the fictional characters, and is in this sense reproduced in the interior of the level of (fictional) story. I am referring mainly to cases where the characters themselves narrate incidents that have already occurred, in such a fashion that their

---

204. Seymour Chatman, *Story and discourse: Narrative structure in fiction and film*, Ithaca, New York, and London: Cornell University Press, 1978, p. 62 ff.

own narration constitutes a significant part of the plot itself.[205] So in the historical novel, occasions where some character narrates or describes an important historical event or condition and his/her participation in it could be considered as examples of how the concept of time, while radically differing between historiographical and fictional discourse, could nonetheless be constituted in such a way that historical time is encompassed within fiction, thereby determining it though in an important manner. The *knowledge* of the *concept* of historical time in the analysis of a historical novel may therefore perform a crucial role in its understanding. And we could obviously bring to mind several other examples of concepts of historiographical knowledge inherent in a historical novel and determining its narrative discourse, like in the case of Marxist historiography the concept of class struggles, the neo-Marxist concept of "centre-periphery", the Hegelian concept of "world-historical individual" etc.[206]

4. *Ideology:* Ideology as a fundamental property of *any* discourse consists in something more diffuse than ideology as a more or less clearly constituted discourse of social taxonomy or as a representation of social relations and practices that guides action. We could accept the latter as a "general definition" of ideology, but ideology also has certain *functions,* and we could say that *by way of its functions* it is indeed present, *as a fundamental property,* at least *potentially,* though *not always actually,* in any sort of discourse. These functions have mainly to do with the fact that ideology is a mode of exercising power but also of expressing antagonism within discourse and by way of discourse.[207] The specific way of locating the ideological property *in this sense* of any discourse consists in tracing some *thematics* that constitute *issues of power*—around which some antagonism is in play, aiming at exercising power (in some direction or other) or at resisting it. In historiographical discourse, a historical event and its interpretation could well constitute such a thematic, in so far as the prevalence of one or another interpretation might justify some corresponding ideological position. Perhaps the most easily understandable such example in Modern Greek historiography is the events of December 1944 and the Greek Civil War that soon followed. In fictional discourse, on the other hand, even though the *antagonistic* element may be *inherent* in relations between characters, the *thematics* constitut-

---

205. In the case of *oral history*, it is obvious that this characteristic also pertains to historiography.

206. On this last concept, see Georg Lukács, *The historical novel* (translated by Hannah and Stanley Mitchell), Harmondsworth: Penguin Books, 1969, and Georg Wilhelm Friedrich Hegel, *Vorlesungen über die Philosophie der Geschichte*, Frankfurt: Suhrkamp, 1970, p. 44 ff. – English translation (J. Sibree): *The philosophy of history*, New York: Dover Publications, 1956, p. 29 ff.

207. See Doxiadis, "Foucault, ideology, communication", pp. 31-34.

ing issues of power and antagonism are inevitably drawn from extra-narrative fields, given the (*relative*) autonomy of the world of fiction. In the case of the historical novel, it is obvious that the main source from which such thematics are drawn is the discourse of historiography with its own relevant ideological stakes. The interweaving of historiographical and fictional discourse will here consist in how, for example, by way of the novel's plot and the antagonisms emerging therein, but also by way of devices like the narrative viewpoint, there may be a justification of some character who has been posited as ideologically leaning towards and/or accordingly acting in favour of a certain side in some antagonistic historical conjuncture.

Chapter 11
The four axes

Referentiality, subjectivity, knowledge, ideology: So having outlined these *four fundamental properties* of *any* discourse, by way of using the relatively simple example of the historical novel, we can now proceed to the listing of *four corresponding axes of analysis*:

1. *Axis of objects* (referentiality): investigation of the discourse's relations with *the outside of discourse*.
2. *Axis of enunciative modes* (subjectivity): investigation of the discourse's relations with *itself*.
   First part: *External conditions of enunciation*
   Second part: *Internal conditions of enunciation*
3. *Axis of concepts* (knowledge): investigation of the discourse's relations with *other discourses*.
4. *Axis of thematics* (ideology): investigation of the discourse's relations with *power*.

Two (interlinked) remarks should be made here. The first one concerns the correspondence of the above with Foucault's *Archaeology of knowledge*. I emphasise that I have stayed on the "spirit" rather than the "letter' of his "methodology", since anyway, as I have already pointed out, we do not have to do with a "methodology" strictly speaking, but rather with a philosophical conception regarding the fundamental properties of discourse. The terms he uses to describe these properties are indeed these four, and they permeate the entire structure of *The archaeology of knowledge*'s text – in different versions, but the basic terms are these: *objects, enunciative modes* (to be precise, Foucault here uses the, misleadingly perhaps, rather obscure term *enunciative modalities*), *concepts, thematics* (here he also uses the alternative term *strategies*, which emphasises more the antagonism/power dimension; I nevertheless prefer the term *thematics* for its simplicity and generality; "strategy" almost inevitably implies some *systematically elaborated* component, which is not always present).[208]

The second remark has to do with the choice on my part of the term *axes*. Even though it is one more instance of a perhaps inevitable "importation" of some term from geometry and the natural sciences, I chose it as the *least taxonomic* term I could think of. More or less similar of course are the terms *dimensions, components* and *aspects*, but I went for the term *axes* because it points more to some sense of an *analytical tool* (especially if one also bears in mind the sense of an "*imaginary* axis") rather than to a notion of some constituent *inherent in the object of analysis itself* (which is possibly the case with the other similar terms).

But why did I wish for a term that was *as little as possible taxonomic* in the first place? That is, why did I opt for *axes* instead of terms like *levels, fields, domains, realms, areas* or *categories*? Above, when I maybe inevitably used the term *realms of existence*, I tried *afterwards* to undermine its classificatory operation by exhaustively emphasising its provisional character through the generalised use of the modifier *per se*: objectivity / referentiality / discourse *per se*. And at this point, with the *axes of analysis* that I propose as analytical tools, I had sought *right from the start* for a term that evades taxonomic logic as far as possible. Why so?

Another matter needs to be settled first, though. Why are axes less taxonomic than the other six terms listed in the previous paragraph? Axes are *less comprehensive*. As a metaphoric figure, the word "axis" implies that something "*revolves around* (an axis)", it is not irrevocably contained (= classed, classified) in it. The conceptual-methodological schema of the axes therefore allows for a greater *flexibility* in our approach, it makes clear from the start *not merely* the *constant interweaving and mutual referentiality* that we find between objects, enunciative modes, concepts and thematics, but also the *inconspicuousness of their being separate*. The term *axes*, perhaps more than any other relevant one, escapes from the logic of *the set and its subsets*. The question is not how to *classify* the elements of a discourse into *four separate categories*, but how to *approach* and *understand* a discourse on the basis of its *four fundamental properties*.

We may now go back to the question of why I am trying to avoid taxonomy. It is certain that as long as we speak and write we cannot entirely dispense with taxonomic logic, that is, with representation, given that we have already referred to speech as the "zero degree" of representation and in

---

208. Foucault, *L'archéologie du savoir*, especially pp. 44-93 – English translation: pp. 31-70.

a non-Derridean manner to (phonetic) writing as a representation of speech. It also goes without saying that, even on a less elementary level, the use of conceptualities and terms deriving from mathematics, the natural sciences and technology, either as metaphoric figures or simply as unavoidable extensions of those practices of knowledge in human affairs, renders taxonomic thought and representation to a large extent inevitable. One cannot be *generally against* representation and taxonomy.

The question of representation specifically concerning *discourse analysis as a critical practice* has to do with the fact that representation, i.e. taxonomic discourse, forms by definition a central constituent of *ideology*. It is one of the two basic ways in which ideological power is exercised. Of the other we have already talked and will talk again, it is *hypostatisation*. Risking an anatomic metaphor, we might say that, if hypostatisation is the *head* of ideology, representation forms its *backbone*. I repeat the "general definition" of ideology we gave above. Ideology is a representation of social relations and practices that guides action, that is, the discourse that classifies or orders social relations and practices and that *thereby* guides action *accordingly*.[209]

It is obvious that there are kinds of discourse in which the representation, that is, the taxonomy of social relations and practices enters in a particularly indirect and by no means evident manner. In the discourse of the natural sciences, for example, social relations and practices are represented—classified or ordered—mainly by means of the institutional framework of the production of scientific discourse, but also by means of the prospects for its possible applications. The "regime of truth",[210] which is in large part constituted by the natural sciences, has also some definitely ideological components, precisely in the sense of the representation of social relations and practices. Issues like "the social role of science and the political responsibility of the scientists", "the social utility but also the political dangers of scientific discourse and technology", "the environmental problems arising from technology and their social consequences", "the possibility or impossibility of access to scientific knowledge by non-privileged social groups", accompany the process of production and application of scientific knowledge from start to finish, and constantly raise, even if not always in an explicitly expressed manner, questions of social relations in general and power relations in particular.

In this sense, we might say that, in the specific case of analysing the discourse of the natural sciences, a crucial role is played by the correlation of the axis of *thematics*, namely of the *directly* ideological axis, especially with the part of *external conditions of enunciation* of the axis of *enunciative modes*. In this correlation, at the "intersection", so to speak, of the two axes, we

---

209. I juxtapose the Althusserian definition: "*Ideology is a 'Representation' of the Imaginary Relationship of Individuals to their Real Conditions of Existence*" - Althusser, *Positions*, p. 114 - English translation: Althusser, *Lenin and philosophy and other essays*, p. 152. I prefer the more "minimalistic" definition here employed, holding the view that one cannot jam the entire relevant theory into one definition.

210. See above, fn. 196.

could discern the constitution of a discourse, not *of* the natural sciences, but rather *about* the natural sciences, in which the classification or ordering of social relations and practices would revolve around the above and other related issues (axis of *thematics*), and which would be formed according to its subjective origin and the conditions of its enunciation and address (*external conditions* in the axis of *enunciative modes*). This discourse, which is to say, this ideology, may not always be expressly uttered or written, but may in fact be implicit in the practice and the conditions of enunciation of the scientific discourse *per se*, as well as in the process of the latter's reception.

As a social classification or ordering that *guides action*, ideology always entails an *evaluative* quality. It is a matter of a *moral* taxonomy, and we could well presume that morality in a broad sense, i.e. morality that does not always present itself as such, that is, as guiding action, is identical with ideology. In the case of the discourse *about* the natural sciences, and in relation to some of the issues (or thematics) I mentioned above as examples, social taxonomy might, for instance, consist in the evaluatively preferential treatment of "experts" as against the "ignorant", or of "practically applicable" scientific fields (i.e. "directly useful to the market or production") as against "theoretical" ones (a classification that might also concern the *interior* of the natural sciences, and not merely the natural/social sciences distinction), or, on the other hand, in the evaluative priority given to "environmentally sensitive" solutions proposed by the natural sciences as against some others, "environmentally harmful". It goes without saying that the classification or ordering of social relations and practices constituted in *any* ideology, as it is quite apparent especially in the last two examples, does not merely consist in the classification or ordering of social *groups* but also of *institutions*. As for the *power effects* brought about by each such classification or ordering, I think they are quite evident.

Having in mind this general framework wherein the axis of thematics interweaves with the external conditions part of the axis of enunciative modes, in which the implicit but important ideological and power-exercising components of the discourse of the natural sciences are demonstrated, it would now be interesting to proceed to some very general *hints* concerning the possibility of utilising the remaining "two and a half" axes: the axis of objects, the internal conditions part of the axis of enunciative modes, and the axis of concepts. On these axes, natural-scientific discourse *per se* returns in its immediacy.

On the axis of objects, the question of the distinction between objectivity *per se* and referentiality *per se* would be posed in relation to the definitive role of the *experiment* in the natural sciences. More specifically with the technological sciences, one might investigate their particularity in comparison to the "pure" natural sciences, which consists in that the constitution of the object *of knowledge* (referentiality *per se*) coincides with the constitution of the *real* object (objectivity *per se*). I am obviously referring to the dual quality of all forms of *machines* as objects (their *design* belonging to referentiality *per se*, and the machines *themselves* belonging to objectivity *per se*). In the internal conditions part of the axis of enunciative modes, the question posed on each occasion concerns the enunciative subject of scientific discourse *per se*. In the broader discursive regime of the natural sciences, we may assume that it is of crucial importance whether the particular scientist who is writing happens to consider him/herself as a member of some scientific group or not, and more generally to what extent he/she belongs to a scientific tradition or some dominant paradigm.[211] Finally, on the axis of concepts, we might say that we are provided with the possibility of investigating the position occupied by the specific scientific discourse under consideration within the broader framework of related discourses, in so far as the conceptualisation of a scientific field forms the main body of its cohesion.

It goes without saying that the critical efficacy of discourse analysis in the case of the natural sciences will depend on the possibility to connect the axes concerning the discourse *about* the natural sciences to those in which the discourse of the natural sciences *itself* is analysed. Since in the "not directly political" axes the question of power and social relations and practices does not enter directly, the connection to the *representation of social relations and practices* would have to focus on the first part: on *representation*, that is, on *taxonomic discourse in its generality*. In particular, and with reference to the above considerations, on the axis of objects, technology as an applied taxonomic discourse could be linked with the classification into socially useful or harmful practices. In the internal conditions on the axis of enunciative modes, belonging or not to a scientific group could be considered as an element of some *potential* social taxonomy concerning the practice and views of that specific group as to the social responsibility of scientists or as to how democratic should be the production of scientific knowledge. And on the axis of concepts, one might investigate a possible categorisation of concepts according to criteria of an *indirectly* political character, that is, whether, for instance, the exclusion of some concepts in favour of some others conceals a preference regarding the social role of science and its applications. I suppose that we could find several examples, but which would be of value merely as examples. Neither *all* classifications or orderings of concepts, nor *all* those of the enunciative subjects of scientific discourse, nor *all* those concerning objects are necessarily susceptible of being attributed some socio-political quality. Here as elsewhere, the challenge for discourse analysis is to demonstrate the *partial* and the *concrete*.

I chose to give some general hints as to the "difficult" case of the discourse of the natural sciences, not in order to show that "even there" discourse analysis may be applied "be it with some difficulties", but, on the contrary, precisely because the "difficulty" with the case of natural-scientific discourse reveals the *limits* of discourse analysis *generally speaking*. As a

---

211. On the concept of "paradigm", see Thomas S. Kuhn, *The structure of scientific revolutions (Second edition, enlarged)*, Chicago, Illinois, and London: University of Chicago Press, 1970, p. 10 ff.

materialist critique axiomatically based on limits and fundamental finitude, discourse analysis has first of all to accept *its own* material component and consequently the fundamental finitude of this component. In accordance with what I have already said, this would amount to, among other things, accepting the *discontinuity* inherent in its conceptualistion and its applications. So if I chose as an analytical tool that corresponds to the four fundamental properties of discourse the term *axes* as *less taxonomic*, it is because it does not allow for *generalised relations of continuity*. The fact that there may be, for example, many elements on the axis of concepts that may not be connected with the (directly ideological) axis of thematics should not be considered as a *failure* of the methodology, but as an instance of its *discontinuity*, which has been anticipated *by the very presuppositions* of the methodology, which include, among other things, the choice of the term *axes*.

Obviously the anticipation of its own discontinuity on the part of discourse analysis does not restrict itself to the noble motives of "philosophical consistency" and "self-criticism". It also has its ulterior motives. The discourse of discourse analysis avoids as far as possible being itself taxonomic, i.e. a discourse that establishes continuity, also in order to be more effective in calling into question the continuity aimed at being established by the taxonomic discourse that it criticises, that is, by representation, either in its directly ideological form, i.e. as a representation of social relations and practices, or as not directly ideological taxonomic discourse, which *may* be linked with ideological taxonomy thereby enhancing it, but which then again it *may not*. Far from aiming to demonstrate and hence to denounce the omnipotence of ideologies and the dominant, scientific or otherwise, representations—an omnipotence that would consist, among other things, in the establishment of an indissoluble and undisruptible (symbolic, of course) continuity between the natural and the moral world—discourse analysis as a critical practice aims on the contrary at tracing their limits and discontinuities, both in the relations between them and in the interior of each.

As a *non-economistic* but *materialist* critique of ideology, discourse analysis does not intend to reveal the determination (in the last instance) of ideologies and representations in general by the economy or by some other *exterior* material force, but to demonstrate the discontinuities and limits *inherent* in them, *first of all* because of their *partly inherent material conditions of existence*. Something which does *not* amount, on the other hand, to consider discourse, representation, knowledge, ideology as *only* material entities, not even as *mainly* material. When referring to language and discourse, I emphasised the *ethical* priority of their subjectivity/conceptuality as against the *ontological* priority of their objective/material aspects. It goes without saying that this also holds for the entities by definition directly based on them. We might suggest that this peculiar (non-economistic) materialism amounts to a *materialist dualism*, precisely in the above sense, which would of course concern existence in general and not merely discourse and directly related entities. It is just that here the dualism is made more evident, since the two basic realms of existence permeate its interior.[212]

We are still in the investigation of one direction of the dualist relationship, of whatever derives from the ontological priority of the objective/material aspects, namely of what concerns the axiomatic belief that concepts cannot exist without their material conditions while the latter can exist without the former. The investigation of the other direction, of what the ethical priority of concepts consists in, will be more easily approachable if we first make some critical comments regarding the Foucauldian conception of the materiality of discourse.

---

212. The asymmetry of the term "materialist dualism" may be attributed to the fact that the dilemma *idealism/materialism* is conceivable only in the realm of ontology and not in that of ethics.

Part III
The Ethical Priority of the Conceptual Component

Chapter 12
The concept of the subject

In some sense, we could suggest that what Foucault loses with his dissociation from signifiers and the linguistic problematic he is trying to gain with the first part of his methodology's title, namely with the use of the term *archaeology*. In a caustic reply to a likewise caustic critique by the American literary critic George Steiner, who ascribes the use of the word "archaeology" "outside its normal field" to Freud,[213] Foucault points out that he has been inspired for this term by one of Kant's texts, in which the German philosopher is discussing the possibility of a philosophical history of philosophy.[214] In the *Archaeology of knowledge* itself, the term "archaeology" is used to emphasise and elucidate in various ways the *materiality* of discourse and knowledge.

The first and probably the main explanation of the use of the term *archaeology* is provided at the beginning of the book, where Foucault is discussing the significance of calling into question the concept of the *document* by way of that of the *monument*: While traditional archaeology sought to

---

213. George Steiner, "The mandarin of the hour - Michel Foucault", *The New York Times, February 28, 1971*, 1998, http://cogweb.ucla.edu/Abstracts/Foucault.html (9 May 2008).

214. Emmanuel Kant, *Les progrès de la métaphysique en Allemagne depuis Leibniz et Wolf* (translated by Louis Guillermit), Paris: Librairie Philosophique J. Vrin, 1990, pp. 107-108, and Foucault, *Dits et écrits 1954-1988, II*, pp. 221-222.

transform silent monuments into historical discourse, there is a tendency in contemporary historiography discerned by Foucault, to which he allies himself, towards a roughly inverse direction. His aim is not to approach monuments as documents that will speak revealing the truth of events, but rather to treat the documents under consideration as monuments connected between them by some rules, thereby constituting *discursive formations*.[215]

Once again I believe that in this case as well, i.e. in Foucault's "archaeology", materiality emerges by way of *discontinuity*. The way in which Foucault conceives of the monument as against the document and the methodological preference he has for the former has to do precisely with the fact that, while documents provide some ground for conceiving historical time as a continuum that has been interrupted by conjunctures and whose restitution should be the historian's central concern, monuments on the other hand constitute a constantly present reminder of the discontinuity of historical time, by way of both their inherent imperfections (monuments are never complete) and the different stratifications that call for discontinuous between them groupings.

In a text published the year he died (1984), in spite of all those maintaining that after *The archaeology of knowledge* he abandoned his archaeological method, patently emphasising the latter's importance for *critique* as he understands it, Foucault will say: "...this criticism is [...] archaeological in its method [...] -and not transcendental- in the sense that it will not seek to identify the universal structures of all knowledge or of all possible moral action, but will seek to treat the instances of discourse [les discours] that articulate what we think, say, and do as so many historical events."[216]

The contrast here of "historical events" with "universal structures" is revealing precisely as to how Foucault conceives of the materiality of discourse. If the concept of the "monument" emphasises more the *discontinuous* dimension of materiality, the "historical event" brings out the materiality of discourse as a *finite practice*: as a practice spatio-temporally limited ("spatio-temporally" here is a pleonasm, given how we defined spatiality and temporality above).

But is discourse eventually, according to Foucault, just *any* material practice, with its discontinuity and its finitude? Is one actually justified in distinguishing between *discursive formations* and *non-discursive domains*, or is it that Laclau and Mouffe are right to reproach him precisely for this distinction?[217] If we accept that the above four fundamental properties of any discourse—referentiality (objects), subjectivity (enunciative modes), know-

---

215. See Foucault, *L'archéologie du savoir*, p. 13 ff. –English translation: p. 6 ff.-, and above, fn. 208.

216. Foucault, *Dits et ecrits 1954-1988, IV*, p. 574 – English translation (Catherine Porter): Michel Foucault, "What is Enlightenment?", in: *The Foucault reader* (edited by Paul Rabinow), Harmondsworth: Penguin Books, 1986, p. 46.

217. See above, fns 171 and 172.

ledge (concepts), ideology (thematics)—are *exclusive* properties of discourse, then the answer has already been given. I suppose that one may easily accept that referentiality, knowledge and ideology could not pertain to any non-discursive practice. As to subjectivity, someone might counter that it lies behind *every* human practice. Foucault himself however would accept that even in non-discursive practices subjectivity is mediated *by way of discourse*. If we accept that the subject is defined as that which forms concepts, we cannot accept that there is subjectivity outside discourse, i.e. subjectivity "immediately" connected to non-discursive practices. I believe that this is the meaning of Foucault's insistence on treating as the main object of the archaeological method "the instances of discourse [les discours] that articulate what we think, say, and *do*".

Some caution is required here though. If we accept that there is discourse in every human practice, then how can we distinguish within this *nexus* of different practices, those practices that in themselves are discourse from those that are non-discursive in the sense that they are linked to subjectivity only *through the mediation* of discourse, only being "articulated" by it? As it was also made evident when discussing the example with the "golden mountain" and "California", I believe the specificity of every practice may be judged from its effects. Discourse as a practice, the practice of discourse, which *on this level of abstraction* does not differ from the practice of speech, has *enunciation* as a direct effect. If we defined above language as the actual *ability* to form concepts, here we could define enunciation as the *effect* of this ability, i.e. simply as *the actual formation of concepts itself.*

At some crucial point of presenting his views on discourse in *The archaeology of knowledge*, Foucault uses the example of the typewriter in order to explain how the *statement* (*énoncé* in French) emerges—in other words, when it is that we have *enunciation* (*énonciation*). According to Foucault, the sequence of letters on the keyboard constitutes no statement. We do have a statement though when this same sequence of letters has been typed on a sheet of paper,[218] thus forming an incoherent "word", as "referent" of which we could consider the sequence of letters on the keyboard itself.

I suppose it has already become apparent that I have assumed the somewhat graceless role of eliciting from Foucault's work definitions which he obstinately refused to formulate. I have no particular problem with this, in so far as I have made clear that the "definitions" I give generally speaking, not merely the "Foucauldian" ones, are usable, flexible and provisional, especially to the extent they refer to mainly subjective entities. Be that as it may, at the specific point with the example of the typewriter, I believe Foucault has "trapped himself", if not into some implicit though quite clear definition, at any event into some implicit though quite clear *conception* of what "statement"/"enunciation" and therefore "discourse" means.

---

218. See Foucault, *L'archéologie du savoir*, p. 116 ff. – English translation: p. 88 ff.

Let us first of all think of the theoretical consequences of his not considering as a statement the sequence of letters on the keyboard. This means that Foucault considers the *material construction* of the keyboard as a *non-discursive* practice, even though he would surely recognise this is articulated with some *discursive* practice, some *technology*, consisting in the *application of certain knowledges* having to do with questions like the *most convenient sequence* in which to place the letters on the keyboard etc. The question now posed is this: what is it that intervenes between the sheer material existence of the letters on the keyboard and their imprint, in the same sequence, on paper, or, to update Foucault's example, on the computer screen? Quite simply, the fact that *someone is typing, someone is writing by using the keyboard.* If some statement/enunciation, and consequently some elementary form of discourse, is to exist, according to Foucault it is not even necessary to have the utterance, written or oral, of some word belonging to any of the existing languages. On the other hand, I do not believe it would be exceedingly arbitrary to suggest that Foucault would exclude from his example the case of having a statement if the typing were done by an ape or some infant. So to have enunciation, that is, actual formation of concepts, there should be *someone who is able to enounce, that is, to form concepts, and who puts into action this very ability*, even if the concept formed in this case is merely the "concept" of the sequence of letters on the keyboard.

But let us see what Foucault himself has to say on this point: "What has happened, then, that a statement should have been made? What can the second group [of letters] possess that is not possessed by the first? Reduplication, the fact that it is a copy? Certainly not, since the keyboards of typewriters all copy a certain model and are not, by that very fact, statements. The intervention of a subject? This answer is inadequate for two reasons: it is not enough that the reiteration of a series [of letters] be due to the initiative of an individual for it to be transformed, by that very fact, into a statement; and, in any case, the problem does not lie in the cause or origin of the reduplication, but in the special relation between the two identical series."[219]

He then goes on to explain what makes up this special relation, which distinguishes the statement both from the relation of signifiers and signifieds and from a phrase or a proposition, and which has mainly to do with the connection "to a 'referential' that is made up not of 'things', 'facts', 'realities', or 'beings', but of laws of possibility, rules of existence for the objects that are named, designated, or described within it, and for the relations that are affirmed or denied in it".[220]

Likewise, in the immediately following pages, he also refers to the "particular relation" of the statement with some subject, which, in brief, consists in the specific, concrete conditions, different in each case, to be fulfilled by the position occupied by an individual if this is to be a subject of enun-

---

219. *Ibid.*, pp. 116-117 – English translation: pp. 88-89.

220. *Ibid.*, p. 120 – English translation: p. 91.

ciation.²²¹ Generally speaking, Foucault's logic in this chapter where he is describing the "enunciative function",²²² is quite consistent with his overall approach, which largely consists, as we have already suggested, in a (non-economistic but nevertheless materialist) philosophical investigation of the field defining his research. Let us go back to the first extract.

We can observe there some "*discontinuity*". With the first remark, that a statement cannot be a simple copy, he is easily convincing. Having already excluded the letters of the keyboard from being statements, he has but to remind us that these in fact are copies (without constituting statements). With the second remark though there is some problem. The problem consists precisely in his pointing out that it is "inadequate for two reasons" to suggest that what mediates (so that there can be a statement) is the intervention of a subject. His first objection is that the intervention of an individual(-subject) *is not enough*. If he left it at that, we could presume that he considers the intervention of a subject as a "*necessary but not sufficient*" condition for the existence of a statement, and we would expect his second objection to consist in pointing out some *additional* "necessary conditions", for example, what he actually says just afterwards about the "special relation" between statement and "referential", as well as what follows, regarding the conditions of involvement of the subject itself.

But this is not so. In the second objection, Foucault will say that, "in any case", *the problem does not lie there* (it lies in the "special relation" etc. etc.). That is, it is *as if he regretted* the fact that he himself posed the question of the subject, *on this primary level, on the level of the distinction between discourse and non-discourse*. Since we are considering a book and not some fleeting remark while chatting with friends, we could hardly accept that he posed the problem of the subject and then changed his mind. In such a case he would have only to erase the relevant question and proceed directly to the "particular relation". Instead, though, he says, "the problem does not lie in the cause or origin of the reduplication [i.e. of the statement]". The words "*cause*" and "*origin*" that he uses here to refer to the subject are, I believe, quite revealing as to the problem Foucault is facing particularly at this crucial point of expanding his theses about the specificity of discourse, and may therefore serve to account for the remarkably *awkward* way he is trying to evade this problem.

On one hand, in the "discursive regime" of the time and geographical area of *The archaeology of knowledge*'s publication (end of 1960s, continental Western Europe), he is obliged to accept the "philosophical blackmail" imposed by a controversy that still prevailed, concerning a quite rigorous demarcation between two possible attitudes towards the subject. *Either* one is on the side of the *constituting* subject, that is, of the subject as (autonomous and self-existent) *cause* or *origin* of discourse, thought and action, *or* one

---

221. *Ibid.*, pp. 121-126 – English translation: pp. 92-96.

222. *Ibid.*, pp. 115-138 – English translation: pp. 88-105.

accepts that the subject is *constituted*, that it is *only* constituted.[223] Given that the main target of his critique throughout the course of his work, at least since *History of madness*, had been the former attitude, it would have been difficult if at all possible to differentiate himself significantly from the latter.

On the other hand, he is aware that he cannot avoid the question of the subject. As I have already said, I suppose that he would have to answer in the negative if someone were to ask him whether there would be a statement in case the keyboard was used by an infant or an ape. These two cases *are not the same* as that of the mad, whose subjectivity we well know he had taken quite seriously[224], but neither as that of drug addicts, whom he explicitly takes into account as possible subjects of enunciation in one of the examples in those very pages of *The archaeology*.[225] I mention the ape and the infant as examples of *non-subjects*, provided, I repeat, we agree with the definition of the subject as that which forms, and therefore *is able* to form, concepts. Quite revealing is the fact that perhaps the most characteristic representative of the latter attitude towards the subject at the time *The archaeology of knowledge* was published, namely Louis Althusser, expressly considers newborn infants, even *foetuses*, as subjects. "That an individual is always-already a subject, even before he is born, is [...] the plain reality, accessible to everyone and not a paradox at all."[226]

The publication of Foucault's *Archaeology of knowledge* coincided with the time Althusser wrote (the largest part of) "Ideology and ideological state apparatuses" (1969).[227] I already said above that I have repeatedly been occupied in the past with the difficult but in my view indispensable correlation of the two thinkers. What concerns me here as to the chronological coincidence of those two particular texts is that they both are, each with its own ideologico-philosophical starting point, characteristic indications of a profound mistrust towards the subject, that was, in those years at least, a commonplace for those directly or indirectly connected to French structuralism and poststructuralism. In the *Archaeology of knowledge*, this mistrust becomes particularly evident in Foucault's polemic epilogue, where the impressive device of a dialogue with an imaginary opponent mainly aims to demonstrate the significance of the archaeological method in further advancing the critique of the concept of the subject in a direction more radical than so far accomplished by structuralism. The radicalness mainly consists in including within the notion of the subject as target of critique the subject

---

223. For a more extensive critical presentation of this controversy, see my Afterword in Barthes, *op. cit.*, p. 342 ff.

224. See above, fn. 90.

225. Foucault, *op. cit.*, p. 119 – English translation: p. 90.

226. Althusser, *Positions*, pp. 127-129 – English translation: Althusser, *Lenin and philosophy and other essays*, pp. 164-165.

227. Althusser, *Positions*, p. 134 - English translation: Althusser, *Lenin and philosophy and other essays*, p. 170.

of knowledge and science itself,²²⁸ something which of course differentiates him from Althusser, who, by insisting, also in his 1969 text, on the separation between ideology and science, restricts the concept of the "constituted subject" in the former and thereby places the latter out of critique's reach. This differentiation, apart from being an indication of Althusser's economism and scientism from which Foucault evidently escapes,²²⁹ is at the same time quite revealing as to the way the two thinkers are posited in relation to the *Kantian* notion of a subject with a *free will*.

Although Althusser could well be considered as the least Hegelian of the important Marxist theoreticians, in this particular matter he remains traditionally Marxist, and consequently Hegelian, insofar as he confines himself to *inversing* Hegelianism. Hegel defines the State as the realisation of freedom, idealising freedom by way of opposing it to reality and coercion on the basis of the oppositional schemes of *infinite antithesis* (unendlicher Gegensatz) and *Realisation*.²³⁰ Althusser utilises the two possible meanings of the term *subject*:

- centre of a free self-will
- that which is *subjected*, which is subjugated

and then proceeds to oppose them and to subordinate the former to the latter, maintaining that the belief in the imaginary entity of the former, a belief that forms the foundation of every "ideological interpellation", leads to the acquiescence to the reality of the latter which is "in the last instance" the existing relations of production.²³¹ The inversion obviously consists in the "materialist" reduction of the idealised entity of freedom in Hegelian idealism. Being an inversion, it remains, as one could expect, entrapped within the oppositional scheme from which it is trying to escape. To be outside ideology presupposes you are aware you are inside it, Althusser will say,²³² thereby reproducing Engels's scheme of freedom based on the knowledge of necessity,²³³ only now the place of freedom has been occupied by science which has the privilege of being a "discourse without a subject".²³⁴ Therefore without subjugation. And without freedom? Without *imaginary* freedom, no doubt. Is there *any other* freedom according to Althusser?

---

228. Foucault, *op. cit.*, especially p. 259 ff. – English translation: p. 199 ff.
229. On these questions, see references in fns 159 and 160.
230. See Hegel, *op. cit.*, pp. 29-74 – English translation: pp. 16-54.
231. See above, fns 57 and 60.
232. Althusser, *Positions*, p. 127 – English translation: Althusser, *Lenin and philosophy and other essays*, pp. 163-164.
233. See above, fn. 61.
234. See above, fn. 202.

To depart from Althusser, or rather, to let him be together with the impasses of "official" Marxism, and before we go back to Foucault, let us pose the question in its more general form. Is there a freedom that is not included in the bipolar schema real/imaginary? Of course there is, freedom as a moral value.

Very broadly speaking, we might say that, on the fundamental issue posed in relation to determinism and freedom, there are three possible responses. The first one is given by traditional Marxism and other trends, and it consists in the *ontological negation* of freedom, as well as in attributing any indeterminacy that may emerge to a *merely temporary* inadequacy of hitherto constituted scientific knowledge. If there is any ethical issue apart from the ontological one, in this response it is posed as an ethics of necessity. Staying in Marxism, the ethics of either the necessity of the class struggle and its inevitable conclusion or the necessity of the findings of Marxism as a science, or of some variation or combination between the two. The second response is given by the various versions of liberalism and/or humanism, and it consists in the *ontological affirmation* of freedom, and in bestowing it additionally with a *moral value*. In this response, freedom is dissociated from the question determinism/indeterminacy, it is considered as existing anyway, *objectively*, as a *hypostasis*, as a basic constituent of *(also considered as a hypostasis) human existence*, irrespective of whether it may be violated or restricted. The third response, given by what I have here called "materialist dualism", which is inspired by a materialist version of Kantianism and in which I would also include Foucault, consists in the *ontological acceptance of indeterminacy* as a general condition of existence. It is a matter of an ontological hypothesis of an indeterminacy deriving from fundamental finitude and the discontinuity that this entails, which is not incompatible with some form of necessity/causality, especially in the realm of material entities, *given that necessity/causality is also finite*, and which in human affairs acquires the *moral* form of freedom.

The hypothesis of a *specifically human indeterminacy* has to do with the *gaps of discontinuity in language* and hence in all practices directly deriving from it: enunciation, discourse, knowledge, reason and will.[235] In other words, it is a matter of the indeterminacy of *concepts or signifieds*. The fact that *this* indeterminacy acquires the moral form of freedom, that is, the form of freedom as a moral value, as a value that guides action, results simply from the fact that, according to all the above assumptions (somehow connected with the "third response"), the subject as *that which forms concepts* and the subject *having a will* (which means also the subject of *action*) are one and the same thing. The indeterminacy of the signifieds that fill in the gaps of discontinuity in language, the subject of enunciation that intervenes between the letters of the keyboard and the printed letters in Foucault's ex-

---

235. We accept here the Kantian definition of the will as *practical reason* - Immanuel Kant, *Grundlegung zur Metaphysik der Sitten*, Frankfurt: Suhrkamp, 1977 (first German edition: 1785), p. 41 – English translation (James W. Ellington): *Grounding for the metaphysics of morals*, Indianapolis, Indiana: Hackett, 1993, p. 23.

ample,²³⁶ and freedom of the will as a moral value, constitute a conceptual and axiological triplet that opens up the passage to the second direction of the dual relation, namely to the ethical priority of concepts as against their material conditions of existence as well as material entities in general.

I insisted on the "aspect of signifieds" so as to connect the linguistic problematic to Foucauldian "archaeology". This connection is mostly neglected due to the fact that Foucault himself, in his attempt to avoid being counted among Saussure's structuralist successors, systematically either ignores it or dissociates explicitly himself from it.²³⁷ This connection is nonetheless indispensable to my mind, if we are to understand Foucault's method within the broader framework of the problematic on language and discourse as well as of the related trends of structuralism and poststructuralism.

The other end of the triplet, the ethics of freedom of the will, may at first glance seem even more provocatively arbitrary if connected with Foucault's thought. My opinion though is that the treatment of Foucault's work as "hostile" towards freedom of the will is based on two assumptions, of which one is correct but only partially valid, and the other rests on false premises from the start.

Let us start with the first. It is true that the text of *The archaeology of knowledge* is *partially* characterised by a "positivistic" sort of "determinism". I use quotation marks for both words at issue, because we have a peculiar kind of "positivism" and an even more peculiar "determinism". Both consist in Foucault's possibly excessive insistence on the concepts of *rule* and *system*, the description of which forms a central concern of the archaeological method if it is to explain the emergence of certain statements or discourses in a particular period and society and the exclusion of certain others. On the other hand, the essence of Foucault's use of these concepts is to be found not so much in the direction of assimilating them to some natural-scientific paradigms but rather in that of the *specific materiality of discourse and knowledge*,²³⁸ a materiality which we discussed at length above, referring, among other things, to the linguistic problematic. Besides, Foucault himself undermines the very "regularity" of the rule and the system by repeatedly using

---

236. Here we should also accept the existence of *internal enunciation*. In correspondence with the –Saussurian- concept of *internal speech* (see above), we should also imagine the Foucauldian equivalent of an *"internal typing"*; that is, thought as a material process –as a function of the brain-, about which, however, we –axiomatically- suppose that it has a subjective basis, and which is inherent –as *internal enunciation*- in every human practice, even in non-discursive practices. It goes without saying that this internal enunciation largely –though not entirely- coincides with the Freudian-Lacanian unconscious.

237. See, for example, his Preface to the English edition of *Les mots et les choses* - Foucault, *The order of things*, p. xiv.

238. See, for example, Foucault, *L'archéologie du savoir*, pp. 131-138 – English translation: pp. 100-105.

the crucially significant term: *systems of dispersion,*[239] a "dispersion" that in this instance indicates both the discontinuity of materiality and the indeterminacy of subjectivity.

The second assumption has to do with the notorious "mistrust towards the subject", which I mentioned above as a "commonplace" of structuralism, poststructuralism and the trends more or less connected with those. It is true that Foucault, both in *The archaeology of knowledge* and in other works, "ranks among the first" of the "critics of the subject". But here lies the root of a huge misapprehension, the responsibility for which rests to some degree with the intransigence or the inexplicitness of many of the "critics" themselves, including Foucault. The critique of the subject is directed against the *hypostatised* subject. It does not deny the *hypothetical* existence of that *conceptual* entity, which thinks, that is, which *hypothesises*, that is, which *forms concepts*, among which is the *concept of itself*, which speaks, enounces discourse, knows, has a will, acts. In other words, the critique of the subject has as its target those multiple versions of modern idealism, including Hegelianism, liberalism and humanism, which are based on the acceptance of an *objectively existing* subject of thought and/or action.

---

239. *Ibid.*, pp. 44-54 – English translation: pp. 31-39. We notice here a possible –mutual, perhaps- influence between Foucault and Deleuze, who considers the "*disperse*" as that element of *difference* that cannot be "tamed" by representational thought – see Deleuze, *Difference and repetition*, especially p. 330 ff. The term "dispersion" is also used by Laclau and Mouffe, but only in order to curtail its significance by way of the concept of "overdetermination" – Laclau and Mouffe, *op. cit.*, pp. 114-122.

Chapter 13
Hypostatisation and representation

The primordial form of the hypostatisation to which I have been referring, a first critique of which we meet in Kant's "Transcendental dialectic" in the *Critique of pure reason* and also in his *Prolegomena*, is to be found in the underlying structure of the "psychological paralogism" that constitutes the Cartesian *cogito*:

I think, therefore I am, I exist.

That is:

I think, therefore that which thinks, that is, the subject, exists.

That is:

I think, therefore the subject exists independently of my thought.

The basic argument for this indeed arbitrary, in a sense, interpretation of Descartes's reasoning is that if he did not mean this, that is, if he meant simply that I who think, that is, the subject, exist *if* I think, the central formulation of his philosophy would be a blatant tautology.[240]

---

240. René Descartes, *Discourse on method and the Meditations* (translated by F.E. Sutcliffe), Harmondsworth: Penguin Books, 1968, pp. 53-54. For the Kantian critique, see above, fns 52 and 54. Also, on this particular point, see especially the interpretation of the Kantian critique of the "psychological paralogism" given by an English translator of Kant - Kant, *Prolegomena to any future metaphysics that can qualify as a science*, pp. 169-170.

The initial formulation, *by itself,* of *I think, therefore I am/exist* at the beginning of the fourth chapter of the *Discourse on method*, and the equivalent conception of the *I* as *res cogitans*, as a *thing that thinks*, at the beginning of the *Meditations*, is indeed tautological. But it is a *justified* tautology, so to speak. Aiming to establish absolute certainty, and starting from absolute doubt against even the simplest cognitions of the external world, assuming these are illusions caused by an "evil demon" (genius malignus),[241] Descartes initially concludes that the only certain knowledge is the knowledge of the thinking self. Initially, that is, he ensures for himself as thinking subject a *space of continuity*, secure against any outside intervention that would lead him to some false knowledge. The very property of lack of extension in the *res cogitans* ensures that absolute continuity reigns therein. The material world, *initially, that is, as it is perceived by the senses*, is a *space of discontinuity*, given the multiplicity and the confusing forms of both the senses and the conditions that make it perceivable.

In this sense, by the passage from the discontinuity of material objects and the senses to the continuity of the pure intellect of the I that thinks, the *idealisation* of the thinking subject is also accomplished. In other words, this idealisation is but another facet of the passage from discontinuity to continuity. The gaps, the doubts, the confusions of the external world and the senses are abolished together with the founding of the Cartesian "*epoché*" and the grounding of representational thought. The body, the senses and material objects provisionally disappear, in order to undergo eventually their classification by the pure intellect, after the latter has "come to terms" with itself, after it has recognised itself as a continuous being in the sense of the removal of any gap into which doubt might insinuate itself. Even if the "evil demon" deceives me, or rather, *because* it deceives me, as *thought, be it as deceived thought, as a thing that thinks even having been deceived*, it is certain that I exist: "There is therefore no doubt that I exist, if he [the evil demon] deceives me; and let him deceive me as much as he likes, he can never cause me to be nothing, so long as I think I am something."[242] So we move from the discontinuity of uncertainty to the continuity of the *cogito*, which is certain of its own existence. The continuity of the *cogito* initially is but *the certainty of thought as doubt.*

But Descartes's reasoning does not stop here. Should this be the case, apart from a simple tautology, we would also have to do with the self-evident right of the storyteller to his/her unhindered storytelling, of the dreamer to his/her peaceful dreams, of someone phantasising to his/her ecstatic phantasies, of the usual forms of cutting off from the discontinuous and thereby

---

241. René Descartes, *Méditations métaphysiques*, Paris: Flammarion, 1992 (bilingual –Latin and French- edition; first Latin edition: 1641, first French translation: 1647), pp. 66-69 – English translation: Descartes, *Discourse on method and the Meditations*, pp. 100-101.

242. *Ibid.*, pp. 72-73 – English translation: p. 103.

problematic and uncertain character of the real world. Descartes asks himself whether there can be certainty *also about something outside* the thinking self.

The I that thinks, the *cogito*, is *a thing or a substance: res sive substantia cogitans*.[243] *Initially* in Descartes "substance" carries the very general meaning of *independent existence*, of the *thing that is by itself able to exist: substantia, sive res quae per se apta est existere*.[244] Descartes, though, takes the notion of *independent* existence "at face value". He is not content with the Aristotelian conception of *hypostasis* (or *substance*) as that which is distinguished from *quality* and *relation*. So considering himself, the thinking I, as an independent existence, he begins to investigate the possibility of the existence of other substances (or hypostases), apart from himself. If they are to be true substances, that is, independent existences, they must be *independent of him, that is, of his thought*. Since the only certain existence is my thought, the criterion for independent existence cannot but be posited as *independence from my thought*. In this way we see that *eventually* in Descartes substance acquires the more specific sense of *objective* existence, that is, of existence *independent of my thought*. *Provisionally*, and we will see further on why *provisionally*, it goes without saying that the subject of thought, even though itself a substance, is exempted from this. It cannot be that I who think exist independently of my thought.

As for material things, and with regard both to the senses (which are confusing anyhow and thereby possibly erroneous) and to the "clear and distinct ideas" that I may have of them, i.e. *duration, number, extension, figure, position, movement*, I have no reason not to assume that they do not derive from myself. Therefore they do not constitute any indication for some existence independent of me and my thought. The only idea that I have within me and that necessarily drives me to recognise something outside my thought and independent of it is the idea of God, that is, the idea of the *infinite substance*:

> "...And consequently I must necessarily conclude from all I have said hitherto, that God exists; for, although the idea of substance is in me, for the very reason that I am a substance, I would not, nevertheless, have the idea of an infinite substance, since I am a finite being, unless the idea had been put into me by some substance which was truly infinite.

> "And I must not imagine that I do not conceive the infinite by means of a true idea, but only by the negation of the finite, in the same way as I comprehend rest and darkness by the negation of movement and light: for, on the contrary, I see manifestly that there is more reality in the infinite substance than in the finite, and hence that I have in me in some way the notion of the infinite, before that of the finite, that is to say the notion of God, before that of myself. For how would it be possible for me to know that I doubt and I desire, that is

---

243. *Ibid.*, pp. 120-123 – English translation: p. 127.

244. *Ibid.*, pp. 112-115 – English translation: p. 123.

to say, that I lack something and am not all perfect, if I did not have in me any idea of a more perfect being than myself, by comparison with which I know the deficiencies of my nature?"[245]

In this sense, the only *original* substance according to Descartes is the *infinite* substance, that is, God. He is the only entity that is a substance with both meanings of the term. He exists independently of my thought, but he also exists independently of everything else. Since he is the cause of all, he does not depend on anything, and, on the contrary, everything depends on him. *Finite* substance, according to Descartes, necessarily means *dependent* substance—dependent not on other finite substances, *neither on my thought*, but on the *infinite substance*. Finite substances are *finite* in the sense that the *infinite* substance is both the cause of their existence *and that in comparison to which they are determined as finite*. Therefore they cannot be substances in the *general* sense of *independent existence*. But they *are* substances in the *specific* sense of *that which exists independently of my thought*, that is, which exists *objectively*.

This *ultimately applies also to the subject of thought itself*. The fact that the idea of the infinite substance of God exists within me *before* the idea of myself as a finite substance, that is, as a substance *that doubts and desires therefore it is not perfect or infinite*, ensures that I exist *before* my thought, that is, *independently of it*, since at this stage my thought is still *identical with doubt*. The thinking subject, while doubting, recognises that something *pre-exists* within it, which is the idea of infinite substance, and in comparison to which, that is, being *based* on which, it *can* doubt, that is, think. I think, therefore I am/exist before, that is, independently of my thought.

If in the first structural stage of the Cartesian *Meditations*, as we have seen, the passage from *discontinuity* (of uncertainty) to *continuity* (of the *cogito*) consisted in the *idealisation* of the subject, we now notice that in the second stage the passage from *finitude* to the *infinite* amounts to *its objectivisation*, that is, to *its hypostatisation* in the *specific* sense of its conversion into an objective existence. At the same time though we see that in this stage the hypostatisation of the idea of God has also been accomplished, both in the *specific* and in the *general* sense of independent existence. If the former hypostatisation, as we have said, constitutes the equivalent of the "psychological paralogism", the latter is the equivalent of the "theological ideal", both of them constituting in common "unavoidable illusions of reason", which the Kantian Dialectic seeks to expose.[246]

The third structural stage of the *Meditations*, as is to be expected, concerns the question of certainty about the existence of *other* finite substances, that is, of *material things*. Being *finite* substances, as in the case of the subject of thought, and for the equivalent reason, they cannot anyhow be considered as substances in the *general* sense. Their existence and their

---

245.*Ibid.*, pp. 114-117 – English translation: pp. 123-124.

246.Kant, *Kritik der reinen Vernunft*, pp. 341-399 and 512-605 – English translation: pp. 233-249 and 334-405.

finitude are dependent on and determined by the infinite substance. As to the *specific* sense, up to this point, until the end of the third *Meditation*, we have seen that Descartes presumes he cannot exclude the possibility that their idea derives from his thought, therefore that their existence depends on it. At the beginning of the fourth *Meditation* though Descartes invokes anew the notion of the infinite substance in order to solve the problem:

> "...Already, then, I seem to discover a path that will lead us from the contemplation of the true God, in whom all the treasures of knowledge and wisdom are contained, to the knowledge of the other things in the universe.
>
> "For, in the first place, I recognize that it is impossible that he should ever deceive me, since in all fraud and deceit is to be found a certain imperfection; and although it may seem that to be able to deceive is a mark of subtlety or power, yet the desire to deceive bears evidence without doubt of weakness or malice, and, accordingly, cannot be found in God.
>
> "Secondly, I am aware in myself of a certain power of judgement, which undoubtedly I have received from God, in the same way as all the other things which I possess; and as he would not wish to deceive me, it is certain that he has not given to me a power such that I can ever be in error, if I use it properly."[247]

As long as I use my judgement correctly, that is, as long as I am based only on "clear and distinct ideas" and not on confused images deriving from my body or my senses, which are but indications of my imperfect nature, that is, of my finitude—and *this is why it cannot be presumed that the erroneous impressions caused by them derive (directly) from God*[248]—it is certain that I will not err, since I am guaranteed for this by the perfect or infinite (*morally as well*) being, namely God. So it is once again on the basis of the infinite substance that we have the passage from the certainty about the existence of the *res cogitans* to that of the objective existence of material things (objective in the sense of independent of my thought, but not of God).

This passage forms a new *threefold* version of the passage from discontinuity to continuity. First, we have a passage from the discontinuity between the finite substance of the *res cogitans* and the infinite substance of God to a continuity between the two: the *will* to perfection, which is expressed precisely by the *correct use* of the ability to judge and therefore by the release from the illusory nature of my material, that is, of my *irrevocably* finite substance, is also an indication that God has created me *as a thinking subject* in his own image,[249] thereby rendering me a *potentially* omniscient subject, even though never *actually* omniscient like him.[250] Second, we have

---

247. Descartes, *op. cit.*, pp. 132-135 – English translation: pp. 132-133.

248. *Ibid.*, pp. 148-153 – English translation: pp. 140-141.

249. *Ibid.*, pp. 138-143 – English translation: pp. 135-137.

250. *Ibid.*, pp. 118-121 – English translation: pp. 125-126. In this *potential* identification between the subject (*res cogitans*) and God (infinite substance), we may notice a first version of the Althusserian specular relation between subject (with small *s*) and Subject (with capital *S*) - Althusser, *Positions*, pp. 129-134 – English translation: Althusser, *Lenin and philosophy and other essays*, pp. 165-170.

a passage from the discontinuity between the *cogito* and the material world to the continuity between the two, which consists in the possibility of certain knowledge of the latter by the former. And third, we also have the passage to the establishment of continuity between the material things *themselves*, namely to *their classification or ordering*. It is quite revealing how the penultimate paragraph of the sixth and last *Meditation* ends. In that paragraph, adopting a somewhat "self-critical" attitude, so to speak, towards the doubts formulated at the beginning of the *Meditations*, which also included calling into question the distinction between sleep and wakefulness, Descartes says the following:

> "...And I must reject all the doubts of these last few days, as hyperbolical and ridiculous, particularly the general uncertainty about sleep, which I could not distinguish from the wakeful state: for now I see a very notable difference between the two states in that our memory can never connect our dreams with one another and with the general course of our lives, as it is in the habit of connecting the things which happen to us when we are awake. And, in truth, if someone, when I am awake, appeared to me all of a sudden and as suddenly disappeared as do the images I see when I am asleep, so that I could see neither where he came from nor where he went, it would not be without reason that I deemed him to be a spectre or phantom formed in my brain, and similar to those which are formed there when I am asleep, rather than a real man. But when I perceive things of which I clearly know both the place they come from and that in which they are, and the time in which they appear to me, and when, without any interruption, I can link the perception I have of them with the whole of the rest of my life, I am fully assured that it is not in sleep that I am perceiving them but while I am awake. And I must not in any way doubt the truth of these things, if, after having called upon my senses, my memory and my understanding to examine them, nothing is reported to me by any of these faculties which conflicts with what is reported to me by the others. For as God is no deceiver, it follows necessarily that I am not deceived in this."[251]

It is quite clear, even the criterion for the distinction between sleep and wakefulness consists in the possibility to establish continuity, a possibility which, in the last instance, depends on the infinite substance.

This close interconnection between *representation as the discourse of continuity* on one hand and *hypostatisation* on the other is something that pertains to modern (in the broad sense) ideology in general. In this sense, the *Meditations* are not merely the grounding text of modern philosophy but also the founding act of modern ideology. Here perhaps the adjectival modifier "modern" may constitute a pleonasm. If there is any meaning in distinguishing between mythology and ideology, this consists in that the latter is not antagonistic to rationalism.[252] The triplet idealisation-continuity-hypostatisation, which, as we have seen, forms a fundamental component of reasoning in the Cartesian *Meditations*, is also the basic organising motif more or less underlying most of the multiple and varied versions of (modern) ration-

---

251. Descartes, *op. cit.*, pp. 208-211 – English translation: p. 168.
252. And in this sense we would not agree with the well-known Althusserian thesis that "ideology has no history" - Althusser, *Positions*, pp. 111-114 – English translation: Althusser, *Lenin and philosophy and other essays*, pp. 150-152.

alism. In mythology too, of course, there are idealisations and hypostatisations, as well as some primordial form of representational classification or ordering and continuity (and doubtlessly we also find the power-exercising and antagonistic *function*).[253] However, what characterises (modern) rationalism as such is the quest for a continuous ideational ordering or classification of the existing world[254] on the basis of a central and/or supreme organising principle that occupies *structurally at least* the position of the Cartesian infinite substance: God, nation, race, people, History (with capital *H*), tradition, nature, science, man, public or individual utility, polity, public opinion etc. The existence of the infinite substance is the guarantee for the ordering continuity, which in turn serves as a guarantee for the *objective existence of itself.* If continuity constitutes the criterion for certainty, the latter also invalidates the hypotheticality, that is, the subjectivity, of thought. I am (absolutely) certain of something, in so far as this "something" is considered as objective, means that my thought of "something" is similarly objective. The completion of the Cartesian and, more generally, of the (modern) ideological programme amounts to the independence not merely of the subject from thought but also of thought from itself.

---

253. See Georges Dumézil, *Mythe et épopée I. II. III.*, Paris: Gallimard, 1995, and above, fn. 177. This is why it goes without saying that the critique (as well as the theory) of ideology *in a broader sense of the term* also includes the critique (and the theory, respectively) of mythology, since, moreover, on one hand, quite often in modern discourse (properly) ideological elements mingle with mythological ones, and on the other, in discourse analysis we cannot in any case distinguish *beforehand* the ones from the others.

254. A quest that appears in its completed form with Destutt de Tracy's "ideology" – see Destutt de Tracy, *Traité de la volonté et de ses effets (Éléments de l'idéologie: Seconde section)*, Paris: Fayard, 1994 (reproduction of the second edition of 1818), and Foucault, *Les mots et les choses*, p. 253 – English translation: pp. 240-241.

Chapter 14
Foucault and freedom as a moral value

The critique of hypostatisation in general and of the hypostatised subject in particular is not at all antagonistic to accepting the existence of a *hypothetical* subject of thought. The fact that indeed the initial formulation of the Cartesian "I think, therefore I am", if considered *by itself*, would constitute a blatant tautology serves at the same time as an indication that if the critique of the subject were also addressed against its *hypothetical* existence we would have an equally blatant paradox, something for which we could hardly reproach not merely Foucault but several other poststructuralists too.

There are of course also some *positive* arguments in favour of the view that *freedom of the will as a moral value* is not alien to Foucault's approach. If Foucault avoids using the *term* "freedom of the will", I believe this could well be attributed to the fact that the term has been identified with idealist and liberal approaches that, together with the *subject* having a free will, also hypostatise the idea of freedom of the will itself. The *essential meaning* of the term though, namely the *concept* or *signified* of the term, is there at some crucial points of his thought, especially towards the end of his intellectual (and biological) life.

I have here in mind the last published systematisation of his views about power (1982), where what is quite revealing is how he approaches the notion of *resistance* to power. This is a notion he had earlier treated in a fashion that could lead to crude, positivistic forms of approaches, with formulations of the sort, "where there is power, there is resistance",[255] which, combined with terms like "microphysics of power",[256] bring to mind "to every action there is always opposed an equal reaction" from physics.[257] I now quote from his *last* systematisation *mentioned a few lines above*:

> "The relationship of power and freedom's refusal to submit cannot therefore be separated. The crucial problem of power is not that of voluntary servitude (how could we seek to be slaves?). At the very heart of the power relationship, and constantly provoking it, are the recalcitrance of the will and the intransigence of freedom. Rather than speaking of an essential 'antagonism', it would be better to speak of an 'agonism'—of a relationship which is at the same time reciprocal incitation and struggle; less of a face-to-face opposition which paralyzes both sides than a permanent provocation."[258]

I believe this passage poses several crucial questions, one of which is the close correlation between the will and freedom. Let us be cautious though. We should not hasten to assume that the connection between the two concepts is equivalent to "freedom of the will". Here we rather have to do with the *will to freedom*. What is more, in this case, as to the "will" in particular, we could hardly accept that it is used in the Kantian sense of "practical reason". I would rather suggest that we have to do with the will as a *Nietzschean* concept, which is more akin to the concept of desire[259]—a Nietzschean concept all right, but a Nietzschean concept led astray. Foucault converts the "will to power" into the "will to freedom". It is not the same thing, and we will see why further down.

However, something which is perhaps more revealing here is the enigmatic rhetorical question posed in brackets, "how could we seek to be slaves?". Why do I say "enigmatic"? Given Foucault's "cynicism" generally speaking, which is apparent both in his (Nietzschean-inspired) "anti-humanism" and in his formulations and analyses concerning power, someone could *easily* ask him, "And why, may I ask, is this so? Why could we not seek to? Is there perhaps something in human 'nature' or 'essence' that does not allow it?"

---

255. Foucault, *The history of sexuality, Volume 1*, p. 95.

256. See Foucault, *Dits et écrits 1954-1988, III*, p. 140.

257. Moreover, it is indicative that in his lectures given at the Collège de France during the same year that the first volume of *The history of sexuality* was published, Foucault developed an approach to the concept of power characterised by an underlying though quite clear in my view tendency to *hypostatise the idea* of relations of power/resistance on the basis of the model of "war" - Michel Foucault, "*Il faut défendre la société*": *Cours au Collège de France (1975-1976)*, Paris: Gallimard and Seuil, 1997.

258. Dreyfus and Rabinow, *op. cit.*, pp. 221-222 (text slightly modified, taking into account the French version - Foucault, *Dits et écrits 1954-1988, IV*, p.238).

259. See Friedrich Nietzsche, *The will to power* (translated by Walter Kaufmann and R.J. Hollingdale), New York: Vintage Books, 1968.

As I have maintained elsewhere,[260] Foucault's philosophical "anti-humanism" mainly lies in his refusal to accept the hypostatisation of the *idea* of "man", that is, of "man" as an *ideational* entity, beyond his/her biological substance, either as "nature" or as "essence" or in any other form. That human beings cannot seek to be slaves, as a *factual* or *ontological remark*, is, in this sense, *as un-Foucauldian as anything that could be said*. Doubtlessly, we should see the *will* or *desire* for freedom as a *moral incitement*, which Foucault, perhaps because of some concern that his attitude might be taken for an idealist or liberal sort of moralism, puts in brackets and in the form of a rhetorical question, possibly hoping we will let it pass. Moreover, it is a moral incitement carrying a *profoundly anarchist meaning*. The theory of "voluntary servitude", which Foucault here expressly opposes, cannot but refer to the Hobbesian "covenant", as well as to all related rationalist legitimations of power from a liberal and/or juridical viewpoint.

On the other hand, as I have already said, this will or desire for freedom, as a moral incitement, should not be equated to the Nietzschean will to power. Desire for power is something characterising the human being *basically as a biological organism*, as well as animals generally speaking (hence Nietzsche's peculiar *biologism*, which Foucault himself recognises[261]). Besides, identifying freedom with power would bring to mind some of the most extreme versions of economic liberalism. For a more thorough understanding of the Foucauldian desire for freedom as moral incitement, we cannot but take into account, by way of context, Foucault's last well-known text (1984), of a similarly programmatic character, to which I have already referred and in which he insists on naming his method "archaeological". I quote the most revealing ending of that last text: "I do not know whether it must be said today that the critical task still entails faith in Enlightenment; I continue to think that this task requires work on our limits, that is, a patient labor giving form to our impatience for liberty."[262]

The *concrete form* of the desire for freedom, which Foucault here designates by using the rhetorical figure "impatience for liberty", is *critical work as work on our limits*. What can this mean?

That whole text by Foucault, bearing the title "What is Enlightenment?" could be considered an attempt at a *reformulation of the terms of critical thought*, which *at once recognises Kantian critique as its starting point and differentiates itself from it*. Having in mind Foucault's work generally speaking, and especially Foucault's "archaeological" stance towards Kantian critique in

---

260. Doxiadis, "Foucault and ideology", p. 27 ff.

261. Foucault, *Les mots et les choses*, p. 353 – English translation: p. 342. See, for example, Nietzsche, *op. cit.*, pp. 37 and 403-404.

262. Foucault, *Dits et ecrits 1954-1988, IV*, p. 578 – English translation: Foucault, "What is Enlightenment?", p. 50.

The order of things,²⁶³ we could actually schematise this ambivalent attitude of Foucault with regard to Kant in the following manner. It is a matter of *substituting the transcendental method of the "analytic of finitude" with the archaeological method of the "work on our limits"*. In other words, while Kant's transcendental method, especially as this is developed in the "transcendental analytic", sought to establish the universal limits of "all knowledge or of all possible moral action", the Foucauldian (archaeological) work on our limits investigates limits as socio-historical, that is, as altering and/or alterable spatio-temporal determinations. In accordance with what we have already said, it is precisely a matter of a *materialist appropriation* of the Kantian notion of (fundamental) finitude, which consists in treating the latter not as a transcendental, that is, beyond experience, deriving from the outside and universally identical form of human existence, which would furtively constitute the foundation of modern humanist hypostatisation, but rather as a fundamental inherent property of material entities, which has as a primary consequence the discontinuity, instability, asymmetry both of knowledge together with its real objects and of every form of practice. Which means that the critical attitude consists in *concretely investigating but also calling into question our limits on each occasion*, and not in the abstract concern with a universal *and thereby self-refuting* form of human finitude that transcends the biological, neurobiological or otherwise material (geographical, environmental) determinations of the human species.

In this sense, the very investigation of the distinction between subjectivity and objectivity in essence coincides with the Foucauldian critique as work on our limits, that is, with *practical thought on limits*. The critique of both hypostatisation and representation involves, on one hand, exposing the subjectivity and therefore non-necessity of ideational entities themselves, and, on the other, demonstrating the discontinuity of the objective aspect of discourse and representation, as well as of the objective world generally speaking—a discontinuity into whose gaps subjectivity constantly intervenes.

In the same text on Enlightenment, just a little below the invocation of the archaeological method, Foucault says, "[This criticism] is not seeking to make possible a metaphysics that has finally become a science; it is seeking to give new impetus, as far and wide as possible, to the undefined work of freedom."²⁶⁴

It would not be overly hazardous to infer that the above formulation contains the core of Foucauldian ethics. The will to freedom in Foucault is the desire for, or *incitement* to, *freedom of critique*. In this sense he is profoundly Kantian and in favour of the Enlightenment. He repeats the incitement "sapere aude" after Kant. Without the condition set by Kant

---

263. See Doxiadis, "Foucault and the three-headed king", and Doxiadis, "Foucault and ideology".
264. Foucault, *Dits et ecrits 1954-1988*, IV, p. 574 – English translation: Foucault, "What is Enlightenment?", p. 46.

though.²⁶⁵ Foucault does not require obedience either to some benevolent, democratic and/or collective sovereign or to some transcendental rules of knowledge and morality. Without, on the other hand, this meaning that he disavows rules in general and consequently rationality in general—and in this he dissociates himself from the "postmodernists"—let alone limits in general, it is just that he recognises the finitude of the former (of rules and rationality) and he investigates the concrete and alterable form of existence of the latter (of limits).

According to a Foucauldian approach, freedom of critique could certainly not be considered as a *precondition* for resistance to power. If this were the case, we would have pure idealism. More specifically, we would have a *hypostatisation* of freedom (of critique), since "precondition" in that case would mean "*ontological* precondition", that is, "*objectively existing* precondition". On the contrary, *resistance to power constitutes an ontological precondition for freedom of critique*. We could define power as the *social setting of limits to the will and to action*, and resistance to it as the *tendency to transgress* this setting of limits. Having in mind these definitions, it goes without saying that freedom of judgement, that is, in accordance with the Foucauldian conception, freedom of the "work" on limits, has as a precondition the *tendency* to transgress them. What specific direction this tendency may assume, or, in terms of the above mentioned Foucauldian formulation, what "form" the "impatience for freedom" may assume, will depend, if conditions so allow, on the "patient" work of critique on each occasion.

However, freedom of critique could be considered as a *moral justification* for resistance to power. So we come to the second direction of the dualist relation, namely to the ethical priority of concepts as against their material conditions of existence and material entities in general. It is self-evident that critique and its free exercise belong primarily to the realm of discourse, of thought, of the formation of concepts, of subjectivity. Freedom of critique, as the Foucauldian equivalent to Kantian freedom of the will, could in fact be seen as a supreme moral value providing the *criterion* for moral justification or repudiation or for a moral attitude in general towards power and the objective/material conditions of existence that go with it. It is a logical consequence of the axiomatically accepted moral priority of concepts, and first and foremost of freedom of critique, that the criterion for a moral attitude will first of all concern the *possibility of the basic precondition* for freedom of critique, that is, the *possibility of resistance* to power. Material conditions are morally judged (not the material conditions themselves, of course, but the subjects considered responsible for them) on the basis of *to what extent they ensure the possibility of resistance*. It goes without saying that miserable

---

265. Immanuel Kant, "An answer to the question: What is Enlightenment?" (translated by James Schmidt – first German publication: 1784), in: James Schmidt (ed.), *What is Enlightenment? Eighteenth-century answers and twentieth-century questions*, Berkeley, Los Angeles and London: University of California Press, 1996, pp. 58-64.

material living conditions and/or violent oppression are to be morally rejected according to this criterion. But obviously moral judgement does not confine itself to such matters.

The circle of the dualist relation subjectivity-objectivity, or of the relation between discourse and its material conditions of existence, now closes as follows. *In the first place*, the axiomatic acceptance of the ontological priority of material conditions is a *consequence* of the likewise axiomatic acceptance of the ethical priority of concepts. The emphasis on material conditions does not have to do with some fetishisation of matter, but precisely with the fact that "matter" means *among other things* "*material conditions of existence of concepts and critique*". *In the second place*, the ontological priority of material entities *which emanates from the ethical priority of concepts and critique* does not consist *only* in the fact that the former constitute the conditions of existence of the latter, but *also* in the fact that *the inverse is not true*. That is, in accordance with what we have said so far, once again axiomatically, material entities, *and only these*, exist objectively, i.e. independently of concepts. This acceptance forms an *inseparable (logical) precondition of the central aim of critique*, which is the *critique of hypostatisation*. In this sense, *the critique of hypostatisation is a practice that on one hand is based on the ontological priority of the material component and on the other serves the supreme moral value of freedom of critique, as well as of thought in general, by constantly demonstrating the non-objective character of the latter*.

I have repeatedly argued elsewhere[266] that the essence of Foucault's work is the critique of hypostatisation. On the other hand, it is surely not without significance that the term "hypostatisation" does not appear in Foucault's work. It would be less forced to argue that the critique of *representation* characterises the largest part of his work. Even the "political technology of the body",[267] the analysis of which is his central concern when dealing with the penal system as well as with sexuality, is a form of representation precisely in the sense of an applied social-taxonomic discourse. On the basis of what has been suggested above, and maybe schematising somewhat excessively, we could assume that the analysis of representation is the "means" while the critique of hypostatisation is the "end": The analysis of representation from the viewpoint of (fundamental) finitude, by demonstrating the gaps, the discontinuities, the asymmetries and the multiple socio-political applications and material components of discourse and representation, reveals at the same time precisely where and how the subjective element intervenes, either as contingency or as strategic choice, thereby exposing it as to its tendency to present itself as objective, i.e. as hypostasis, either in the form of some inescapable scientific necessity (not always false in itself) or as some compulsory moral imperative (not always oppressive or

---

266. See above, fn. 263.

267. Foucault, *Discipline and punish*, p. 24 and fn. 2 (p. 309).

prohibitive). In correspondence with the correlation between "archaelogical method" and "genealogical design" that Foucault effects in a relevant passage of his text on the Enlightenment mentioned above,[268] we could suggest that the analysis of representation "leads" to a critique of hypostatisation.

However, apart from the *term* "hypostatisation" which is absent from Foucault's texts, something more essential is also missing. The *mechanism* of hypostatisation is missing. I am referring to the conceptual tools that would allow us to understand the process by which individuals as subjects *accept* and/or *constitute* hypostatisation, or are *constituted* by it, since hypostatisation largely consists in the hypostatisation of the subject. Even though Foucault, in his misleading attempt to dissociate himself from the use of the term "ideology", also disavows the term "illusion",[269] it is certainly a matter of the *illusion* of hypostatisation — be it not "illusion" in the sense of simple error, be it illusion in the *Kantian* sense of "unavoidable illusion" of reason,[270] at all events it is a matter of illusion. As I have argued elsewhere,[271] Foucault himself treats hypostatisations as illusions, even though without explicitly admitting it. The non-explicit acceptance, and what is more the explicit *non*-acceptance of the term "illusion", is what allows him not to be concerned with conceptualising its mechanism. Not without cost though.

Kant attributes the (hypostatising) "illusions of reason", which form the target of his critique in the "Transcendental Dialectic", namely the "psychological paralogism", the "cosmological antinomies" and the "theological ideal", to the hypostatisation of the "idea" or "regulative principle" of the "systematic" or "in conformity with aims [zweckmäßigen] unity". Having accepted the existence of the transcendental realm in itself, he does not have to provide a materialist explanation for this hypostatisation.[272] Foucault on the other hand, even though he expressly and repeatedly rejects transcendentality,[273] at some key points in his work invokes some *emotive* background to human thought and practice, which he does not attribute, and which he *could not* attribute, to some sort of *biological* impulsive tendency (as Nietzsche does). The result is that this invocation is carried out either in the form of provocatively arbitrary rhetorical questions, or in some unexplained metaphoric figures. An example of the former was already given

---

268. Foucault, *Dits et écrits 1954-1988, IV*, p. 574 – English translation: Foucault, "What is Enlightenment?", p. 46.

269. Foucault, *Dits et écrits 1954-1988, III*, pp. 148 and 160 – English translation: Foucault, *Power/knowledge*, pp. 118 and 133.

270. Kant, *Kritik der reinen Vernunft*, pp. 339-340 – English translation: pp. 232-233.

271. Doxiadis, "Foucault and the three-headed king", p. 537 ff.

272. See also Kant, *op. cit.*, p. 585 – English translation: p. 389.

273. See, for example, above.

and commented on above: "how could we seek to be slaves?", he wonders (in brackets). And in one of his most famous formulations on power, he asks his readers, "Would power be accepted if it were entirely cynical?"[274]

An example of the latter is when he tries to describe the efficacy of the gaze of Panoptic surveillance: "An inspecting gaze, a gaze which each individual under its weight will end by interiorising to the point that he is his own overseer, each individual thus exercising this surveillance over, and against, himself."[275] It is quite obvious that the "interiorised gaze" could only be conceived as a metaphoric (that is, not literal) figure. In particular, the metaphor consists in invoking a similarity between an altogether material-bodily situation, wherein the overseer or supervisor sees (*without quotation marks*) and thereby exercises surveillance over the supervised, and a situation in which the supervised "sees" (*in quotation marks*) and thereby exercises surveillance over him/herself. And it is also obvious that in the latter situation we have to do with the illusion of hypostatisation: the supervised accepts as objectively existing the *idea of him/herself* as supervisor of him/herself. If someone were to ask Foucault about the existential status of the self as supervisor, I very much doubt he could reply.

In *The order of things* and in *The archaeology of knowledge* itself, remaining, as he himself claims,[276] purely on the level of discourse, perhaps he does not feel obliged to fill in the conceptual gap of the mechanism of hypostatisation. However, in his later writings, even though he retains the archaeological method, and in this sense keeps having discourse as a *main field* of concern, he also addresses questions more directly concerning various ways of *applying and putting to work* discourse and knowledge, as well as their *material conditions of production*. The "political technology of the body" is discourse, but discourse *materially applied*. This process of application, since we have to do with the *body*, and thereby with human *practice* in all its manifestations and interactions, and consequently with *power*, involves various *moral* and *political* issues, perhaps most fundamental of which is one that Foucault *constantly takes aim at in his critique but is in no position to explain*: why, or in any case how, do people accept as objectively existing and necessary some entities that are but discursive constructs?

---

274. Foucault, *The history of sexuality, Volume 1*, p. 86.
275. Foucault, *Power/knowledge*, p. 155.
276. Foucault, *L'archéologie du savoir*, p. 101 – English translation: p. 76.

Chapter 15
Psychoanalysis and linguistics

It is quite well-known that Foucault's relationship with psychoanalysis is a complicated and controversial matter, which has provoked several discussions and disagreements in different theoretical and ideological directions. Even Derrida devoted a considerable part of his dispute with Foucault (after the latter's death) to investigating this issue.[277] Displaying their annoyance in a fashion similar to the way official (Althusserian) Marxists had reacted to *The order of things* (1966) feeling Marx had been disparaged because Foucault had posited in Ricardo the essential break in political economy,[278] psychoanalysts reacted to the first volume of the *History of sexuality* (1976) feeling that psychoanalysis is disparaged because Foucault had dared to imply a parallel between psychoanalytic therapy and the Christian practice of confession. Foucault himself had tried to do away at least with some part of the "misunderstanding", when, in a discussion with Lacanian psychoanalysts (1977),[279] he recognised Freud's (and Lacan's) enormous contribution as to the *logic of the unconscious*, suggesting though at the same time that the

---

277. Derrida, *Résistances de la psychanalyse*, pp. 89-146.
278. See, for example, Sheridan, *op. cit.*, pp. 70-71.
279. Foucault, *Dits et écrits 1954-1988, III*, pp. 298-329 – English translation: Foucault, *Power/knowledge*, pp. 194-228.

psychoanalytic theory of sexuality is less important in so far as it is implicated in the broader complex of knowledge and power relations around which modern Western discourse about sex had been articulated.[280]

As to the former part, it was actually not merely some "polite statement". In a text that is quite revealing with regard to his methodology, namely in the Preface to the English edition of *The order of things* (1970), Foucault had introduced the most enlightening term "*positive unconscious* of knowledge" precisely to describe the field of his own research.[281] The modifier "positive" indicates that it is not a matter of the *opposite* of knowledge that for some reason has been repressed and that constantly threatens knowledge and its validity, but of discursive rules constituting knowledge itself, which are *productively* related to it, and which just remain unconscious to its enunciating subjects.

We could well consider this (Foucauldian) concept of the "positive unconscious" as being quite close to the Lacanian conception of the Freudian unconscious, according to which the latter is largely *thought* and not "impulses" or "instincts", which means it is not something necessarily *opposite* or *hostile* to human rationality.[282] On the other hand, of course, the fact that he deems it worthwhile to use the term "*positive* unconscious" probably conveys some reservation concerning the psychoanalytic concept of the unconscious generally speaking, which is quite possibly due to the predominance of interpretative models mainly influenced by Freudo-Marxism, which do actually approach the unconscious as a reservoir of repressed "impulses" or "instincts". In his eagerness to keep his distance from every version of Hegelianism, and in his insistence, at the same time, on explicitly dissociating his views from the structuralists, Foucault perhaps fails to recognise the contribution of mainly Lacanian psychoanalysis to the de-Hegelianisation of Freud,[283] largely brought about by the conjunction of psychoanalysis with the linguistic problematic, to which we will return further on.

---

280. Foucault, *Dits et écrits 1954-1988, III*, p. 315 - English translation: Foucault, *Power/knowledge*, pp. 212-213. Furthermore, it is quite indicative that at the beginning of *Discipline and punish* (1975) –see above, fn. 267- Foucault names as a source of inspiration Deleuze and Guattari, who, in *Anti-Oedipus* –Gilles Deleuze and Félix Guattari, *Anti-Oedipus: Capitalism and schizophrenia* (translated by Robert Hurley, Mark Seem and Helen R. Lane), New York: Viking, 1977- and elsewhere, radically differentiate themselves from psychoanalysis on one hand, while being in *constant dialogue* with psychoanalytic theory and terminology on the other.

281. Foucault, *The order of things*, p. xi ff.

282. See, for example, Jacques Lacan, *Écrits*, Paris: Seuil, 1966, p. 495 ff. – English translation: *Écrits: A selection* (translated by Alan Sheridan), London: Tavistock, 1977, p. 147 ff.

283. It goes without saying that nowadays, with Žižek's prevalence in the reading of Lacan, the recognition of this contribution has gone down the drain.

More significant than the fact that Foucault's attitude perhaps "does injustice" to psychoanalysis is that, irrespective of his own intentions or interpretations, psychoanalytic theory, again in mainly its Lacanian version, is capable of filling in the gap he leaves open as to the mechanism of hypostatisation. I am referring to a conceptualisation that is neither directly related to the "logic of the unconscious" nor on the other hand could it in any way be included in the (psychoanalytic) "theory of sexuality". My view is that it is a conceptualisation of at least equal importance to that of the unconscious, precisely in terms of its considerable *philosophical* significance, even though it has largely been "misunderstood".

The ego in Freud's theory and in the technique of psychoanalysis is the title of the second (1954-1955) and perhaps most important of Lacan's *Seminars*. We might say that, at least in some sense, this whole *Seminar* is an analytical elaboration of some concepts inherent in Lacan's theory of the "mirror stage", which he had presented some years earlier (first in 1936 and in a revised version in 1949). It is quite important to point this out, because the theory of the mirror stage has played a crucial role in the part of post-war French thought that is connected to the critique of the subject.[284] Lacan himself had ascribed to this theory a directly philosophical significance, by "programmatically" declaring, at the very start of his text, that the mirror stage "sheds [light] on the formation of the *I (je)*" in a way that drives him to oppose "any philosophy directly issuing from the *Cogito*".[285]

I briefly summarise the central theme of the theory of the mirror stage. The human infant, at the age of between 6 and 18 months, constitutes a perception of itself as a uniform entity by way of its identification with the image of its body in the mirror, in the first place, and in the second place, by way of its identification with the image of the body of the *other* in the mirror, of the "other" who holds it and shows to it "itself" in the mirror (of its mother or of any "other"). The decisive significance of this experience for the constitution of subjectivity is made evident by the fact that before the mirror stage the infant perceives of itself as unconnected bodily parts, thereby being incapable of coordinating its movements.[286]

The importance of Lacan's contribution mainly lies in his demonstration of how an experience of crucial significance and its equally significant outcome, which is the primary and entirely indispensable independence of the individual as subject, is based on an *identification with an image*. About this image, by the identification with which the individual is initially constituted

---

284. See especially Althusser, *Positions*, pp. 129-134 – English translation: Althusser, *Lenin and philosophy and other essays*, pp. 165-170.

285. Lacan, *op. cit.*, p. 93 – English translation: p. 1.

286. *Ibid.*, p. 96 ff. – English translation: p. 3 ff.

as subject, in his second *Seminar* he will say that it is *the ego (moi) itself.* The (Freudian) ego, according to Lacan, is but the –internalised- image of the body, in the experience of the mirror stage.[287]

Let us be reminded of the opening sentence of Kant's *Anthropology* (which Foucault had translated into French in 1964): "The fact that the human being can have the 'I' in his representations raises him infinitely above all other living beings on earth." And a few lines further down: "But it is noteworthy that the child who can already speak fairly fluently nevertheless first begins to talk by means of 'I' fairly late (perhaps a year later); in the meantime speaking of himself in the third person (Karl wants to eat, to walk, etc.). When he starts to speak by means of 'I' a light seems to dawn on him, as it were, and from that day on he never again returns to his former way of speaking. Before he merely *felt* himself; now he *thinks* himself."[288]

I have argued elsewhere that Foucault's critique is directed not only towards classical or pre-Kantian thought, but also towards Kant himself, to the extent that the latter, in his *Anthropology* but elsewhere too, hypostatised the idea of man in a manner similar to that in which Descartes, according to Kant's own critique, had hypostatised the ideas of the thinking subject and of God.[289] In this particular (first) passage from *Anthropology*, in the formulation "infinitely above" we notice the hypostatised infinite being restored in the form of "infinite superiority" of man over every other biological species. I believe that the Lacanian interpretation of the Freudian ego may serve as a concrete philosophical support for the critique not merely of philosophies directly deriving from the Cartesian *cogito*, but also of all modern, including Kantian and post-Kantian, forms of hypostatisation. In the Lacanian theory of the mirror stage we find a theory of *how the process of hypostatisation itself takes place at a temporally and structurally primary stage*, of how, in other words, it may be explained that people believe in the *illusion* of hypostatisation in any of its forms.

If we accept the Lacanian theory of the mirror stage but also more generally the related interpretation of the (Freudian) ego, we might say that at the *basis* of all hypostatisations, as, so to speak, their *pre-rational receptor*, there is the *hypostatising illusion of the ego*. In place of the (Kantian) transcendental acceptance of the hypostatisation of the "idea" or "regulative principle" of the "systematic" or "in conformity with aims [zweckmäßigen] unity", (Lacanian) psychoanalysis posits the *findings from the experience of an*

---

287. Jacques Lacan, *Le Séminaire, livre II: Le moi dans la théorie de Freud et dans la technique de la psychanalyse*, Paris: Seuil, 1978, pp. 66-72 – English translation (Sylvana Tomaselli): *The Seminar of Jacques Lacan, Book II: The ego in Freud's theory and in the technique of psychoanalysis, 1954-1955*, Cambridge, New York and Melbourne: Cambridge University Press, 1988, pp. 49-53.

288. Emmanuel Kant, *Anthropologie du point de vue pragmatique* (translated by Michel Foucault), Paris: J. Vrin, 1991 (first edition: 1964, first German edition: 1798), p. 17 – English translation (Robert B. Louden): Immanuel Kant, *Anthropology from a pragmatic point of view*, Cambridge: Cambridge University Press, 2006, p. 15.

289. Doxiadis, *op. cit.*, p. 539 ff., and Doxiadis, "Foucault and ideology", p. 31 ff.

identification with an image and of the process of its internalisation. These are the findings of an observation situated *at the limits* between biological determination and mental autonomy, between ethology (or comparative psychology[290]) and psychoanalytic theory, between objectivity and subjectivity. The term "*specific prematurity of birth*", which explains "motor unco-ordination"[291] of the new-born human *before the mirror stage*, is but some basis for a materialist way of explaining the objective conditions for the primary constitution of subjectivity. According to this explanation and its corollaries, the hypostatisation of the "idea" or "regulative principle" of the "systematic" or "in conformity with aims [zweckmäßigen] unity", that indeed pertains to human thought, is descended from the *illusion* of the *idea of absolute completeness and unity* acquired by the infant for itself during the mirror stage.

More precisely, and in accordance with what we have said so far with regard to related issues, the image of the self as an absolutely complete and uniform entity is an illusion that the subject, primarily constituted as such during the mirror stage, has internalised *in a lacking manner*. Its finitude as a biological being, initially, and later as a social being, does not allow it to identify *completely* with its image. Hence the psychoanalytic term "*ideal* ego" or "*narcissistic* ego" as a more accurate description of the ego (*per se*). The ego as an illusion is the *ideal* self, the self as the subject *desires* it to be. If we define desire in terms of the conceptualisation of finitude and limits, one definition could be, the "tendency to transgress limits or to suspend finitude". In the case of animals this quite simply amounts to their tendency to satisfy their biological needs. The self-preservation instinct is what drives them to transgress their limits, that is, the obstacles to be superseded in order to find food, for example. *Their limits are both the fact that they must feed themselves if they are to survive and the fact that finding food is not easy*. In this sense, animals "learn to live" with their finitude, with the fact that they are not absolutely complete or uniform, i.e. perfect, *provisionally* suspending it, by satisfying some of their *specific* desires or needs.[292]

The human subject, with the mirror stage, has one more bother. Its desire does not merely aim at the (provisional) transgression of those (specific) limits that will allow it to subsist as a biological being, but also at the transgression of the limits that differentiate it from *its ideal self*, from itself as an absolutely complete and uniform i.e. perfect being. The *ultimate* desire of the human subject aims at the *abolition of its finitude in general*, hence the *central* significance of the *infinite* in every form of hypostatising illusion, starting from the illusion of the ego.

---

290. Lacan, *Écrits*, p. 93 – English translation: p. 1.

291. See above, fn. 286.

292. Running the risk of provoking a "conceptual scandal", I deliberately use here the term *desire* as roughly synonymous with *need*. An approach based on the concept of finitude leaves no room for a radical distinction between the two. On the other hand, as it will be seen further on, I most radically differentiate *specifically* human desire from that of animals, therefore I could hardly be reproached for biologism.

Indispensable and primary illusion, but *illusion it is*. In accordance with our own terms, the idea of the ego is the primary hypostatisation, indispensable not merely for the constitution of subjectivity but also for all further (ideological) hypostatisations, that which constitutes the *receptor*, as we have already said, of all the other ideas that are to constitute the individual as subject of one or more ideologies.

The role of the "receptor" is undertaken by that part of the ego that psychoanalysis calls "*super*-ego" or "ego *ideal*".[293] The "infinite" in the ego ideal initially appears in the form of the image of the "other" at the mirror stage, and afterwards in the form of any idealised "other", whether it is a love object or the supreme ideal of some ideology. The "infinite" in the ego *per se* or ideal ego is the idealised, narcissistic self. The coexistence of different "infinites" in the ego ideal and the ideal ego, which, moreover, may often be antagonistic to each other, on one hand, is feasible because of the *pre-rational* character of the ego in general, and on the other, explains the fact that the constitution of subjectivity, even on this primary level, is *multiple, asymmetric and differentiating*. Let us see though what the primary hypostatisation that constitutes the "ego *per se*" or "*ideal* ego" consists in.

As in most hypostatisations, its first phase is the idealisation of a material entity. In this case, according to the Lacanian analysis of the mirror stage, the individual is seduced by the image of its body in the mirror (hence the "primary narcissism" that characterises this experience). The material entity that is idealised here is therefore the human body, the body of the self. At the second phase of hypostatisation though, the idealised image of the self is objectivised, it is considered as objectively existing, and this is something that accompanies the individual's unconscious thought in its entire further development. The human subject, unconsciously at least, does not conceive of its psyche as a hypothetical entity that thinks, but as something objectively existing, in a mode *analogous* to the objective existence of its body.

At the same time though, since the origin of the ego as to the perception of the self *before the mirror stage* initially emerges from the condition of the "small human *animal*", the characteristics of that "animal" are carried over to the constitution of the ego *being accordingly idealised and then objectivised*. So not only the basic senses of pain, hunger, warmth, cold, fatigue, but also every bodily pleasure, and all *needs and desires* relating to the senses, are idealised and then objectivised, that is, they are accordingly hypostatised and they constitute the basic characteristic properties and tendencies of the hypostatised idea of the ego. What we call "emotions" are but the effects of precisely this hypostatising process: sorrow, anger, affection, sympathy, distaste, hostility, boredom, joy, love. Philosophically, psychoanalytic theory could remain in the realm of the ego and the hypostatising process of its constitution in order to explain what it designates with terms like "object

---

293. On the terms *ideal ego, super-ego* and *ego ideal*, see Laplanche and Pontalis, *op. cit.*, pp. 201-202, 435-438 and 144-145.

cathexis", "psychical energy",²⁹⁴ etc., without having to fall itself into the illusion of hypostatisation by considering as objectively existing entities what it calls "drives".²⁹⁵ Quite revealing is Freud's *implicitly* self-critical statement in his *New introductory lectures on psychoanalysis*, "The theory of the drives is so to say our mythology."²⁹⁶

But let us be somewhat more analytical: What is the difference between the ego and the drives (or the "id"²⁹⁷) as to hypostatisation? In both cases we are dealing with hypostatised ideas. But in the former case, with the ego, it is a matter of a hypostatised idea that we accept as a concept, because it explains the primary constitution of subjectivity. In the latter case, with the drives, it is quite important to notice that it is not merely a matter of a hypostatisation, but of a hypostatisation that largely diminishes the critical sharpness of psychoanalytic discourse as well as of the philosophical discourses inspired by it.

In other words, with the ego, we have a concept (and a conceptualisation) that explains a crucial and fundamental point of the ideological process. While with drives, we have a concept that does not adequately explain anything. By being presented as belonging to a scientific discourse it serves as a constant alibi for the attribution of conditions and trends definitely having socio-historical causes to innate and omnihistorical human inclinations. A structural difference between the ego and the drives may perhaps clarify further the distinction with reference to the question of hypostatisation.

Hypostatisation is a social-ideological phenomenon, and as such on one level at least it is treated as an *effect*. The ego, even though itself constitutes a *cause* for many other things, on a quite fundamental level it is also treated as an *effect*. The ego is *constituted, according to psychoanalysis itself*. In this sense, however we may use it as cause to demonstrate its significance in the emergence of other phenomena, it is at the same time easily made evident that we have to do with a *construct*, i.e. with an *illusion*, a *hypostatised idea*.

On the contrary, the drives, while they are distinguished from (biological) instincts and thus are not considered as material entities, are nevertheless promoted by psychoanalysis *as primary causes, and not as effects*.²⁹⁸ It is therefore quite impossible to retain them as a psychoanalytic conceptual-

---

294.*Ibid.*, pp. 62-65.

295.*Ibid.*, pp. 214-217.

296.Sigmund Freud, *New introductory lectures on psycho-analysis* (first German edition: 1933), *The Standard Edition of the complete psychological works of Sigmund Freud* (translated by James Strachey, Anna Freud, Alix Strachey and Alan Tyson), London: The Hogarth Press and the Institute of Psycho-Analysis, 1953-1974, *Volume XXII*, p. 95 (translation slightly modified).

297.Laplanche and Pontalis, *op. cit.*, pp. 197-199.

298.What is nonetheless quite indicative is the theoretical awkwardness brought about by the highly ambiguous meaning of the drive as *"psychical representative"* - *ibid.*, pp. 364-365.

isation (that is, as a conceptualisation generally speaking) and at the same time to treat the entities to which they refer, i.e. the drives themselves, as illusions and hypostatised ideas. Very simply phrased, the main difference is this: *The concept "ego" is the concept of a hypostatisation, while the concept "drives" is a hypostatised concept.*

The Lacanian mirror stage, the conceptualisation of identification, and more broadly the erotic component of the conceptualisation of the ego do not need to be based or grounded on the conceptualisation of the libido,[299] nor on that of the aggressive drive (and the related terms).[300] Lacan himself is responsible for a variation of the latter, when he uses the term *"imagos of the fragmented body"* to describe a mental condition prior to the mirror stage, which, according to him, accompanies the development of subjectivity even after the mirror stage and accounts for aggressivity as something that constantly threatens the unity of the ego effected by identification.[301]

The theory of the drives, even in its Lacanian variation, is, I believe, a concrete manifestation of an underlying Hegelianism in psychoanalysis, which pertains both to the psychoanalytic theory of sexuality and to the Freudo-Marxist conception of power as merely repression, towards which Foucault also directs his critique. On the other hand, I will try to show how the connection of psychoanalysis to the linguistic problematic, a connection of which the basic pioneer of course is Lacan, may lead to a de-Hegelianisation of Freudianism—something which Foucault, for the reasons we mentioned above, was in no position to see.

There is a quite well-known precedent as to the correlation between Freudian theory and the linguistic terms *metaphor/metonymy*. I am referring to the analogy pointed out by Lacan between *condensation and metaphor* on one hand and *displacement and metonymy* on the other. It has been several years now, since I started to be systematically concerned with metaphor and metonymy mainly, though not only, in my work as a teacher. I have begun to consider this analogy as rather forced. As *former students of Lacan* Laplanche and Pontalis point out in their *Vocabulary*, "The term 'displacement' does not for Freud imply the singling out of any particular type of associative connection—such as association by contiguity or association by similarity—as characteristic of the chain along which the process of displacement operates."[302] To put it more simply, a displacement may be either metonymic or metaphoric. And we could say the equivalent about condensation.[303]

The correlation between the terms *metaphor/metonymy* and Freudian theory should rather be investigated in the conceptual direction of *identity-opposition-difference*, where, in my view, the *more essential philosophical value* of

---

299. *Ibid.*, pp. 239-242 and 417-418.

300. *Ibid.*, pp. 16-17, 97-103 and 116-117.

301. Lacan, *op. cit.*, pp. 101-124 – English translation: pp. 8-29.

302. Laplanche and Pontalis, *op. cit.*, p. 123.

303. For the definition of condensation, see *ibid.*, pp. 82-83.

these two terms is to be found, according to my arguments above. What is mainly of interest here is a conception of the three concepts that avoids the Hegelian subordination of difference to opposition and the consequent reduction of opposition to identity. A subordination-reduction that, as we maintain, largely constitutes a *dominant version* of the process by way of which the ensuring of representational *continuity* is inseparably connected, as I have argued, to the hypostatising operation of modern ideology. In this case this takes place by way of the virtual *undermining of discontinuity* brought about by *abolishing the initial effect* of the latter, i.e. by abolishing precisely *non-reducible difference*. It is just that here the structural position of the *infinite substance* is taken over by the hypostatised (dual) idea of a *Principal Contradiction*. Examples: capital/labour, imperialism/anti-imperialism, sexual repression/sexual liberation, populism/modernisation, corruption/rule of law etc. The ordering or classifying process in such cases is more complicated, since there are two central and/or supreme organising principles rather than one, but this is precisely why it is more effective. The essential point remains. Even the idea of God implies its contradiction by the idea of the Devil.

So let us start "backwards", in some sense. Let us first consider the terms *identity-opposition-difference* and find the psychoanalytic terms to which these correspond, and let us then investigate how the conceptual pair *metaphor/metonymy* may serve to allow the corresponding psychoanalytic terms *as well* to "float" easily, each in its own relative functional autonomy, without there being any (Hegelian) sort of reduction of one to another.

Let us start with the pair *identity-opposition*, which is contained in the concept of *metaphor*. The corresponding psychoanalytic pair of terms is *identification-aggressivity*. In the Hegelian reduction of opposition to identity, two conditions are in force simultaneously: (a) *general mutual necessity* and (b) *specific logical symmetry and equivalence*. That is, (a) generally speaking, if *there is* identity there is opposition and vice versa. (b) Within a given system of relations where there is identity-opposition, in the instances where there is *no* identity it logically follows there is opposition and vice-versa (in other words, the identity-opposition relation takes the form of the *being/non-being* relation), and the instances of identity and opposition are *in principle* equivalent, quantitatively and/or qualitatively. The Hegelian reduction of opposition to identity presents both as being the two sides of the same coin. None exists without the other, and if one does not occur the other will, with an *in principle* equal distribution of probabilities (which of course varies according to circumstances).

A schematic example from Hegelian Marxism: in the capitalist system, the identity-opposition relation becomes *capitalists-workers* in the sense that there is an *identity of interests* between the capitalist system and capitalists and an *opposition of interests* between the capitalist system and workers. (a) Generally speaking, in social reality in general, if there are capitalists there are also workers and vice versa. (b) In the capitalist system, when someone is not a capitalist he/she is a worker and vice versa, and there is a *qualitative* equivalence between capitalists and workers (at least in the sense that they are both equally necessary for the existence and functioning of the capitalist system). Due to the patently much more complicated and asymmetric development of socio-historical reality itself, many Marxists have abandoned this simplistic Hegelian schema, without having to resort to the Saussurian conceptualisation related to metaphor and metonymy. For example, as to (a), in actually existing socialism there were workers without there being capitalists, and as to (b), in the capitalist system there is also the "new" petty bourgeoisie (see Poulantzas's analysis[304]).

In psychoanalysis though, since we have to do more with "internal", i.e. subjective relations, (Hegelian) things cannot so easily be overturned. In the Hegelian version of psychoanalysis, the identity-opposition relation, that is, the corresponding psychoanalytic identification-aggressivity relation, becomes *tendency towards unity / tendency towards dissolution*.[305]

The movement by each the conversion of the identification-aggressivity relation to the *tendency towards unity / tendency towards dissolution* relation is executed mainly follows two paths, one in Freud's own work and one in Lacan's.

- In his texts from 1920 onwards, and especially in *Civilisation and its discontents* (1930), Freud reformulates his theory of the drives in a fashion that tends to be absolutely bipolar. On one hand: Eros, life drives, sexual drives or libido / tendency towards unity. On the other: Death, death drives, aggressive or destructive drives / tendency towards dissolution.

- As we saw above, in the Hegelian dimension of his theory of the mirror stage, Lacan puts forth, as the other facet of the process wherein the ego is constituted by way of its identification with the image of the self and that of the other and its consequent constitution as a *unity*, the *imagos of the fragmented body*, which pre-exist the experience of the mirror stage, which nonetheless continue to co-exist with identification in all stages of the subject's development, and which form the basis for all its aggressive tendencies, that is, for its *tendency towards dissolution*, towards a (real or imaginary or symbolic) *fragmentation of the body*.

In both its versions, Freudian and Lacanian, the *tendency towards unity / tendency towards dissolution* bipolarity is Hegelian precisely in the above sense of the two conditions we described: (a) *General mutual necessity:* Generally speaking, in subjective-emotive relationships, if there is tendency towards unity there is (unconsciously, at least) tendency towards dissolution and vice versa. (b) *Specific logical symmetry and equivalence:* within a given system of subjective-emotive relationships where there is *tendency towards unity / tend-*

---

304. Nicos Poulantzas, *Classes in contemporary capitalism* (translated by David Fernbach), London: NLB, pp. 191-336.

305. Freud, *Civilization and its discontents* (first German edition: 1930), *S.E. XXI*, p. 118 ff. See also Freud, *An outline of psycho-analysis* (first German edition: 1940), *S.E. XXIII*, p. 148 ff.

ency towards dissolution, e.g. in a family or in a love relationship or in any other systematic human interaction, in the instances where there is no tendency towards unity there is tendency towards dissolution and vice versa, and the two tendencies are more or less equivalent. In *Civilisation and its discontents* Freud is quite clear. Humanity perpetually oscillates between these two tendencies, and the outcome of the conflict between them remains uncertain, since both are very (i.e. in principle equally) powerful.[306] Accordingly, similarly necessary for the constitution of the subject are these two tendencies in Lacan, in what he himself mentions as a "dialectic" (obviously meaning a *Hegelian* dialectic), an "example" of which is the mirror stage, and which accompanies the subject in all stages of its constitution/development.[307]

Now how could the concept of *metaphor* de-Hegelianise, or, even better, retain as non-Hegelian, the *identification-aggressivity* relation? Suppose we started from the general approach I mentioned above, that is, to consider as given that, in the case of identification as the psychoanalytic equivalent of identity, the concepts similarity-comparability-substitution are more "in play", while in the case of aggressivity as the psychoanalytic equivalent of opposition, this holds for the concepts disjunction-substitution-comparability, with roughly this priority sequence in each case.

I will apply the above approach to two crucial points of psychoanalytic theory: As for identification, to the Lacanian mirror stage, without though taking into account its "dialectic" (i.e. Hegelian) dimension, and as for aggressivity, to the Oedipal antagonism towards the father, without taking into account the bipolar (or any other) theory of the drives.

- So we start with considering the relations that the subject has, while being primarily constituted, with the images in the mirror and with the other as metaphoric relations. Quite simply: The (*"imaginary"*) identification *with the image of the self* is based on *similarity*. The infant discovers that the image of its body is *similar* to its body (constitution of the ideal ego). The (*"imaginary"*) identification *with the image of the other* (of its mother) is based on *comparability*. The infant *compares* the image of the other with its own and discovers they are similar though not quite (constitution of the ego ideal). The "*symbolic*" identification with the other is based on *substitution*. The subject *substitutes* itself with the other, in the sense that it *recognises* it is interchangeable with others (entrance into the "symbolic" field).

- Now let us take the antagonistic Oedipal relation with the father as a metaphoric one. In the above case, the priority of each concept was determined by the primacy of each stage in the identification/constitution process. Here, priority is determined by the intensity of each component

---

306. See Freud, *Civilization and its discontents*, p. 145.

307. See Lacan, *Le Séminaire, livre II*, p. 66 – English translation: p. 50.

of the antagonism, i.e. of aggressivity. *Disjunction* forms the *direct manifestation* of the antagonism, the violent overthrow of the paternal *yoke*, or the struggle to the death, disjunction in the sense of "*it's either him or me*". *Substitution* implies the *aim* of the antagonism: "to *substitute* father (in relation to mother)". And *comparability* designates the *cause* of the antagonism: "I *compare* myself with father and I find out he has something I don't".

In the above approach, I believe one quite effectively avoids any reduction of aggressivity(-opposition) to identification(-identity) or vice versa, in the following manner. It is a matter of a different usability of concepts. The four concepts in each case are used in an inverse priority sequence, with the first in priority concept being entirely omitted in the other case (we omit *disjunction* in *identification* and *similarity* in *aggressivity*). Perhaps more significantly as to the concepts, even with concepts used *in common* (*comparability, substitution*) there is a *different nuance* of the terms in each case. This means we have to do with *common* terms, *common* concepts, and more generally with a *common group* of concepts (with *metaphor*), thus identification and aggressivity *are not unrelated between them*, but there is quite simply no way that one may be reduced to the other, neither by mutual necessity, nor symmetry or equivalence. Generally speaking, in subjective-emotive relationships, there may be identification without aggressivity and vice versa. Furthermore, in a family or in a love relationship or in any systematic human interaction where there is both identification and aggressivity, there may be instances where there is neither identification nor aggressivity but something else: friendship, fondness, sheer sexual attraction, any positive, i.e. not aggressive emotions that certainly derive from the subject's ego by definition but that are not such as to constitute it in the sense of identification. Lastly, in a relationship there may be an intense identification and some *little,* let us say occasional, aggressivity or vice versa. You may generally identify with your brother but he may also get on your nerves now and then (prompting occasional aggressivity), and with an enemy you may hate his/her guts but if something terrible happens to him/her you may feel pity in the sense of not wanting to be in his/her place (occasional identification). Someone might say, fine, but are not all those self-evident things accepted by Hegelian Freudians-Lacanians? They themselves may accept them all right, but their *conceptualisation* does not.

Let us go now to *difference*, which is contained in the concept of *metonymy*. I quote an extract from Laplanche and Pontalis (last lines in the entry *displacement*): "... for Lacan, human desire is structured fundamentally by the laws of the unconscious, and its nature is metonymic *par excellence.*"[308] Here we have a connection of psychoanalytic theory with the term *metonymy* certainly more essential and less unfortunate than the equation of this term

---

308. Laplanche and Pontalis, *op. cit.*, p. 123.

with the term *displacement* (an equation which Laplanche and Pontalis mention just a few lines above, having though, as we have seen, implicitly but definitely dissociated critically themselves from it).

Lacan has defined *desire* as *a relation of being to lack (of being)*.[309] I have elsewhere argued that this definition of desire is equivalent to equating desire with *finitude*.[310] In this text, I maintain that this definition is false, but that nonetheless desire could be defined *in relation* to finitude. *Desire is the tendency to transgress limits, that is, the tendency to suspend finitude*. Parenthetically, we could here suggest that Lacan's error is *once again Hegelian*. He equates desire with finitude, by virtually *reducing finitude to the opposite of desire and then to desire itself*. Let us see though how the definition of *desire* given here in relation to *limits* and *finitude* could be linked to both *difference* and *metonymy*.

Some caution is needed at this point. Having said that difference is a *primary effect* of fundamental finitude and the discontinuity that this entails, we should not lead ourselves to re-introduce reductionism through the back door. That is, we should not equate (reduce) difference to fundamental finitude. Difference is not identical to limits, in the sense that it may not cease to exist *even after limits have been transgressed*. A body is united with another, and in this sense limits between them are abolished and continuity between them is established. *This does not necessarily mean that they identify or that they cease to be different*. Similarly, in language, letters-phonemes-signifiers unite and acquire continuity between them in forming e.g. a word, without this meaning that the differences between them are abolished.

At this point precisely, I think it pertinent to "put into play" the concept of *desire*. *Desire, as tendency to transgress limits, that is, to suspend finitude, is not necessarily tendency to identify, nor to suspend difference*.

At issue here is the avoidance of the Hegelian scheme, according to which desire appears as the equivalent of identity-identification, and the limits that desire tends to transgress appear as the equivalent of opposition-aggressivity, with the relation between the two sides assuming the form of (Hegelian) *negation*: on one side, the form of *libido* or some of the other hypostatised versions of sexual desire, and on the other side, the (internalised aggressive) repressive mechanism called *super-ego* or the (manifestly aggressive) repressive mechanism of *state and society*. In other words, at issue is a theoretical conception of desire and of its relations to limits and power that would not fall into the (Hegelian) model of *repression and prohibition* that Foucault notoriously criticised—without however being able to, or in any case without being concerned with putting anything else in its place.

A general answer has already been given. As to desire, its non-reducibility to identification and identity is given by the principle of retaining difference and non-identity even after the transgression of limits. And as to limits (and power as the *social setting of limits to the will and to action*), their non-reducibility to aggressivity and opposition is given by the general conception of

---

309. Lacan, *op. cit.*, p. 261 – English translation: p. 223.

310. Doxiadis, *Subjectivity and power*, p. 128.

limits (and power) as a fundamental condition of existence of all material entities (and social relations and practices). A limit between two entities *may* define an oppositional or aggressive relation, but then again it may not. It may simply be an instance of a (non-oppositional) relation of difference. And the equivalent holds for desire. Desire *may* lead to identification and identity, as in the process of the ego's constitution by way of identification, but then again it may not. Most sexual relations are *not* relations of identification. But the *inverse* cases *may* also apply. A limit may play some part in the ego's constitution by way of identification since it is a matter of a *power-exercising* process *par excellence*, and desire quite often is an *aggressive* desire as is the case in sexual sadism and elsewhere.

A somewhat more specific answer may be given if we examine how the concepts of desire, finitude-limits and difference may "float", in common and within the conceptual framework of the terms describing metonymy: contiguity-combination-conjunction. *The terms contiguity-combination-conjunction are quite simply the terms that describe the (subjective) condition after the transgression of limits (and the suspension of finitude) that is not necessarily equivalent either to identification-identity and the abolition of difference, or to aggressivity-opposition.* In other words, the *general (subjective)* form of desire as tendency to transgress limits is *the tendency towards contiguity, combination and/or conjunction.*

If in Foucault's well-known formulation, "where there is power, there is resistance", "resistance" is conceived as *opposition*, this would amount to accepting that Foucault introduces Hegelianism through the back door. By conceiving of the relation between desire on one hand and limits and power on the other within the conceptual framework of metonymy and difference, I believe we could avoid the risk of a Hegelian "relapse". Desire as tendency to transgress limits *in relation to power* could be considered as *resistance* to power, in the sense of the tendency to transgress the *social setting of limits* (to the will and to action). But once again, not necessarily in the sense of an *opposition* to the social setting of limits, but rather in the sense of the tendency towards a *social* contiguity, combination and/or conjunction, in other words, in the sense of the tendency to *cohabit, cooperate and/or interact*, in an *alternative manner*—that is, not necessarily in a manner *opposed* to the existing social setting of limits, but *different* from it. Therefore *metonymy* is the linguistic term that may describe the *subjective aspect* of both desire in general and resistance to power.

Chapter 16
Desire and understanding

For a more thorough understanding of the subjective aspect of desire, some more things should be said about the ego. In the ego there may be a coexistence of (hypostatised) forms of infinity, either in the ego ideal (by external supreme ideals that constitute it) or in the ideal ego (as narcissism), with (also hypostatised) forms of finitude, once again either in the ego ideal (by external *non*-supreme ideals that constitute it) or in the ideal ego (as a finite image of the self). The coexistence of infinity with finitude in the ego ideal is feasible anyway, since the ego ideal may internalise entire ideological systems or parts of them, in which the hierarchical relations are given from the start between supreme, infinite ideals and non-supreme, finite *though non-fundamentally finite ideals, that is, determined as finite by the former*. The coexistence of infinity with finitude in the ideal ego is more problematic, insofar as we have a uniform entity, the self *par excellence*, the ego *per se*. However it is also feasible because of the pre-rational nature of the ego generally speaking, which, as we have already said, may also explain the possible coexistence of different, perhaps even antagonistic, internalised ideas in the ego ideal. Let us explain more adequately the relation between the infinite and the finite part of the ideal ego, as well as the *kind* of finitude of the finite part.

I will start with the latter, since its explanation will also clarify the former. Since we have to do with a subjective (even though hypostatised) entity, in accordance with what we have said so far, we cannot talk about fundamental finitude. It is a *non*-fundamental finitude, determined as finitude both by the infinite part of the ego ideal and by the infinite part of the ideal ego itself. At the same time though, *the finite part of the ideal ego is the part of the ego that desires.* It desires under its *dual* property as:

- *Desiring therefore finite* being. The *finite* part of the ego is *primarily* located in the *ideal ego* in the sense that with the constitution of the ego ideal we are already on the side of perfection, i.e. infinity.
- *Non-fundamentally* finite being.

The ego's *desire*, even though we have the desire of a *non-fundamentally* finite being, *in the first place* cannot but be subject to the property of *discontinuity and asymmetry* effected by *fundamental* finitude. The realm of desire *in the first place* is that of *fundamental* finitude. As a *non-fundamentally* finite being though, it differs from animals in that its desire is determined *not only* by *itself, its limits and the possible objects of its desire*, but *also* by those infinities that determine it as finite, by the infinite part of both the ideal ego and the ego ideal. As to the former, we encounter narcissistic desire. As to the latter, depending on each case, we may be dealing *either* with ideological desire (determined by the supreme ideal of some ideology), *or* with erotic desire (by the idealisation of some love object), *or* with neurotic desire (by fear of a cruel super-ego). It goes without saying that the coexistence of fundamental with non-fundamental finitude as to the *desire* of the finite part of the ideal ego may once again be explained by the pre-rational nature of the ego in general.

There are some desires that are specifically human, and these are the desires of the ego, that is, of the finite part of the ideal ego. Apart from something tautological and self-evident, that they are the desires that exist because human society does, we can approach them merely descriptively (and once again tautologically) saying that these are the desires human beings *do not* have in common with animals—always supposing, of course (wrongly, perhaps), that animals do not have ego, subjectivity or language (having defined the subject as the entity that forms concepts and language as the active ability to form concepts). In this sense, perhaps the most fundamental specifically human desire, the most fundamental desire of the ego, is the desire that is inherent in language.

So let us consider the ego as a desiring being in language. Someone hears a language he/she does not understand. This is always annoying and awkward. We could regard it as a blow to narcissism (that is, to the ideal ego). If we accept the universality of this negative example, we may also accept that the basic desire in language is the desire to *understand*. What does it mean to say, "I understand a sentence, a formulation, a statement, a discursive formation"? It means that I am able as a mind, as a thinking being, as a subject, *to pass from one concept to another, so as to constitute some meaning, to form concepts, that is, simply, to think something that the other or others have constituted, or formed or thought, before me.* So the basic desire in language, that is, the desire to understand, is *the tendency to transgress the limits between concepts.* If someone speaks some language well enough, this transgression to some degree takes place automatically, so to speak, since language, as *the zero degree of representation*, is the "representation" of thought itself, in the following sense: language means *placing in a continuous sequence the concepts themselves, by uniting initially discontinuous material elements (signifiers)*. In other words, the continuity between concepts, and thereby the passage from one to another, is ensured by the very process of enunciation, either as simple speech or in more complex forms. And this process, precisely to the extent that it ensures continuity, is something that comes within the jurisdiction of formal logic.

To the extent, however, that it ensures continuity. I am working here with the *basic meaning* of introducing the (Saussurian) linguistic problematic in discourse analysis of a Foucauldian (but also psychoanalytic) inspiration, mainly in relation to the conceptual pair metaphor/metonymy. That is, my focus is on the relation to what I mentioned above as "Saussure's non-reductionist connection between identity, opposition and difference". This is an attempt to disengage ourselves from the exclusive authority of formal logic as the theoretical discourse that deals with relations of meaning. The advantage of linguistics in relation to this is that it is concerned with a *raw material that is not strictly logical*, that is, it accepts there are material, objective, fundamentally finite and initially discontinuous elements (signifiers) that on one hand *form* thought and on the other *pre-exist* it (structurally, if not temporally). *This is not the case with the symbols of formal logic*. Hegelianism, apart from the fact that, according to Foucault, is but a continuation of classical representation, or perhaps *because* of this fact, largely draws its reductionism on the continuous and symmetric conception of meaning production provided by the approach of formal logic.[311]

Perhaps the main phenomenon of meaning in which one notices a specificity of language that cannot be approached by formal logic is that of *nuance*. This is a phenomenon empirically observed in its generality first of all by the fact that dictionaries never, or in any case almost never, give exactly the same definitions. Nuance is the instance wherein *the continuity of language as "representation" of thought stumbles*. When we use the term "nuance", we mean that it cannot be determined where one meaning or concept of a word ends and where some other meaning or concept of it begins. That is, that there is no general determining authority or principle (which may be simply the subject of enunciation or something superior to it like the rules of logic) that may define the limits between meanings/concepts so that they form limits of *continuity* between them (like numbers); which leads us to accept that we have to do with limits of *dis*continuity.[312]

---

311. On this issue, see especially the relevant passage in Foucault's essay on Deleuze, "Theatrum philosophicum" (1970), in Foucault, *Dits et écrits 1954-1988, II*, pp. 89-90 – English translation: Foucault, *Language, counter-memory, practice*, pp. 183-185. See also above, fn. 67.

312. Quite indicative of the awkwardness of analytic philosophy and formal logic when faced with the phenomenon of nuance are the texts included in the volume edited by Rosanna Keefe and Peter Smith, *Vagueness: A reader* – see above, fn. 148.

Some further explanation is required here. It is true that the *image* of "nuance" is that of *indeterminate continuity*. In this sense, the word "walls", which I chose above to describe discontinuity in general as a direct consequence of fundamental finitude, in the case of nuance is rather unfortunate. But what matters is that the emphasis here is on *indeterminate* and not on *continuity*. In some sense, *indeterminate* continuity is a form of discontinuity. It is just that a more appropriate word to describe limits would be not *walls* but *seas*. Having once again the *image* of nuance in mind, to pass from *definitely blue* to *definitely green*, one must cross the *sea of turquoise*. The limits of discontinuity in the realm of thought, of meaning, of subjectivity, themselves possess a fundamental property of that realm, namely *flexibility*, without ceasing however to be limits of *discontinuity*. In what we call "nuance", we can "see" thought, meaning, subjectivity, following (*in its own fashion*) the discontinuity of objective, material, fundamentally finite entities. *The flexibility of thought could be considered as the most effective means of facing the (fundamental) finitude of material entities.*

Let me treat the above formulation as an example. *Thought, meaning, subjectivity.* I used three words (perhaps I could find some more) to say *roughly* the same thing. This *roughly* marks the phenomenon of nuance. The fact that, in this case, it cannot be determined how to separate the meanings/concepts of each of the three words that make them conceptually identical to each other from those that differentiate them. At the same time, we have three *signifiers* that differ radically between them as material entities. The initial discontinuity that is responsible for this radical differentiation as to their material substance is brought about, as we have said, by their fundamental property as material beings, namely by fundamental finitude. It is a discontinuity that does not cease to pertain *between them* even after they are constituted as words, that is, even after they have contributed to the production of meaning or the formation of concepts, whatever that may be. It is thus to be expected that the property of discontinuity will also accompany the concepts that the (material) signifiers have formed, even though the former (the concepts) remain by definition subjective, non-material, non-fundamentally finite, or even infinite. The "irony" of language is that the fundamental finitude and consequently the discontinuity of its objective aspect is that which ensures for its subjective aspect its infinity, that is, its freedom.

The instances of nuance, that is, the instances of *conceptual discontinuity*, are so many that we cannot talk about exceptions. In fact, there are not just "many instances" of nuance. According to what we have said, *nuance in its generality is a property of language inherent to it at least as much as its logical continuity*. But what does all this mean then, that there is no understanding in nuance since there is no conceptual continuity? That is, that there is no "passage from one concept to another", no transgression of limits between concepts?

There are two kinds of understanding:

- *Understanding on the basis of representation.* This is a case of an understanding that rests on the rules of (formal) logic, and which presupposes the existence of a (logical) continuity between concepts. In this case, the *desire* to understand, that is, the tendency to transgress the limits between concepts, is "automatically" satisfied, so to speak.

- *Understanding on the basis of desire.* In the instances of nuance, where there is no conceptual (that is, logical) continuity, the transgression of limits between concepts, that is, understanding, takes place solely on the basis of desire. How is this feasible? But who said the only way to surpass walls is to knock them down, or, in the case of seas, to open them like Moses did with the Red Sea? You may also climb (the walls), or swim (the seas), or go round (either of the two). *Climbing or swimming*, in this case, means you accept *the difficulty* and *the dangers* of understanding. *Difficulty:* toil and effort is needed to understand some formulation containing nuances (but it might be worth the trouble). *Dangers:* you may understand some entirely wrong meaning (but then again you may not). And *going round*, in this case, means that *practice*, that is, *experience* with language and discourse in general is required. Someone who is now learning to speak a language or who is now being introduced to a kind of discourse (or to a "discursive practice", to use a Foucauldian term) is not very likely to understand the slightest when hearing or reading some nuance. One hardly grasps *right away* the meaning of the *first* nuance one hears; one usually needs to have heard several. In the field of nuances, concepts are not so much grasped after definitions, which provide *limits of continuity* (with other concepts), but rather *by way of their practical usability*. Moreover, it is quite indicative that the above metaphoro-metonymic sequence walls-climbing-seas-swimming-going-round was obviously not used to display some sort of lyrical eloquence, but rather to describe the understanding of nuances with its risks and difficulties *as effectively as possible*. In other words, the use of metaphor and metonymy is in this case justified precisely by the fact that these two dimensions of language, which demonstrate, as we have seen, the specificity of its materiality, are at the same time what ensures the *flexibility of its conceptuality*.

It goes without saying that most kinds of discourse require both kinds of understanding. If however we had to choose one of the two as more basic, that would be understanding on the basis of desire. Even in mathematics and the natural sciences, and even if we accept something highly questionable, that there are no nuances to be found in them, understanding on the basis of representation *presupposes the desire to understand*. Someone who detests mathematical equations and formulas of physics is not likely to understand either. On the other hand, in non-representational forms of art, as in abstract painting, for example, in improvisational music, or in avant-garde poetry, *only* (or in any event *almost* only) understanding on the basis of desire is required. This is why, in some sense, understanding is more difficult there. The complete absence of rules that could be reduced to the rules of formal logic shifts the whole burden of understanding to the existence of desire, which cannot be taken for granted about anything, insofar as we have anyhow departed from the realm of objectivity.

Someone of course might object by saying that desire too is *determined* by representation; and that, as we have accepted with regard to the ego and according to (Freudian and Lacanian) psychoanalysis itself, apart from cause it is also effect. The response to both is to be expected: *yes, but*.

Both the ego ideal and the infinite part of the ideal ego, since they are constituted themselves within a nexus of representations, however complex, differentiated, heterogeneous and asymmetric, starting from the images of the mirror stage and moving on to all forms of ideological internalisations, representationally determine the *(non-fundamentally) finite* part of the ideal ego as such and consequently its desire too. To put it more simply, what we desire with regard to both our ideological or erotic preferences and the satisfaction of our narcissism is indeed to an enormous extent determined by symbolic systems and external prototypes and does not depend on some inherent spontaneity. *On the other hand though*, the desire of the ego follows the indeterminacy pertaining to the realm of desire generally speaking. Starting from the desire of animals, which, as we have accepted about all material entities, is determinable all right, but (fundamentally) *finitely* determinable. Whether some tiger will have a yearning for some deer may depend on the place of both in the "food chain", but also on conjunctural and largely unpredictable factors, like how long it has been since the tiger's last meal, the environmental conditions of living at that particular area and time period etc. In the case of the ego, the indeterminacy of desire is crucially enhanced by the complexity and indeterminacy of social relations, which means, *in this case*, mainly by the indeterminacy of *language*. The ego, apart from the mirror stage, which is responsible for its initial constitution, is mainly constituted in language. It is an indeterminacy which, as we have seen, even though initially a *material* indeterminacy, is responsible for the indeterminacy, that is, for the *freedom* of subjectivity.

Can there be *rules of (human) desire*, rules of the ego's desire, which are not rules of logical continuity, which do not obey the rules of formal logic and/or representation? We could in fact accept that there are such rules, provided we accept at the same time that they share in common with the material dimension of language and nuances the properties of discontinuity, asymmetry and indeterminacy. They would be rules that would help us to *understand desire*; first of all, in accordance with what we have said above, to understand a specifically human desire, namely to *understand the desire to understand*.

In relation to this, we could pinpoint four such rules, which at the same time constitute *four basic methodological principles of discourse analysis*, four *motives* for discourse analysis, as we propose it here, since the latter cannot but be based, first and foremost, on the desire to understand. Therefore, understanding the desire to understand would at best coincide with the answer to the question, *Why discourse analysis?* Moreover, these *four rules of the desire to understand*, which I will presently list below—in a somewhat belated manner for which I will hopefully be forgiven—summarise what has been said so far on the basis of the two mutually complementary axiomatic assumptions of *the ontological priority of material entities (therefore also of objectivity)* and *the ethical priority of concepts (that is, of subjectivity)*. These two assumptions, also in accordance with the above, are specified respectively *in the material dimension of language and discourse* on one hand and *in freedom of critique as a supreme value* on the other. In this sense, the following four rules of the desire to understand convey, in the realm of desire, some philosophical and ultimately ideological choices, without however being constituted by some ideology as representation, since it is precisely a matter of *axiomatic* assumptions.

- mistrust towards power
- emphasis on the relation to referents
- emphasis on socio-historical conditions
- emphasis on the multiple and asymmetric constitution of subjectivity

The second and the third of the above rules are more related to the material dimension of language and discourse, the first is related more to freedom of critique as a supreme value, and the fourth is shared more or less equally between the two. Even though there is a "quantitative" imbalance in favour of the material dimension, the first rule, as will be shown below, is the most basic. About the other three, enough has been said so far and they need no further explanation. I should merely clarify one point with regard to the emphasis on socio-historical conditions, namely that these do not include only the external conditions of producing discourse, but also *other (related) discourses*, as well as the *materiality of signifiers*. From the *etymology of words* to the *technological development of the media*, it becomes obvious that this materiality cannot but constitute itself an inseparable part of socio-historical conditions. And something concerning all three last rules: the word "emphasis" is perhaps quite revealing as to how nuance insinuates itself into the very rules (of the desire to understand). There is no way to "define" emphasis, that is, to understand it beforehand on the basis of some logical continuity. It becomes understandable only in "its practical usability", that is, on one hand, in the application of the rules, and on the other, obviously enough, in the importance that has actually been given, throughout the theoretical elaboration of the relevant concepts, to the relation with referents, to socio-historical conditions, and to the multiple and asymmetric constitution of subjectivity.

We now come to the first rule of the desire to understand, to the first basic methodological principle of discourse analysis. Perhaps we could have some first "taste" of what mistrust towards power might consist in our case if we bring to mind the following formulation by Foucault in one of his interviews (1983): "My point is not that everything [that is, every relation of power] is bad, but that everything [every relation of power] is dangerous, which is not exactly the same as bad."³¹³ "Dangerous" obviously is something that *may* be or may *become* "bad", but that then again it may not. As a "bad" relation of power, if we take into account more generally Foucault's views on this matter, I assume we could consider a relation of power that is non-reversible, a relation of power in which even though there is also some *confrontation* between the two sides of the relation it is not possible for the one over whom power is exercised to release themselves from it. According to Foucault's own term, a relation of power that is also a relation of *domination*.³¹⁴ I suppose that relations of capitalist exploitation, relations of state oppression, relations between men and women in a patriarchal society, relations of racial discrimination in racist regimes would be included in the category of relations of domination or "bad" relations of power.

The problem with discourse analysis is that it is concerned with the exercise of power in *discourse* and by way of *discourse*, that is, primarily though not exclusively, with the exercise of *ideological* power. Ideological power has the peculiarity that, when effectively exercised, it by definition *eliminates* any sort of confrontation between the two sides of the relation that might arise. However, the non-reversible element is there too, and it is the element of *hypostatisation*. The acceptance of some ideas as *objectively* existing amounts to the belief that such ideas are *indisputable*. Therefore, what is reprehensible in ideology is precisely that it *deprives* of the possibility for resistance and confrontation. Having already given a *philosophical* definition (derived from Foucault's formulations) of critique as *practical thought on limits*, we could now give an equivalent *ideological* definition of critique as *resistance in discourse and by way of discourse*, something which of course mainly means *resistance to ideological power*. The critique of ideology, which forms the *critical thrust* of discourse analysis (which is in turn the *methodological framework* for the critique of ideology), *aims first of all at the restitution of the possibility for its own existence*.

If the main (negative) target of critique is hypostatisation, the same goes for mistrust. In a manner equivalent to the jealous lover's question, "Is my partner cheating on me?", the key question the discourse analyst constantly asks him/herself is, "Is this a hypostatisation?". Of course the answer hardly ever comes immediately, it does so only in cases when the question is posed with regard to the supreme ideal of some ideology itself. To the question whether God is a hypostatisation, an atheist or a materialist would obviously reply immediately, "Yes", while a believer would immediately say "No". Generally speaking though, as we have already said above, as a rule the *aim* of the *critique of hypostatisation* is achieved by *means* of the *analysis of representation*.

---

313. *The Foucault reader*, p. 343.

314. Dreyfus and Rabinow, *op. cit.*, p. 226. In this case, *confrontation*, in so far as it is *resistance to power* and in accordance with what we have already said, does not necessarily always assume the form of *opposition*.

Now to approach this means-aim relationship somewhat more concretely, we could say that the analysis of representation aims to demonstrate how hypostatisation is accomplished *by way of representation*. That is, how representation acts on people's thought in such a manner that they conceive of some ideas, some concepts, some subjective entities, as objectively existing. According to what we have said above, the main characteristic of representation, namely classification and ordering, that is, the establishment of *continuity*, is the primary means by which the illusion of hypostatisation is accomplished (without this meaning that the establishment of continuity or representation *always* leads to hypostatisation). Some theoretical approaches in contemporary philosophy, contemporary physics and contemporary mathematics notwithstanding, the *discourse of continuity* persists as the *predominant model* for the presentation of the natural, *i.e. the objective* world: the discourse of formal logic, of (traditional) natural and mathematical sciences, as well as of their multiple applications and extensions. Moreover, the hypostatising operation of continuity is also inherent on a *pre-rational* level, that of the *primordial constitution of the ego*. The perception of the *coherence/continuity of the body*, which, at the mirror stage, is responsible for the primordial hypostatisation of the image of the *uniform ego*, is also responsible for further hypostatisations precisely in so far as it matches *the property of continuity with that of objective existence*.[315]

So the discourse analyst's mistrust is first and foremost *mistrust towards the continuous*. In this sense, the discourse analyst's mistrust is *the inverse* of the detective's (or the jealous lover's). The latter asks him/herself, "X was at work till five and at home since seven. But what was he/she doing between five and seven?" In other words, in this case there is mistrust towards *discontinuity*. The search is for the "*missing piece of the puzzle*". The aim is to restore continuity at all costs. The detective puts his/her mind at rest when he/she is capable of replying, "Between five and seven, X was paying a visit to some friends." Therefore innocent. Or, alternatively, "...was committing adultery" or "...was murdering Y". Therefore guilty of adultery or murder. The *false* alibi, in case, for example, the "friends" X was "visiting" were "in on it", is but a *false* continuity. It goes without saying that the aim is to restore *true* continuity. The existence of discontinuity, or the existence of *suspect*, that is, *unconvincing* continuity, thus possibly *concealed dis*continuity, is the detective's equivalent to Cartesian *doubt*. The detective's thought *on one hand has it as its starting point and on the other aims at its removal*. The *certainty* provided by the *continuity* of the final solution to the mystery is *by itself, potentially at least, a form of hypostatisation*. The final *narrative* of the crime, in which there are no logical gaps, in which every event, every action, can be explained on the basis of motives and the cause-effect relation more generally, as well as the inescapable laws of the continuity of natural time-space (*every* person at *every* point in time must be *somewhere*), is considered

---

315. Lacan: "The image of his [man's] body is the principle of every unity he perceives in objects." - Lacan, *op. cit.*, p. 198 – English translation: p. 166.

as constituting a *faithful representation* of *objective* reality, that is, of the real (material) events that have actually occurred (murder, adultery) and that in this sense their existence as already accomplished facts does not depend on anybody's subjectivity. For this reason *the representation-narrative is itself considered objective*.

The discourse analyst, on the other hand, will not rest if he/she cannot manage to *subvert continuity*. For the discourse analyst, discovering discontinuity in something presented as continuous, is not a problem to be solved. It is not realising that a "piece of the puzzle" is missing and must be found in order to restore continuity; it is an "end in itself" and at the same time a *means*, a keystone for the critique of hypostatisation.[316]

To avoid being taken to imply that discourse analysis should intervene in the procedure of justice and take over the work of police or detectives, but also to clarify further the difference of the former from the latter, I will give an example where detectives' logic and discourse analysis may coexist "on equal terms", so to speak. A fictional narrative with a "detective" plot would be an appropriate example of this sort, since fiction by definition creates a distance from reality, thereby providing the preconditions of a situation where the only essential issues are *ideological anyhow*.

---

316. It goes without saying that, as a means and keystone for the critique of hypostatisation, the concept of discontinuity should not itself be involved in some hypostatising process, such as, for instance in the constitution of a "philosophy of History" on the basis of discontinuity. Foucault had repeatedly and explicitly dissociated himself from this sort of discontinuity's conceptual use. See Foucault, *Dits et écrits 1954-1988, III*, pp. 142-144 –English translation: Foucault, *Power/knowledge*, pp. 111-113-, and Michel Foucault, *Politics, philosophy, culture: Interviews and other writings 1977-1984* (translated by Alan Sheridan et al), New York and London: Routledge, 1988, pp. 99-100.

Part IV
Applications

Chapter 17
Chinatown

Roman Polanski's film *Chinatown* (1974) is among the most narratively complex, symbolically rich and ideologically polysemous films ever to have come out of Hollywood. Therefore, since I have chosen to use it here merely as an example, which means I will inevitably be brief in my treatment of it, I am bound to do blatant injustice to all that complexity, richness and polysemy, which would need a separate book to be adequately shown in a critical-analytical approach. Nevertheless, this film is a challenge, because it is justifiably considered as one of the most important and well-made films of all time, but also because, as to what mainly concerns us here, it could hardly be reproached for ideological conservatism or for any sort of socio-political conventionality.[317]

---

317. Several studies on *Chinatown* have been published, I mention here two of them that might in some ways be related to my approach: Vernon Lionel Shetley, "Incest and capital in *Chinatown*", *MLN*, Volume 114, Number 5, December 1999 (Comparative Literature Issue), pp. 1092-1109, and Ian S. Scott, "'Either you bring the water to L.A. or you bring L.A. to the water': Politics, perceptions and the pursuit of history in Roman Polanski's *Chinatown*", *European journal of American studies* [Online], 2 | 2007, document 1, Online since 17 October 2007, connection on 28 February 2011. URL : http://ejas.revues.org/1203.

I quote the summary of *Chinatown* from *Wikipedia*:

A Los Angeles private investigator named Jake 'J.J' Gittes (Nicholson) is hired to spy on Hollis Mulwray, the chief engineer for the city's water department. The woman hiring Gittes claims to be Evelyn Mulwray, Hollis' wife. Mr. Mulwray spends most of his time investigating dry river beds. Mr. Mulwray also has a heated argument with an elderly man. Gittes finally catches Mulwray during an outing with a young blonde and photographs the pair in a kiss, which becomes a scandal in the press. After the story is published, Gittes learns that the woman who hired him was not the real Evelyn Mulwray.

Clues suggest a scandal in the city government: Despite a serious drought and an expensive proposal to build a new dam, the Water and Power department is dumping fresh water into the ocean at night.

On a tip, Gittes seeks out Mr. Mulwray at a reservoir but finds the police there instead, investigating Hollis Mulwray's death from drowning. When the police speak to Mrs. Mulwray about the death, they assume she hired Gittes, which Gittes corroborates. She thanks him and hires him to investigate what happened to her husband.

Later that night, while breaking into the reservoir's secured area, Gittes is confronted by water department security, Claude Mulvihill, and a thug (a cameo by Polanski himself), who slashes Jake's nose for being a "very nosy fella." Gittes receives a call from Ida Sessions, the woman who was hired to pretend to be Mrs. Mulwray, who suggests that Gittes look at the obituary column. At the water department, Gittes notices photographs of the elderly man Mulwray quarreled with a few days before his death, Noah Cross (Huston). Cross, who is Evelyn Mulwray's father, used to own the water department as Mulwray's business partner. Cross ended his association with the department when the partners sold it to the city.

Cross hires Gittes to find the blond girl Hollis had been seeing, saying that she might know what happened to him. Acting on a hint from Sessions, Gittes begins to unravel an intricate water scandal. Cross and his partners have been forcing farmers out of their land so they can buy it cheap, after which a newly-built (and controversial) dam and water system would start redirecting much of L.A.'s water supply to that land, dramatically increasing its value. Since Cross wants no record of such transactions, he has partnered with a retirement home community in such a way that many of the eldest residents within (one of whom is mentioned in the obituary column) would legally, but unknowingly, own the land.

Gittes follows Evelyn to a middle-class house and sees Mulwray's girlfriend crying. Evelyn claims this is her sister, who was crying because she had just learned about Hollis' death. Later that night, Sessions is murdered. Escobar points out that the coroner's report proves that salt water was found in Mulwray's lungs even though the body was found in a freshwater reservoir.

Gittes returns to Evelyn's mansion, where he discovers a pair of eyeglasses in a garden saltwater pond. Gittes confronts Evelyn, who reveals that the blonde girl, Katherine, is both her sister *and* her daughter; Gittes asks Evelyn if her father raped her and she shakes her head no but it is insinuated through her body language and frequently expressed fear of her father that she is not being wholly truthful. Gittes then chooses to help Evelyn escape. Evelyn remembers that the eyeglasses could not have been her husband's because they are bifocals. Gittes arranges for the two women to flee to Mexico and instructs Evelyn to meet him at her butler's address in Chinatown. Evelyn leaves, and Cross arrives with Mulvihill under the pretext that Gittes has found the girl, however, Gittes confronts Cross with the accusation of murder and the glasses. Mulvihill takes away the eyeglasses that are the only physical evidence. Cross forces Gittes to take him to the girl. When Gittes arrives at Evelyn's hiding place in Chinatown, the police are already there.

When Cross approaches the girl, demanding custody of her, Evelyn pushes him back, shoots him in the arm and starts her car. The police arrest Gittes, and as Evelyn drives away, they open fire and Evelyn is shot and killed. Cross clutches Evelyn's shrieking daughter as a devastated Gittes is comforted by his associates, one of them saying, "Forget it, Jake. It's Chinatown."[318]

Now to investigate the question concerning the continuity of narrative representation, let us start from the axis of enunciative modes. From the first part of this axis, namely from the external conditions of enunciation, we are informed of an important detail concerning the second part, i.e. the internal conditions: While initially in the script it was specified that there would be a voice-over narration by the central character, namely the private detective Jake Gittes (Jack Nicholson), Polanski removed the voice-over, and "filmed the movie so the audience discovered the clues at the same time Gittes did".[319]

We know that the voice-over is a device by which to accomplish in film the "subjective" type of narration, i.e. the mode of narrative enunciation in which the narrator clings to the subjectivity of a certain character and narrates the story from his/her viewpoint.[320] It is rather a "literary" and not a purely filmic device, in the sense that language itself, in fact speech itself is used, instead of some cinematic means.[321] It is, nonetheless, quite effective, since it is equivalent to the most directly "subjective" narrative mode in literature, which is narration in first person singular.

In this case, however, what do we notice? Polanski justifiably abandons the voice-over device in order to achieve an *even closer proximity* between Gittes and the narrator's position. This is quite a revelation: Both the voice-over in film and the first person singular narration in literature, even though both based on a *complete identification*—always fictitious anyhow, of course—between the narrator and one of the characters, *create some distance* between on one hand the narrating character who identifies with the narrator and on the other the character *of the story itself*, that is, of the character who *experiences directly* the events at the moment they take place. Even though we have to do with the same person, their subjectivities differ in that they are separated *by a temporal distance*: the character-narrator of the "present" that is "now" narrating to us the story is supposed to know it as a whole including its end. This is not the case of course with the reader or the viewer, and this creates some distance between them and the character-narrator. There is also some distance though produced between the

---

318. "Chinatown (film)", *Wikipedia*, 4 May 2008, http://en.wikipedia.org/wiki/Chinatown_(film) (9 May 2008).

319. See *ibid*.

320. See above, fn. 185.

321. See Doxiadis, *Ideology and television*, p. 102.

reader/viewer and the character who is directly experiencing the story, since the action of the latter is presented to us as a *past*, as something that *has already happened*; moreover, at least in cases of the *conventional* use of the first person or the voice-over, we know something about him/her that he/she does not know about him/herself: that he/she is not going to die at least till after the end of the story.

So we end up with something that at first glance might seem paradoxical: The most "subjective" narrative mode, that is, the mode of narrative enunciation by which to accomplish the closest proximity between the narrator and one of the characters, and by extension between the character-narrator and the reader/viewer, is ultimately *not* the first person singular in literature and the voice-over in film. What matters in the narrative mode as to the relations between characters, narrator and reader/viewer is not so much the *persons' identity* but rather the *narrative function,* which is first and foremost a function of *knowledge*. Narration, before it becomes anything else, is *acquisition and transmission of knowledge*. So when Polanski's basic concern in shooting the film is that "the audience discovers the clues at the same time Gittes does", this means that he has grasped the most effective way of diminishing the distance between character (Gittes), narrator and viewer. The film's impersonal narrator, that hypothetical entity that "says to us" the story, which is there in every sort of narrative and determined according to the filmic (or literary or any other) "medium" that narrates in each instance,[322] in the case of such an immediately "subjective" narrative mode like *Chinatown*, is *crushed*, so to speak, within the relation of near identification between character (Gittes) and viewer. I say "near" because obviously there can be no absolute identification. Even "near" may be an exaggeration. Perhaps a more appropriate term would be "*functional* identification". Gittes and the viewer identify in particular as to the *narrative function*, which, as we said above, is first of all a function of *knowledge*.

More specifically, in the case of *Chinatown*, what does the narrative function performed by Gittes and consequently by the viewer actually consist in? Quite simply, in the function of Gittes's *profession*, which is the private detective's profession. Polanski wanted the viewer to discover the *clues* together with Gittes. Clues that lead to the unraveling of the mystery, clues that make up the narrative as a process of knowledge—in this case, one and the same thing. The narrative-knowledge function, as in many other films and novels with a detective plot but perhaps here in an especially systematic way, entirely coincides with the private detective's investigation process. At this point lies the film's *basic cohesive joint*, that is, the element that forms the main factor in the *continuity* of narrative representation.

The film, on a first level of viewing, has a highly asymmetric and discontinuous narrative structure—the acquisition of knowledge of the mystery's clues, on the part of Gittes and consequently of the viewer, occurs fragmentarily, unpredictably, in a fashion initially disjointed, with guesswork os-

---

322. See *ibid.*, p. 108.

cillating between confirmation and disproval—the latter keeping on till a little while before the end.

For a large part of the narrative, Gittes is inclined to believe that Cross is responsible for Mulwray's death. Having gathered some clues about the former's financial foul play, at some point he surmises that Mulwray found out about it and Cross eliminated him so he wouldn't talk. At some moment towards the end, after having been pursued by Cross's men and after having made love with Cross's daughter Evelyn, he starts suspecting that the latter is keeping some important secrets from him. In one particular scene, masterfully inventive as to its narratively subversive efficacy and its ironic symbolisms, his suspicions about her husband's (Mulwray's) murder are directed almost exclusively towards her. He in this way sides with the police's version—so much so that he phones them to come and arrest her. After this, there follows the scene where Evelyn's terrible secret is revealed, that she had had an incestuous relationship with her father and that the girl whom her husband was seeing is both her daughter and her sister. At the end of the same scene, in a manner that shows she has no awareness of the gravity of her words, Evelyn provides Gittes with a piece of information that leads him to interpret differently the clues that had made him suspect her, and that drives him anew to believe Cross is the culprit of Mulwray's murder, this time with certainty.

The film is notorious for its outrageously pessimistic ending. Evelyn, the woman with whom Gittes had started an affair and whom, after having eventually been convinced of her innocence, he tries to save, gets killed by a policeman's bullet in her attempt to escape with her daughter-sister, Cross gets off being just slightly wounded after Evelyn desperately shot at him, and Evelyn's daughter-sister and Cross's daughter-granddaughter comes under the "protection" of Cross, who we assume will "take care" of her as he had "taken care" of Evelyn—and who, moreover, remains "above suspicion" with regard to Mulwray's murder. Once again drawing on the information provided in the external conditions part of the axis of enunciative modes, we learn that the scriptwriter wanted a "happy end", but Polanski disagreed and insisted on the ending eventually chosen.[323] In this sense, there is certainly some "discontinuity" with the dominant conventions of Hollywood film production, and this is indeed one basic reason that differentiates the film not only morphologically but also ideologically from the prevailing cinematic discourse.

On the other hand though, Polanski's pessimistic ending may be discontinuous as to Hollywood's *more general* conventions, but it is *continuous* as to the *genre* of *film noir*—in fact more continuous than proper film noir productions (of the 1940s and '50s), many of which did not exactly have a "happy end" but still had a sort of *conciliatory* ending; tragic, but at least with a partial predominance of justice and some punishment of the culprits. More precisely, many of Hollywood's *film noir* productions were obliged (even by

---

323. See "Chinatown (film)", *op. cit.*

law: by the notorious Production Code[324]) to reconcile between, on one hand, the general Hollywood convention that in the end the "good" must win and the "bad" must be punished and, on the other, the *narrative-ideological structure of the film noir itself*, which presented the "dark" side of American society in a hopelessly pessimistic manner. In this sense, *Chinatown* (like other films produced after the film noir period *per se*) forms an exception.[325] An exception, however, which, having dispensed with the obligation to reconcile, restores the continuity-consistency with film noir's *inherent* characteristics as a film genre.

Let us now come back to the narrative mode. As we have said, Gittes as character-narrator constitutes the basic cohesive joint that ensures the narrative's continuity. In the end of the story, he finally knows everything. Even though he has "lost" on all levels, even though his own version has not been accepted by the corrupt policemen, what matters is that in his mind as at once private detective and narrator, and consequently in the mind of the viewers, he has completely restored continuity, he has found all the "missing pieces" of the puzzle. And obviously we have to do with a puzzle concerning not merely a crime—Mulwray's murder—but also enormous financial scandals involving Los Angeles water department authorities, the corruption of the police and of public figures, and, above all, the shattering secret of Evelyn and her relationship with her father. All this immense nexus of narrative and thematic elements, initially dispersed and unconnected, this confusion of heterogeneous pieces of information that almost till the end bewilder the viewer as well as Gittes himself with their apparently asymmetric complexity, towards the end of the narrative come to be assembled into a uniform, however complex, structure of cause-effect relationships.

If on the level of discourse the main joint of continuation is Gittes, on the level of story the main joint is Cross. He is not merely the culprit of Mulwray's murder, but the person responsible for all the important events and situations of the narrative, the solution hiding behind all the puzzle's dark points. His name is symbolic in at least a twofold manner. His surname by itself signifies a *cross*: between financial, political and sexual corruption. His first name and surname taken together signify *discontinuity*: *Noah Cross → No Across*. That is: *Crossing (through) is forbidden*– or *is impossible*. Ultimately Noah Cross is a personification of the *lack of transparency*, that is, of corrupt power in all its manifestations, discontinuity as the *absolute negation of the continuity* that would be effected by the intervention of justice and the restoration of truth, either at best in the form of a well-governed state of justice, or at worst, as it actually happens eventually, in the form of a stubborn but powerless private detective: Gittes restores continuity, but only narratively-representationally – not as the law, not as the state of justice, because he may be just but he is not the state.

---

324. See "Film noir", *Wikipedia*, 6 May 2008, http://en.wikipedia.org/wiki/Film_noir (9 May 2008).

325. See *ibid*.

As the negation of the continuity of justice and truth and at the same time as a "cross" in the above sense, Cross is therefore a symbol for the *continuity of corruption*: a representation-classification *of the various sorts of corruption*, admirable in its horrendous magnificence. So in the *axis of concepts*, the continuity that Cross stands for is established as a *conceptual continuity* of the three above mentioned sorts of corruption. Noah Cross, as No Across, as an absolute *Dis*-continuity, as the negation of the continuity of Law, constitutes the absolute Continuity of his own *Anti*-Law, of the Law of Corruption, on all three corresponding levels of social life. On the economic level, by illegally irrigating areas of land so as to raise their value excessively; and by having adroitly (and illegally) arranged for those areas to come to his own possession. Here the Anti-Law of Corruption consists in the *complete perversion* of well-meant, legitimate investment activity, that is, of the Law of Exchange. On the political level, by buying off public servants (the people in charge of the water department, except for Mulwray) and policemen ("He *owns* the police!", Evelyn desperately yells at Gittes in the final scene). The Anti-Law of Corruption is here designated by the *disgrace* of the state of justice, that is, of the Law of Democracy. Political power serves the interests of one at the expense of the many. And finally, on the sexual level, by having an incestuous affair with his daughter. On this level, which from a dramatic viewpoint is the most important, the Anti-Law of Corruption is particularised in a *perfectly symmetric inversion* of the Oedipal structure, that is, of the Law of Desire. Oedipus kills his father and afterwards has intercourse with his mother, Cross has intercourse with his daughter and afterwards kills her husband.

The unifying principle of all three manifestations of the Anti-Law of Corruption, of the Law that *at once abolishes and substitutes* the existing Laws of Exchange, Democracy and Desire, that which ensures the *continuity* between them, is Cross's own *threefold* figure as Father-Master-Tycoon. The element that serves to sustain the cohesion between the three levels of Corruption is Cross's *perversely insatiable desire*. When asked by Gittes why an already extremely powerful and wealthy man would want more power and more wealth, Cross replies with disarming self-awareness that he wishes to *control the future*. Gittes obviously in his question is referring to the politico-economic dimension of Cross's powerfulness, but Cross's reply also covers his sexual-procreative activity: By procreating with his daughter, and possibly (why not?), after the story's ending, with his daughter-granddaughter, he perpetuates his paternal authority, becoming an *intergenerational Father-Master*. Dominating the future, both on the politico-economic level and on the familial-sexual, in other words, *ensuring continuity in time*, is indeed the key to the acquisition of a representational and at the same time real (in so far as the latter is determined by the former) omnipotence.

So on the axis of concepts, as far as the symbolic significance of the figure of Cross is concerned, we notice the articulation of a *peculiar form of Hegelian Freudo-Marxism*. Cross's insatiable desire for power represents three *negations* of a Hegelian type that are joined to form a uniform *negative* schema of domination as Corruption: Capitalist Economy as negation-corruption-perversion of Exchange, Capitalist State as negation-corruption-disgrace of Democracy, Repressive Familial-Sexual Morality as negation-corruption-inversion of Desire. Ultimately, Cross stands for a (Hegelian) negation of Modern Western civilisation, as it is designated by the values of Justice and Freedom, which would be served by a correct combination of desire, exchange and democracy (dissolution of the Oedipus complex in the symbolic field,[326] legitimate competition on equal terms in the economy, respect towards rights and the rules of justice in politics), but which are instead disgraced, perverted and inversed by the capitalist politico-economic system and repressive (and thereby *deeply hypocritical*) sexual-familial morality.

We might therefore presume that if Gittes, in parallel to the private detective's profession, had (Hegelian) Freudo-Marxist social theory as a hobby, notwithstanding his chagrin caused by his lover's death and by the multiple and blatant injustice being committed as Cross prevails, should be quite satisfied with the confirmation of the antithetical representational schema: Justice and Freedom on one hand, necessary and symmetrically equivalent Negation of both on the other. In its *continuity* and *consistency* this schema gives an impression of objectivity, in the sense of an *historical and ethical necessity*; perhaps an overly pessimistic formulation as to its Marxist component, but then let us not forget the first part of Gramsci's famous dictum[327]. As a *basic issue* of the narrative, we could say that the above antithetical schema emerges on the *axis of thematics*. The film's ideological position, at least on a first level of reading, consists on one hand in the recognition of the schema's necessity and on the other in the renunciation of its latter part by its former. It is an instance where a Freudo-Marxist critique of capitalism and repression (and in so far as this is not carried out explicitly in the name of either Marx or Freud or anyone of their successors) coincides with the ideological sensitivities of an "average" liberal viewer.

Now we, as (non-Hegelian) mistrustful discourse analysts, not satisfied with the schema's irrevocable continuity, and inversely to the detective-narrator's work, will obstinately seek for discontinuities, not to restore a more truthful and even more irrevocable continuity, but rather because of our in the last instance axiomatic *mistrust* of continuity: a mistrust which, as we have said, serves as a ground for the analysis of representation and consequently as a means for the critique of hypostatisation.

The axis of concepts, as we have seen, is permeated by a Freudo-Marxist discourse that lies behind the nexus of politico-economic power and sexual-familial repression. Let first investigate the *Marxist* component of this discourse. The crucial question as to this component is the interweaving of

---

326. See Freud, *S.E. XIX*, pp. 171-179.

327. "Pessimism of the intelligence, optimism of the will." The initial formulation belongs to Romain Rolland. See Antonio Gramsci, *Selections from the Prison Notebooks* (translated by Quintin Hoare and Geoffrey Nowell Smith), London: Lawrence & Wishart, 1976, p. 175, fn. 75.

economic might and political power. Apart from the realm of theory and the concept of "determination by the economy in the last instance", there is the issue of the *historical references* of this interweaving. So we inevitably move over to the *axis of objects*, in order to see whether or not there is some correspondence of the events in the *fictional plot* (referentiality *per se*) to the *real historical* events (objectivity *per se*) of the society and period to which the narrative refers.

On a first, general level, the corruption of police and a large part of the public sector in the United States during the inter-war period is more or less well-known and taken for granted. In this sense, the film might be seen as a cinematic renunciation of that corruption, taking place with some forty years' delay, a delay perhaps accountable by the Production Code, which came into force in 1934 (the same decade with the film's story time) and stopped being implemented in 1968 (six years before the film's discourse time).[328] The film's historical references though are far more specific.

I quote a brief history of the "Water Wars" from *Wikipedia*:

Los Angeles Aqueduct: the beginning of the water wars

> The water wars began when Frederick Eaton was elected mayor of Los Angeles in 1898, and appointed his friend, William Mulholland, the superintendent of the newly-created Los Angeles Department of Water and Power (LADWP).
>
> Eaton and Mulholland had a vision of a Los Angeles that would become far bigger than the Los Angeles of the turn of the century. The limiting factor of Los Angeles' growth was water supply. Eaton and Mulholland realized that the Owens Valley had a large amount of runoff from the Sierra Nevada, and a gravity-fed aqueduct could deliver the Owens water to Los Angeles.

Irrigation in the Owens Valley in 1901

> Most of the 200 miles (321.9 km) of canals and ditches that constituted the irrigation system in the Owens Valley in 1901 were in the north, while the southern region of the valley was mostly inhabited by people raising livestock. The irrigation systems created by the ditch companies did not have adequate drainage and as a result oversaturated the soil to the point where crops could not be raised. The irrigation systems also significantly lowered the water level in the Owens Lake (a process that was intensified later by the diversion of water through the Los Angeles Aqueduct). Around the turn of the century the northern part of the Owens Valley turned to raising fruit, poultry and dairy. The discovery of new mining fields in the northern region of the valley also aided in an economic turn-around of the area.
>
> The southern region of the Owens Valley greatly differed from the northern region of the valley. In the south the climate was drier, irrigation was less developed and small farms were unable to compete with livestock owners with large land holdings. Most irrigable land in the south of the Owens Valley could

---

328. See "United States Motion Picture Production Code of 1930", *Wikipedia*, 6 May 2008, http://en.wikipedia.org/wiki/Production_Code (9 May 2008).

not have water diverted to it by small, individual ditch systems. The land in the southern part of the Owens Valley required a system of canals and ditches capable of diverting part of the large Owens River. John Wesley Powell criticized laws that promoted settlement and development on the individual level and suggested than the magnitude of water diversion necessary for successful agriculture could only be achieved though many homesteaders joining together and creating irrigation districts with large-scale aqueduct systems. Each district would create its own rules and regulations for the use and division of the water for the parcels within the district. The failure to create a system of this scale resulted in the limited and inefficient settlement in the southern part of the Owens Valley and made this region increasingly vulnerable and attractive to Los Angeles authorities as a source of water.

Water rights and profit

At the turn of the century, the United States Bureau of Reclamation was planning on building an irrigation system to help the farmers of the Owens Valley. However, the agent of the Bureau was a close friend of Eaton, so Eaton had access to inside information about water rights. Eaton bought land as a private citizen, hoping to sell it back to Los Angeles at a vast profit. Eaton claimed in an interview with the *Los Angeles Express* in 1905 that he turned over all his water rights to the city of Los Angeles without being paid for them, "except that I retained the cattle which I had been compelled to take in making the deals ... and mountain pasture land of no value except for grazing purposes."

Eaton lobbied Theodore Roosevelt and got the local irrigation system cancelled. Mulholland misled residents of the Owens Valley, by claiming that Los Angeles would take water only for domestic purposes, not for irrigation. By 1905, through purchases and bribery, Los Angeles purchased enough water rights to enable the aqueduct.

The aqueduct was sold to the citizens of Los Angeles as vital to the growth of the city. However, unknown to the public, the initial water would be used to irrigate the San Fernando Valley to the north, which was not at the time a part of the city. A syndicate of investors (again, close friends of Eaton, including Harrison Gray Otis) bought up large tracts of land in the San Fernando Valley with this inside information. This syndicate made substantial efforts to the passage of the bond issue that funded the aqueduct, including creating a false drought (by manipulating rainfall totals) and publishing scare articles in the Los Angeles Times, which Otis published.

The building and operation of the aqueduct

From 1905 through 1913, Mulholland directed the building of the aqueduct. The 233 mile (375 km) Los Angeles Aqueduct, completed in November 1913, required more than 2,000 workers and the digging of 164 tunnels. The project has been compared in complexity by Mulholland's granddaughter to building the Panama Canal. Water from the Owens River reached a reservoir in the San Fernando Valley on November 5. At a ceremony that day, Mulholland spoke his famous words about this engineering feat: "There it is. Take it."

After the aqueduct was completed in 1913, the San Fernando investors demanded so much water from the Owens Valley that it started to transform from "The Switzerland of California" into a desert. Inflows to Owens Lake were almost completely diverted, which caused the lake to dry up by 1924. Farmers and ranchers tried to band together to sell water rights to Los Angeles as a group, but again through what historians called "underhanded moves", Los Angeles managed to buy the water rights at a substantially reduced price.

So much water was taken from the valley that the farmers and ranchers rebelled. In 1924, a group of armed ranchers seized the Alabama Gates and dynamited part of the system. This armed rebellion was for naught, and by 1928, Los Angeles owned 90 percent of the water in Owens Valley. Agriculture in the valley was effectively dead.[329]

As we may notice from the above historical information, the problem of water in Los Angeles during the first decades of the twentieth century was an enormous and many-sided socio-economic issue, which did not merely consist in some tycoon's grand fraud. In actual fact, it was about the conflict between urban and rural sector, and the "inevitable" (emphasising the inverted commas) sacrifice of the latter in favour of the development of the former. In the film, the purely social dimension of the problem appears at only three points, in a way that clearly downgrades it: in the beginning, when the farmers disrupt Mulwray's public speech by entering the lecture hall with their livestock shouting protests, at the scene where the water department's vice-president explains to Gittes they have hired a (corrupt) policeman to cope with the watertanks' sabotage by indignant farmers, and when the farmers attack Gittes believing he is a water department agent. The enormous social and regional-planning issue of supplying water to Los Angeles at the expense of the rural region is almost suppressed, and the story focuses on something which in reality was an important but of a rather secondary significance aspect of the problem: on the scandalously preferential (secret) irrigation of a rural area near Los Angeles (of San Fernando Valley in real history) with the aim of profiteeringly exploiting its steeply increased value.

The analogies and non-correspondences between the fictional characters and the historical personages and groups may be quite revealing as to the signicance of the film's divergence from the real story. We may easily assume that Cross is a "condensation", so to speak, or a "cross", between Fred Eaton and the syndicate of San Fernando, while *Holl*is *Mul*wray, as given away by his symbolic name and surname,[330] is a fictional metaphor for *Mulholl*and. From what we can see in the historical facts, the fictional conflict to the death between the two is a far cry from the real events. Mulholland was not the honest chief engineer who discovered and fought against Eaton and the syndicate of San Fernando's fraud. Rather, he participated himself in its cover-up and its carrying out, albeit with the excuse of promoting the city of Los Angeles's vital developmental interests.

---

329. «California Water Wars», *Wikipedia*, 27 March 2008, http://en.wikipedia.org/wiki/California_Water_Wars (9 May 2008).
330. See Scott, *op. cit.*, and "Chinatown (film)", *op. cit.*

The discontinuity that emerges does not consist of course in the non-correspondence between referentiality *per se* and objectivity *per se*, such a non-correspondence in the case of fictional discourse is given by definition. But rather it consists in the fact that here the film *deliberately invokes some historical events*, only to diverge from them considerably in their presentation. More accurately, we should perhaps talk not about a non-correspondence between referentiality *per se* (fictional persons and events) and objectivity *per se* (real persons and events), but rather about a non-correspondence between *two kinds of referentiality per se*: the referentiality *per se* of *fiction*, and that of *historical discourse*, with which fiction *deliberately articulates itself*, thereby constituting, so to speak, a "historical film" (by analogy to the "historical novel"). The discontinuity between the two discourses emerges precisely in their fashion of articulating with each other.

The fictional narrative does not merely choose to situate itself within the framework of a historical discourse describing conditions and important events in Los Angeles before the Second World War, which included the "Water Wars" among other things. On the contrary, it refers directly to those historical events, constituting a considerable part of its plot as a *detective story, by including part of the historical events within it and by constituting certain of the fictional characters on the basis of specific real individuals and groups who participated in them.* In other words, the relation of articulation between fictional and historical discourse in this case consists in a *peculiar appropriation of part of the latter by the former*. The discontinuity therefore emerges as a specific *intervention* of fiction in the field of historiography, certainly not with the aim of *distorting* the specific historical events—fiction by nature cannot make truth claims regarding historical facts anyhow—but rather within the framework of a strategy concerning a representational conception of (real) history generally speaking.

Here one notices perhaps an ironic element of our analytical approach. The *discontinuity* revealed between fictional and historiographical discourse can be accounted for by the attempt to constitute an overall representational *continuity*, the continuity of History as a conflict between two qualitatively, if not quantitatively equivalent opposite forces. The intervention in the historical discourse consists in *concealing the discontinuities of real history*. Discontinuities that in this case could be more effectively understood if one tried to "judge" morally or ideologically or politically the real individual William Mulholland. He is neither Noah Cross, insatiable in his lust for power and absolutely ruthless, nor Hollis Mulwray, honest and incorruptible in all respects. He is a key figure who played an important part in the development of the city of Los Angeles, most possibly motivated by personal ambition but also by some sense of responsibility, a motive force for great pubic works but also partly liable for great disasters, implicated in the insoluble dilemmas and the asymmetric and uneven developments of real history. And of course, relatively speaking, something similar applies to the real individuals and groups that are "condensed" in Cross: Fred Eaton and the syndicate of San Fernando, always in accordance with the information provided by historical discourse.[331]

Let us now go to the *Freudian* component of the Freudo-Marxist discourse that prevails on the axis of concepts. As we have seen, this mainly consists in the symmetric inversion of the Oedipal structure disclosed when Evelyn's terrible secret is revealed. In so far as we are referring to the Oedipus *complex* and not the myth or the tragedy, it is not only a matter of a generational (and temporal) inversion, that is, of substituting the erotic relationship with the mother and the killing of the father with the erotic relationship with the daughter and the killing of the daughter's husband (and of changing the temporal sequence between the killing and the start of the erotic relationship), but also of inverting the realms of existence where the drama takes place. In the Oedipus complex we have subjective procedures, while in *Chinatown* we have "objective" actions (in inverted commas since it is fiction). The "objectivity" of the actions supplies an additional dramatic gravity, insofar as we have the violation of two "age-old taboos" of Western civilisation, incest and killing a close relative. Accordingly traumatic are the subjective *consequences* of these ("objective") actions for the persons immediately involved. Here we are interested mainly in Evelyn as a central character of the narrative. Her daughter-sister we hardly see at all. Mulwray gets killed fairly early, and Cross is the ruthless culprit of both violations. We are also interested in someone not initially involved but eventually involved by way of the narrative, Gittes.

Let us go back to the internal conditions part of the axis of enunciative modes. The scene where Evelyn's secret is revealed is particularly interesting from a filmic viewpoint. Let us remind ourselves that before this scene Gittes was almost certain that it was she who killed her husband. He was almost certain of the cause too; he thought that the girl Mulwray was seeing before he got killed was his mistress and therefore that Evelyn made a scene, they had a row and she killed him by mistake. So the crucial question was that girl's identity. Having already called by phone the police to arrest Evelyn, he starts questioning her about this, hoping to find some mitigating circumstances in order to help her. Evelyn had already told him the girl is her sister, and she repeats this. Gittes does not believe her, she tells him she is her daughter, so he goes livid and starts slapping her. With each slap her reply alternates between "My daughter!" and "My sister!". Finally in desperation she reveals to him the whole truth: "She is my sister *and* my daughter!".

The incest taboo prohibits the conjunction of the two. With each slap she gets, Evelyn repeats the disjunction. The relation between (the sign) "my daughter" and (the sign) "my sister" cannot but be metaphoric. Both being metaphors of the girl's true identity, *substitutions,* Gittes thinks. Therefore both of them seem mere lies, and between the two, Evelyn cannot

---

331. See Kevin Neal, "The Los Angeles Aqueduct and the Owens and Mono Lakes", *TED case studies*, 12/18/96, http://www.american.edu/ted/mono.htm (9 May 2008).

choose which is more convincing. This is what Gittes believes, what he *wants* to believe. Until the conjunction arrives, the emphasised "*and*", the *combination*, a metonymy fully stretched out in front of him, desperately uttered by Evelyn, as if she is yelling sarcastically right to his face: "Yes, such things do happen!".

Let us now notice the camera angle. The moment Evelyn reveals the girl's dual identity, and therefore Gittes stops slapping her, the camera stays (almost) constantly on her. A few seconds later, we hear Gittes (voice-off) asking, "Did he rape you?". Then we watch Evelyn shaking her head in denial, but with such desperation that we cannot be sure if she is just imploring Gittes to stop questioning her or if it is indeed a negative answer to his question. We discover here a slight but important discontinuity.

Throughout the rest of the film, camera movements follow the usual filmic conventions regarding the presentation of the characters' subjectivities. In emotionally intense scenes, in the scenes where some character's strong emotional charge must be shown, there is an *alternation of point-of-view shots and close-ups*. Viewers are invited to see things from a particular character's viewpoint *as well as* to observe his/her reaction as it can be manifested by his/her facial expressions. In this particular part of that scene, as far as Gittes's subjectivity is concerned, the shot remains steadily subjective: we only see Evelyn (roughly) as he sees her, and his face is not shown, for quite some time after Evelyn has uttered the shocking metonymy. After a very brief shot of his face, we hear him asking if her father raped her. Initially, we have no image of his facial expression, which would have been rather more revealing than his tone of voice, especially the first few seconds after Evelyn's phrase, the seconds in which he realises precisely what the metonymic relation "my sister *and* my daughter" means, and before he composes himself enough to ask her about rape. Would it not be much simpler if the camera just showed us a close-up of Gittes's profoundly shocked face? Nicholson is a marvelous actor and the shot would have been most effective.

But no. In that scene's particular segment, which is perhaps the most crucial of the whole film both plotwise and dramatically, Polanski prefers to remain strictly on the point-of-view shot. Once again, we have to do with a discontinuity which is there so as to enhance continuity. The continuity enhanced in this case is the basic cohesive joint of the narrative: *Gittes's position and function as narrator*. At this crucial moment, viewers must experience the revelation of Evelyn's secret "exactly" like Gittes. By not showing his face and by keeping the camera steadily at his viewpoint, Gittes's shock *is implied and precisely for this reason becomes more effective*. The viewer sees and hears Evelyn uttering the horrendous metonymy, "my sister *and* my daughter!". This will do. The shock is universal, self-evident, it goes without saying, "anyone" in Gittes's place would be shocked, no facial expressions need be shown. In this way, it is not just that the viewer gets into Gittes's place, but rather the inverse—Gittes "gets into the place" of the viewer, of "any civilised person", whose hair would stand on end on hearing of the ghastly incestuous deed.

Let alone if, like Gittes, he had started an affair with a woman who at the age of fifteen, as Evelyn herself says after a while, had fallen victim to this abhorrent crime. The point-of-view shot of Evelyn's confession acquires traumatic dimensions for Gittes. Since we are already within Freudian conceptualisation, it would not be far-fetched to consider it as some sort of perverse repetition of the "primal scene" in which the inversed Oedipal structure mingles with the "proper" one: with the latter, Evelyn and Cross constitute (unconscious, of course) parental figures for Gittes who experiences traumatically their having intercourse. The ambiguity of Evelyn's head shaking at Gittes's question enhances this interpretation: for the child at the primal scene the father exercises violence on the mother, which is something not necessarily so in reality.[332]

Even though Polanski pays special attention to the viewer's *audio-visual* identification with Gittes in this shot of the traumatic repetition of the "primal scene", this does not change the fact that it is a shot of a *verbal narration*. Evelyn *tells him what happened* when she was fifteen, he does not see the scene itself, he does not watch her live having intercourse with her father, not even in a photograph. In this sense, the trauma of the "primal scene's" repetition experienced by Gittes, even though it constitutes the central dramatic moment, the climax, so to speak, of the film's narrative, and at the same time Gittes's most essential consolidation at the narrator's position, it is rather "light", comparatively speaking. Comparatively, that is, according to standards set by the film itself.

So we come to the most significant discontinuity as to the narrative mode (internal conditions part of the axis of enunciative modes) that our unremitting mistrust has discovered, in the very first of the film's shots. The film starts with a definite point-of-view shot, which, *first*, is not from Gittes's viewpoint but from *someone else's*, and *second*, is a *most patently obvious* traumatic repetition of the "primal scene", definitely more intense that Gittes's with Evelyn and Cross, because here we have to do with photographs. To be precise, the photographs we see at the film's first shot are point-of-view shots from Gittes's viewpoint *in the past but now* from someone else's. They are photos taken by Gittes (or by one of his partners but Gittes himself has certainly seen them) and they are now in *the moment we see them as viewers* being seen by the person "directly concerned", by the deceived husband, who with these photos has irrefutable evidence that his wife has cheated on him. In accordance with the well-known joke, the pictures are in fact so revealing that we can hardly imagine his wife telling him, "It's not what you think".

---

332. Laplanche and Pontalis, *op. cit.*, pp. 335-336.

The film's first shots are an inventive introduction to Gittes's *profession*. In the frame of the last photo that we see, Gittes appears looking inquisitively as well as awkwardly at the husband who keeps watching the photos, and then the camera moves over to Gittes's viewpoint, and with him we observe the lamenting husband tossing away the photos in disgust and desperately shouting abuse about his wife. It is an inventive and at the same time *cynical* introduction. It introduces us to the banal reality of the profession, reminding us that it is cases of this sort that are usually undertaken by private detectives, a reality that tends to be disregarded by the various embellishing and hero-worshipping representations this profession often enjoys in literature and film. In this case, Gittes's client, who is the first we see in the film and who as a character will participate in the main story very little and entirely circumstantially, does not even have something of the usual "glamour" exhibited by private detectives' clients in fictional narratives. He is a poor "little man", who cannot even pay Gittes for his services. They are related as friends, and Gittes generously grants him some credit. Literally a "little man", short and chubby, with a gullible baby face. These latter characteristics may be of some symbolic significance, precisely since we have a repetition of the "primal scene".

While we are watching –together with him- the photographs, we hear his sobbing, which sounds like some small child crying. Before Gittes appears we do not see the husband's face at all, we just hear him sobbing. The whining becomes stronger the moment we see a photo showing his wife and her lover doing it "from the back"; the well-known *coitus a tergo, more ferarum*, which according to Freud marks the violence of the sexual act as it is understood by the child who is watching his/her parents copulating.[333] So the *discontinuity* in the film's narrative mode consists in the film starting with an evident and emotionally charged point-of-view shot from the viewpoint of some character who not only is not Gittes but is nearly irrelevant to the main story. I believe that this discontinuity, apart from being a cynical and inventive introduction to the private detective's profession, also attributes to the film's beginning some symbolic narrative importance. It is as if the whole filmic narrative that is about to follow is presented as a repetition of the "primal scene". The photos viewed by the deceived husband in the film's first shot are a metaphor for the film's narrative, and the "little-man"/husband a metaphor for the viewer. The cohesive link of the two is once again Gittes as detective-narrator. He provides the husband with the photos, he will provide the viewer with the film's narrative. The difference is that in the former case there is a time lag. Gittes already knows about the infidelity of the "little man's" wife, and even though he shows sympathy he is definitely aloof. He treats him condescendingly, almost as if the whole affair bores him, while he will directly experience himself the main narrative and will be shaken and shocked by it "simultaneously" with the viewer.

---

333. See Freud, *S.E. XVII*, pp. 29-47.

There is a fourth discontinuity, also emerging in the narrative mode and related to the Freudian component of the axis of concepts (like the two previous ones). After having sex with Evelyn, she asks him about his past, about the time he served in Chinatown as a policeman, and Gittes gives an enigmatic reply that is unconnected to the rest of the film: "I was trying to keep someone from being hurt ... I ended up making sure that she was hurt." If we were to consider this remark by itself, and given it is perhaps the only occasion where Gittes refers to something he knows and the viewer does not and will not ever know (hence the sense of discontinuity), we might even take it as a clumsy attempt on his part to impress his mistress by playing it "the man with the obscure past".

This is not the case, of course. Gittes's enigmatic reply has a specific narrative function. It is a warning of *exactly* what Gittes is about to do to Evelyn. In the narrative's last part, he does everything he can to save her and to help her and her daughter-sister to escape from Cross and the police, but eventually it is he who leads them to her, with the result of herself getting killed and her daughter-sister coming under Cross's "protection".

In this way there emerges in the film a specifically psychoanalytic leitmotif. From the beginning of the narrative, Gittes carries a psychic trauma from his past, about which we learn only from the enigmatic and incomplete confession he makes in a very personal moment with Evelyn. According to the psychoanalytic concept of the "compulsion to repeat", he is doomed to repeat the trauma that tortures him.[334] The film's tragic ending, in this sense, is but the dramatic consummation of the trauma's repetition.

We are led to a fifth discontinuity, which concerns the at first glance asymmetric relation of the film's title to the plot. Since it is a matter of the plot, the discontinuity initially emerges on the *axis of objects*; a fictional narrative's plot, being *par excellence* an instance of "referentiality *per se*", belongs to this axis. (The title by itself is not included in any axis.) But there is also a link with the axis of concepts by way of the previous discontinuity concerning Freudian discourse. If the importance of Gittes's traumatic past were not pointed out, Chinatown's significance as to the plot would be disproportionately small for the title to be explained. The fact that the ending scene takes place in Chinatown is almost accidental and would not suffice by itself. Psychoanalytically-symbolically, however, it is the *place of the trauma*. Gittes is doomed to *return* to it, in order to *repeat* his trauma.

In investigating this discontinuity though, we are reconnected to the politico-economic part of the axis of concepts, since Chinatown's symbolism is twofold. This region of Los Angeles is metonymically linked not only with the *trauma of Gittes*, but also with the *corruption of police*. It is an instance where two metonymic connections lead to a metaphoric relation. Both the former and the latter take place in Gittes's subjectivity, and more particularly in his *memory* and in his *present experience* as central character-narrator.

---

334. Laplanche and Pontalis, *op. cit.*, pp. 78-80, 161-162 and 470-473.

More analytically, both in the case of Chinatown and trauma and in that of Chinatown and police corruption, the connections in Gittes's memory as well as in his experience are relations of *combination*. Gittes combines in his memory the fact that he served in Chinatown, on one hand, with the traumatic story of the woman he tried to help and eventually hurt, and on the other, with patent police corruption which, serving in Chinatown, he had the opportunity to know first hand. The same combinations are repeated in his present experience, during the film's final scene; Chinatown as a place is combined both with the consummation of the drama of his unwillingly disastrous intervention in Evelyn's story and with one more, ultimate, glaring manifestation of police corruption.

The repetition of the twofold (metonymic) combination inevitably leads to the *comparison* between the two sides combined with Chinatown. In some sense, here the film's *central meaning* is condensed. On one hand because the two sides are condensations of the two corresponding components of the film's prevailing Freudo-Marxist discourse (on the axis of concepts), and on the other because all these conceptual-symbolic relations are constituted by, and in turn constitute, the central cohesive link of the narrative (in the internal conditions part of the axis of enunciative modes), namely Gittes as character-narrator.

What do we find by comparing the two sides? We discover a *common structure of intervention/non-intervention*. Gittes's *trauma,* together with its repetition, consists in his *intervention*, disastrous for his mistress. He intervenes to save her with the result of destroying her. The *corruption of police* consists in its *non-intervention*, disastrous for justice. At the end of the film, one of his partners tries to "bring him down to earth" saying "Forget it, Jake. It's Chinatown". Before this, looking at Evelyn's dead body, he anticipates him, bitterly mumbling to himself, "As little as possible." He is referring to something he has already said in a previous scene (to Evelyn, a little while before they had sex), that the "advice" to the police in Chinatown was to intervene as little as possible, thereby allowing, of course, the various mafias to do their job unhindered.

The metaphoric relationship emerges from comparing the two sides—on one hand, Gittes's trauma resulting from his intervention, and on the other, corruption of police consisting in its non-intervention. By itself this is a discontinuous conceptual expression of some similarly discontinuous and asymmetric realities—Gittes's personal history and subjectivity, socio-political conditions instigating corruption. This is unified and acquires continuity once again by way of Gittes's position as character-narrator. Gittes's trauma is twofold. Its other facet is identified with police corruption. He intervenes *disastrously* as Gittes because he can *not* intervene as state of justice. Besides, there is an implication that in the past the reason he left the police had been its non-intervention (i.e. its corruption).

We may thus notice three pairs of concepts being formed, initially arising from the complex and asymmetric metaphoric relation between the two sides (Freudian and Marxist) we pointed out above, but eventually developing into a Hegelian schema of identity/non-identity, with its symmetry and its equivalences:

- (Disastrous) Intervention / Non-Intervention
- Personal Trauma / Political Corruption
- Gittes / (Absent) State of Justice

The discontinuities so far pointed out are the disjointed relation to the real (and asymmetric) socio-political conflicts on the axis of objects, the three discontinuities in the narrative mode, and the disproportion to the film's title. These are condensed and eventually cancelled (until our mistrust makes them re-emerge), in the above continuous, idealised (by being mediated through Gittes's subjectivity) and hypostatised (by being presented as an irrevocable account of an equally irrevocable objective reality) conceptual ensemble. This does not mean that the prevalence of Freudo-Marxist discourse on the axis of concepts is annulled, but that the discontinuities linking this discourse to the first two axes are concealed. If the process of establishing continuity, and thereby of idealisation and hypostatisation in accordance with the "triplet" of (modern) ideology generally speaking, consists first and foremost in concealing discontinuities, it is to be expected that the analytical-critical process will follow an *at once parallel and inverse* path, mainly consisting in revealing them.

As we have already said, discontinuities are what gives rise to non-reducible differences. Concealing discontinuities is therefore coextensive with the process of reducing (non-reducible) differences to symmetric and equivalent antithetical pairs. The symmetry and equivalence of the latter also ensures the ultimate reduction of differences to identity. The (Disastrous) Intervention (by Gittes) *is* Non-Intervention (by the police), the Personal Trauma (of Gittes) *is* Political Corruption (of the police), Gittes (as a private detective) *is* the (Absent) State of Justice (in the American society of that time).

We have yet to see though the ultimate form these oppositions/identities acquire on the *axis of thematics*, that is, to understand the *implicit strategic incorporation* of the above conceptual ensemble within an ideological field of conflict. We have seen that, on a first level of reading, in which we simply recognised the Freudo-Marxist discourse, the basic ideological issue of the film is the conflict between Justice and Freedom on one hand and Capitalism and Repression on the other. We will now have to see how the eventual representational continuities, deriving from concealing the discontinuities we have pointed out, transform this conflict into something not altogether irrelevant but in any event ideologically more questionable.

We discover a sixth discontinuity. In the external conditions part of the axis of enunciative modes, we are provided with the information that "Gittes" was named by the film makers after a friend of Jack Nicholson, producer Harry Gittes.[335] This is something entirely contingent, carrying no symbolism in the film that the viewer may be aware of. This is not so with the most important character after Gittes, namely Noah Cross. The discontinuity that in this instance provokes our mistrust consists in the fact that, unlike the case of Gittes, here we have symbolisms that are enticingly obvious.

I referred above to two of the symbolisms of this name, deliberately postponing the treatment of the more evident ones. Noah is the man who survived the Flood, who providently built the Ark, thereby controlling the future of mankind and the world—an ironic parallelism (comparison, metaphor) of Cross's megalomania to the well-known Biblical story. But another extra-textual reference, even though at first glance of a somewhat "joking" sort, is perhaps more important. Once again this rests in external conditions that are part of the axis of enunciative modes. Noah Cross is played by the well-known director John Huston. In the Hollywood film *The Bible* (1966), made by this director, Noah's part had been played by himself. I believe this reference to another film is something more than a mere "wink" at the viewer. In that film, Huston, apart from Noah, had also played the narrator, God, and the serpent.[336] In other words, Noah, in the person of John Huston as an actor, is combined with the Bible's narrator, God, and the incarnation of the Devil. The relation between the first two is one of similarity and ultimately identity. The Bible is the word of God, its narrator *is* God. The relation between God and the Devil is a relation of substitution and disjunction, ultimately of a symmetrically equivalent opposition. Where God does not govern, the Devil rules.

Ultimately, the relationship between the three, in the film *Chinatown* and by way of Noah Cross/John Huston, is one of identity. Noah Cross is the film's omnipotent/omniscient true Narrator, in whose hands Gittes is a *totally powerless* character-narrator. He is a mere pawn, from start to finish. In the beginning, he unwittingly becomes Cross's agent, unjustly exposing Mulwray to a scandal. In the end, he once again unwittingly leads Evelyn and her daughter-sister to Cross. At the same time, Cross is the Devil: The incarnation of Evil, who intervenes disastrously, through Gittes or otherwise, precisely because the police do not intervene, because the State of Justice, the (Just) Law, the force of the Good, ultimately (Good) God, is Absent. If we take into account the whole name of Noah Cross, which is but a metonymy of Judaeo-Christian, i.e. Western civilisation, it turns out that this character is its ironic Negation, not just from a Freudo-Marxist viewpoint, but also, on a more profound level, from a Judaeo-Christian one. Chinatown, as a place of Non-Intervention (by the Good), as a field where

---

335. See "Chinatown", *op. cit.*

336. See "The Bible: In the Beginning", *Wikipedia*, 14 June 2008, http://en.wikipedia.org/wiki/The_Bible:_In_the_Beginning (7 July 2008).

Absolute Corruption prevails, as land where the Primal Scene and the Trauma are transformed into the Original Sin and the Fall, is Hell on earth, or, in terms of Protestant political philosophy, the *state of nature*.[337]

Of course there is no way in which this masterful and extremely elaborate from a narrative, aesthetic and ideological viewpoint film could be likened to *Dirty Harry* (1971), where police violence and arbitrariness are justified in a most grossly unreserved manner. Nevertheless, when we talk about *strategic incorporation* (axis of thematics), we should inevitably take into consideration the general ideological regime within which the text to be analysed appears. *Chinatown*, for all the indisputable particularity (and artistic merit) of its maker, from an institutional viewpoint belongs to a multitude of Hollywood films of the decades following the `sixties "anti-authoritarian" protests, which, starting with *Dirty Harry*, all had *as a central thematic* the issue of the justification of police intervention or non-intervention.

In this sense, and even though *Chinatown*'s time of reference is the pre-war period, the film should be viewed in relation to its position with regard to this ideologico-political issue. The "bad guy" in *Dirty Harry* is a "perverted" serial killer and rapist, in *Chinatown* an omnipotent, ruthless, incestuous magnate. Furthermore, in the former film, the inadequacy of police leading to its non-intervention is not so blatantly connected to corruption, and is rather presented as using the "excuse" of being obliged to abide by some rules of legitimacy (respect for the suspects' rights etc.). Apart from all other important differences, the Freudo-Marxist component which is definitely there in the ideological position of *Chinatown* is totally absent in *Dirty Harry*. The latter's *negative* ideological target is entirely different, it is the supporters of human rights who protest against police arbitrariness.

Even so, the *positive* target is common, *We need more police intervention.* And the justification for this, on a more profound level, is also common. "Evil", or crime, is not just some transgressive behaviour that under different social conditions might not exist or might be approachable by means other than suppression by the police; it is *Absolute Evil*, which may assume a variety of different avatars,[338] and which is diffused throughout the state apparatus and society as (some form of) *corruption*, which can be combated only by policing means.

However, I will not say that *Chinatown*'s ideological position is *by itself* reactionary, or even conservative. As a demonisation of big politico-economic power, the narrative might be considered even as "idiosyncratically progressive"— "idiosyncratically", taking into account Polanski's particular predilections, somewhat more evident in his other American film, namely

---

337. For a remarkably interesting comparison of the philosophy of Hobbes to Protestant theology, see Leopold Damrosch, Jr., "Hobbes as Reformation theologian: Implications of the free-will controversy", *Journal of the History of Ideas*, Volume XL (1979), Number 3, pp. 339-352.

338. It is indicative that in *Dirty Harry* too the religious-demonological element in presenting "evil" is quite strong, but to demonstrate this a separate study would be needed.

Rosemary's baby (1968). However, placed within the general ideological regime of the Hollywood film industry, the film cannot but also have the above described ideological functioning. Besides, what we are looking for in discourse analysis is not to end up classifying texts into conservative and progressive. How could we, given that we question every classification? What we are looking for is to carry out critique: resistance in discourse and by way of discourse, (practical) thought on limits, questioning continuity and discovering discontinuities, exposing multiple forms of hypostatisation.

One more thing regarding the principle of mistrust. There is the question of *aesthetic judgement*. Discourse analysis as critique in the above sense cannot but take into consideration even this question in accordance with the basic methodological principle of mistrust. The facile version of this approach would consist in treating as "suspect" some cultural product that appeals to many people. Our mistrust in such a case would be directed towards those mechanisms that are responsible for constructing some *dominant criteria* for aesthetically accepting or not some artistic creation. The methodology we are proposing though aims at the analysis of *specific properties of discourse* and of how these act on the formation of subjectivity. This means that we should once again take into account the issue of (representational) continuity. I believe that whether one "likes" a cultural product or not directly derives *also* from the extent to which that product is congruous with some continuities already existing—either as ideological systems, in which case there is an enhancement of the continuity inherent in the subjects' ego ideal, or as images of the self, which play up to the immanent narcissism of the ideal ego, or, in most cases, as a combination of both: an attractive character with whom a film's viewers tend to identify also enhances the ideological continuities he/she stands for.

The fact that many people liked the film *Chinatown* may be accounted for (*among other things* - I am not maintaining that the *only* aesthetic criteria are ideological and/or identificational) both by Gittes/Nicholson's engaging and likeable presence, and by the fact that this character, constantly occupying the central narrative position, presents to us a narrative that, in the manner we have shown, fully satisfies, even though extremely pessimistically, the ideological expectations of an audience broadly influenced by some sort of Freudo-Marxist and/or liberal discourse. The issue of course is that at the same time it also promotes some other continuities, to which we have referred at length.

I liked a lot this film myself. For many years I have considered it as one of the best films I have seen, and I still do. The principle of mistrust should lead us to the, perhaps not so easy, but more interesting ideological investigation of films that are liked not by "many", or by the "commercial film-going public", but by *ourselves*. Perhaps a useful first version of our methodological mistrust might be, *Why do I like this film?* That is, what continuities of my ego is it congruous with and does it satisfy, and what others does it promote (by way of concealing what discontinuities on which these are based)?

Chapter 18
Two award-winning films

Much more briefly, I will refer to two much more recent cases of films I particularly liked. They are both European films, one is in French, *Caché* (*Hidden* – 2005, directed by Michael Haneke) and the other in German, *Das Leben der anderen* (*The lives of others* – 2006, directed by Florian Henckel von Donnersmarck).

Even though they are entirely different films, they have some basic things in common. First, with regard to the axis of objects, they both have some real politico-historical references. In *Hidden*, an important role is played in the narrative's past tense by the massacre of Algerian demonstrators by French police in 1961, and in *The lives of others*, the best part of the narrative's present tense takes place in East Germany in the period of actually existing socialism (1984). Furthermore, as to the external conditions part of the axis of enunciative modes, it is of some importance that both were broadly and enthusiastically received in terms of reviews but also awards, the former mainly in Europe, and the latter both in Europe and America.[339]

---

339. Significantly, both won the award of Best European Film (2005 and 2006 respectively), and the latter also won the Academy Award for Best Foreign-Language Film (2007).

I will not analyse either film's many merits. I will come straight to the question of why I *mainly* believed I liked them from an *ideological* viewpoint. In the case of *Hidden*, I interpreted the film as a particularly sensitive allegory about the problem of racism. The relation between the two children, before the young Algerian boy is betrayed by the young French one, is a *brotherly* relation. Racist hatred is in this way likened to the rivalry between brothers; *human*, but unjustifiable for *mature* human beings. In *The lives of others*, I favourably viewed the fact that the film recognised there were some people in the regimes of actually existing socialism, who actually supported them, even though in a ruthlessly authoritarian fashion, out of a genuine ideological devotion to socialist ideals. The Stasi agent regarded dissidents as enemies of socialism, and his faith towards the regime starts to falter when he realises that the writer's surveillance he has undertaken has absolutely nothing to do with the defence of socialism.

On the other hand, as to the first film, I recognised that the allegory might be congruous with my "anti-racist sensitivity", but it has a problem common to all allegories: oversimplification of the real situations that they symbolise. Racism can hardly be dealt with by appeals to "universal fraternity" and the "maturity of Enlightened societies". And as to the second, while I was pleased with the lack of a one-sided anti-communism expressed in the way I mentioned, on the other hand, I was thinking that the problem in those regimes was not *only* the extremely authoritarian corruption of state power (as personified in the film with the character of the uncontrollably indulgent minister), but also, perhaps more importantly, an authoritarianism emerging *mainly* from a particular *genuine ideological devotion*, which absolutely identified the ideals of socialism with the interests and commands of those countries' state apparatuses. So I was wondering if after all it is possible that in the first film we have the *continuity of humanist ideology* that conceals the real power conflicts and asymmetric ideological confrontations, and in the second one once again we have the reproduction of the *ideological continuity* of a commonly accepted bipolarity – *on one hand:* good state = democratic state = state of justice, *and on the other:* bad state = authoritarian state = corrupt state.

After having seen both films, I started being concerned with a continuity *between them*, expressed in a *latent common thematic structure*. Both films are about *surveillance*—by the anonymous person who sends the videotapes to the "successful" bourgeois French intellectual and his wife in one case, and by the Stasi agent who spies on the dissident writer in the other. Moreover, in the second film, we have a perhaps deliberate and ironic inversion of the famous "surveillance novel", namely *1984*. While in Orwell's book (1948) the year of the title refers to an *imaginary future*, in *The lives of others* (2006) the same year (the main part of the story takes place in 1984) refers to a *real past*. Furthermore, the continuity between the *fictional* surveillance in the two films and the *real* surveillance of our time, increasingly intensifying after 11 September 2001, set in motion my principle of mistrust for good, and thereby drove me to start searching for discontinuities.

In *Hidden* I had already pinpointed a discontinuity, the widely discussed enigma, *unsolved by the film itself*, of who was sending the videotapes; in other words, of who was doing the surveillance, of who was the supervisor. An enigma remaining unsolved throughout the narrative is a blatant discontinuity, a "piece of the puzzle" that is never found. I had given an interpretation for this discontinuity, being based on a crystal-clear, in my view, symbolism in the film's beginning. The first videotape that the film's central character has received from the anonymous sender and is watching with his wife is *the film's opening shot, the shot in which titles fall*. Initially we do not know it is a videotape, we think that the still shot of the house's front is the start of the *plot itself*, the *establishing shot*, in filmic terms. We therefore have every reason to suppose that the director, or rather the film's *narrator*, whoever this may be, the camera, the "voice" of the script,[340] in any event the film's *subject of narration* (we are on the thin line between external and internal enunciative conditions) is self-presented to us from the very start as the real perpetrator of the anonymous sending of the tapes, therefore as the real supervisor. The film, apart from an anti-racist allegory, is at the same time an allegory about the *democratically supervising* role that should be played by the mass media, including the cinema.

Initially, I had just thought we were seeing an ingenious symbolic device, without paying any further attention ideologically speaking. Considering however the issue within the broader framework of strategic incorporation, I could not help but take also into account the second film, so I sought for some discontinuity there as well, once again in relation to the thematic of surveillance.

In *The lives of others* I found discontinuity on the axis of objects, but with some assistance from the external conditions part of the axis of enunciative modes. I am referring to the question of the relations between fictional plot (referentiality *per se*) and real occurrences (objectivity *per se*). In the particular case of this film, the question is exceptionally crucial, since real occurrences belong to an especially "harsh" reality, that of the regimes of actually existing socialism, a reality which is furthermore fairly recent, and thus a reality to which one can have access rather easily, drawing evidence from living persons' accounts. In particular, during the last few years the organisation and operation of the notorious Stasi has been the object of much scrutiny in numerous ways, journalistic and otherwise. Already while watching the film, I had thought that the way in which the specific agent manages to disengage from his colleagues' and superiors' control the writer's surveillance so as to save him from certain arrest and conviction is presented as too easy. My suspicion was justified by a comment on the film (external conditions of enunciation) made by a researcher who has done work specifically on Stasi.[341]

---

340. See above, fn. 322.

341. See "The lives of others", *Wikipedia*, 4 May 2008, http://en.wikipedia.org/wiki/The_Lives_of_Others (9 May 2008).

It is a matter of a "factual ineptitude" of an otherwise especially well-made and carefully produced film, and precisely here lies the discontinuity that confirmed and thus further encouraged my mistrust. The Stasi agent does not merely save the writer by withholding information derived from his surveillance that would lead to his arrest. *He actively intervenes* in his life, in at least three crucial ways. And perhaps it is of some importance that all three ways are directly related to the writer's wife, about whom we know she cheats on him with the corrupt and ruthless minister.

- Acting like a private detective "ex machina", he "informs" the writer of his wife's infidelity.

- Playing the part of a self-appointed marriage counselor, he urges the writer's wife to stop seeing the minister.

- And finally, as a well-meaning and, under the circumstances, heroic interrogator, he extracts from the writer's wife the information of the typewriter's hiding place not to use it against the writer, but, on the contrary, to be able to eliminate the basic incriminating piece of evidence before his colleagues and his chief can find it (with the result of losing his job, since the latter has some suspicion of what has happened).

And all these he does *in his capacity as a supervisor: without this privileged position, he could not possibly in any way intervene (in favour of the writer)*.

So a conclusion may be drawn, which complements *Hidden*'s allegoric incitement for democratic surveillance by the media, and which serves together with it the strategic aim of justifying surveillance in contemporary Western societies. There are, or at least there *can* be, good supervisors; and moreover, if they are good indeed, these supervisors can fulfil a role redeeming for democracy and justice. The symbolic title of the book that the writer dedicates in gratitude to the Stasi agent who saved him, *Sonata for a good man*, might also be, *Sonata for a good supervisor*. *Hidden*'s anti-racist humanism and *The lives of others'* liberal humanism both serve to establish between them an ideological continuity that is incorporated in that of the contemporary demand for increasingly more effective "well-meaning", "democratic" surveillance in our societies.

Index

A

Althusser, Louis 6, 29-30, 91, 113, 119, 132-134, 141-142, 155
Aristotle 40
Austin, J.L. 96

B

Bachelard, Gaston 108
Balibar, Étienne 6
Balzac, Honoré de 108
Barthes, Roland 10-11, 21, 54, 108, 113, 132
Barwise, Jon 97
Bassakos, Pantelis 47
Benveniste, Émile 9, 12, 16, 18, 38-39, 51, 77-78, 109
Boole, George 72
Brown, Beverley 94
Butler, Judith 24, 86

C

Canguilhem, Georges 108
Carus, Paul 28
Cavafy, C.P. 25
Cavaillès, Jean 108
Caygill, Howard 69
Chatman, Seymour 114
Cousins, Mark 94

D

Damrosch, Leopold, Jr. 199
Deleuze, Gilles 70, 107, 136, 154, 169
Derrida, Jacques x, 32-33, 37-47, 49-51, 53-55, 57-59, 61-66, 68-72, 75-76, 86-87, 89, 92, 101, 153
Descartes, René ix, 46, 55, 57, 137-142, 156

Destutt de Tracy, Antoine Louis Claude 143
Disraeli, Benjamin 7
Doxiadis, Kyrkos 6, 27, 29, 46-47, 63-64, 89-90, 108, 115, 147-148, 151, 156, 165, 181
Dreyfus, Hubert L. 63, 91, 107, 146, 174
Dumézil, Georges 143

E

Eaton, Frederick 187-189, 191
Engels, Friedrich 30, 133
Erasmus, Desiderius 66
Etchemendy, John 97

F

Foucault, Michel xi, 16, 21, 27, 33-34, 46, 51, 63-65, 68, 87, 89-94, 101-105, 107-111, 113, 115, 117-118, 127-136, 143, 145-156, 160, 165-166, 169, 173-174, 176
Freud, Sigmund 43, 127, 153-156, 159-160, 162-163, 186, 194

G

Gittes, Harry 198
Gramsci, Antonio 186
Guattari, Félix 154

H

Halle, Morris 10
Haneke, Michael 201
Hegel, Georg Wilhelm Friedrich 21, 25, 33-35, 40, 46, 64-66, 115, 133

Heidegger, Martin xi, 64, 68, 92
Henckel von Donnersmarck, Florian 201
Hjelmslev, Louis 54
Hobbes, Thomas 199
Houdebine, Jean-Louis 37, 39, 43
Husserl, Edmund 40, 54-59, 62-65, 68, 92
Huston, John 180, 198

J

Jakobson, Roman 10, 76

K

Kant, Immanuel 27-29, 63-66, 68-69, 127, 134, 137, 140, 148-149, 151, 156
Keefe, Rosanna 72, 169
Klein, Naomi x
Kouzelis, Gerassimos 47
Koyré, Alexandre 108
Kristeva, Julia 40, 43, 71
Kuhn, Thomas S. 121

L

Lacan, Jacques ix, 24-26, 30, 64, 153-157, 160, 162-165, 175
Laclau, Ernesto x, 3-10, 12-21, 23-35, 38-39, 42, 51, 75, 78, 83, 86-87, 89, 93-94, 103, 128, 136
Laplanche, Jean 26, 158-160, 164-165, 193, 195
Le Carré, John x
Lecourt, Dominique 108
Leibniz, Gottfried Wilhelm 33-34, 127
Lenin, Vladimir Ilyich 29, 32, 39, 113, 119, 132-133, 141-142, 155

Lévi-Strauss, Claude 100
Lukács, Georg 8, 91, 115
Luther, Martin 66

M

Mannheim, Karl 109
Martinet, André 10
Marx, Karl 29-30, 47, 153, 186
Meinong, Alexius 102
Merleau-Ponty, Maurice 63, 91-92
Metz, Christian 10
Mouffe, Chantal x, 3-10, 12-21, 23-34, 38-39, 42, 75, 78, 83, 86-87, 93-94, 103, 128, 136
Moore, A.W. 100
Moses 171
Mulholland, William 187-190

N

Neal, Kevin 191
Nicholson, Jack 180-181, 192, 197, 200
Nietzsche, Friedrich 146-147, 151

O

Orwell, George 202
Otis, Harrison Gray 188

P

Plato 40
Poe, Edgar Allan 58, 62, 76
Polanski, Roman 179-183, 192-193, 199
Pontalis, J.-B. 26, 158-160, 164-165, 193, 195

Poulantzas, Nicos 162
Powell, John Wesley 188

R

Rabinow, Paul 63, 91, 107, 128, 146, 174
Ricardo, David 153
Rolland, Romain 186
Roosevelt, Theodore 188
Rousseau, Jean-Jacques 40, 51
Russell, Bertrand 72, 102

S

Saussure, Ferdinand de 8-13, 18, 38, 41, 53-54, 69-70, 76-78, 80, 89, 109, 135, 169
Scarpetta, Guy 37, 39, 43
Schmidt, James 149
Scott, Ian S. 179, 189
Searle, John R. 6, 96, 98-100
Shannon, Claude 72
Sheridan, Alan 26, 107, 153
Shetley, Vernon Lionel 179
Smith, Peter 72, 169
Stavrakakis, Yannis 26
Steiner, George 127

T

Todorov, Tzvetan 106, 113

W

Weber, Max 5
Wittgenstein, Ludwig 6, 100

Z

Zeno 48
Žižek, Slavoj x, 23-35, 39-40, 86, 154

www.ingramcontent.com/pod-product-compliance
Lightning Source LLC
Chambersburg PA
CBHW070830300426
44111CB00014B/2507